Criminal Testimonial Injustice

Criminal Testimonial Injustice

JENNIFER LACKEY

OXFORD
UNIVERSITY PRESS

OXFORD
UNIVERSITY PRESS

Great Clarendon Street, Oxford, OX2 6DP,
United Kingdom

Oxford University Press is a department of the University of Oxford.
It furthers the University's objective of excellence in research, scholarship,
and education by publishing worldwide. Oxford is a registered trade mark of
Oxford University Press in the UK and in certain other countries

First Edition published in 2023

Published in the United States of America by Oxford University Press
198 Madison Avenue, New York, NY 10016, United States of America

British Library Cataloguing in Publication Data
Data available

Library of Congress Control Number: 2022945372

ISBN 978–0–19–286410–9

DOI: 10.1093/oso/9780192864109.001.0001

Printed and bound by
CPI Group (UK) Ltd, Croydon, CR0 4YY

To Paula Aiardo, Quayshaun Bailey, Shurese Bailey, Stephanie Bonds, Robert Boyd, Michael Broadway, Elbonie Burnside, Jeffery Campbell, Lester Carroll, Justin Cavazos, Robert Cloutier, Vanecha Cooper, Corzell Cole, Demetrice Crite, Demetrius Cunningham, Tyrone Daniels, Taurean Decatur, Margaret DeFrancisco, Regina DeFrancisco, Bonnie Diana, Travis Dortch, Edmond Duffin, Anthony Ehlers, Tiffany Fassler, Shareaf Fleming, Amanda Fredrickson, Maria Garza, Lynn Green, Shawnette Green, Craig Harvey, Broderick Hollins, Pierre James, Albert Kirkman, James Lenoir, Brian McClendon, Antonio McDowell, Joyce McGee, Benard McKinley, Todd Mandoline, Flynard Miller, Paul Modrowski, Ramon Montague, Abdul-Malik Muhammad, Patricia Ouska, André Patterson, William Peeples, Chelsea Raker, Erika Ray, Leon Robinson, Irene Romaniuk, Kevin Scott, Rochelle Sephus, Charles Serrano, Cindy Shepheard, LeShun Smith, Bianca Solis, James Soto, Anthony Triplett, and Orlando Watkins.

You are among the most talented, courageous, and inspiring students I have had the privilege of knowing in my 21 years of teaching. Thank you for opening my eyes to forms of harm and injustice I had never before seen, and for breathing new life into philosophical questions I've been asking for the entirety of my career. It is one of the greatest gifts of my life to be on this journey with each of you.

Contents

Acknowledgments

My work on this book—from the earliest moments of envisioning the framework to the final stages of editing the individual chapters—has been inspired, nurtured, and championed by so many exceptional people that I truly regard myself as one of the luckiest authors on the planet.

First, and foremost, I have crossed paths with countless students over the years at Stateville Correctional Center, Logan Correctional Center, and the Cook County Department of Corrections who have, through profound acts of generosity, shared with me their often harrowing personal stories of being violated and traumatized in various ways by the United States criminal legal system. I am not only extremely grateful to each of them, I am also deeply moved that they entrusted me with such pain and vulnerability. I am especially indebted to Demetrius Cunningham, whose own experience of falsely confessing first challenged me to think through the distinctively epistemic wrongs inflicted on him; to Albert Kirkman, whose wrongful conviction based on an eyewitness misidentification motivated me to see how suspects and witnesses are often subject to the same interrogation tactics and, thereby, the same kind of testimonial injustice; and to William Peeples, whose tragic account of pleading guilty to a crime he did not commit reinforced my sense that the plea-bargaining process itself is frequently coercive and thus results in a kind of epistemic injustice that is systemic in nature.

Just as importantly, many of my students in the Northwestern Prison Education Program supported, expanded, and added nuance to my understanding of the framework that I first began developing in this book. For their courage in recounting their personal experiences of being subject to manipulative, deceptive, and coercive interrogation techniques in the United States criminal legal system, my heartfelt gratitude to Anthony Ehlers, Todd Mandoline, and Abdul-Malik Muhammad.

Some students, friends, and colleagues went to heroic levels to read a draft of the entire manuscript. For providing compelling and insightful feedback on a project that is so meaningful to me, I will be forever grateful to Lester Carroll, Tyrone Daniels, Regina DeFrancisco, Alex Guerrero, Benard McKinley, William Peeples, and James Soto.

Many thanks also to friends, students, and colleagues who provided thoughtful, incisive feedback on various ideas in this book, as well as deeply-valued support during the writing process, including Nathaly Ardelean Garcia, Beth Barker, Jessica Brown, Daniel Donadio, Steven Drizin, Catarina Dutilh Novaes, Miranda Fricker, Sandy Goldberg, Thomas Grundmann, Regina Hurley, Jason Kawall,

Chris Kelp, Albert Kirkman, Nathan Lauffer, Whit Lilly, Michael Lynch, Kevin McCain, Veli Mitova, Peter Momtchiloff, Jesús Navarro, Alex Papulis, Laurie Paul, Spencer Paulson, Kathryn Pogin, Bradley Rettler, Alessandra Tanesini, Mohammed Tayssir Safi, Mona Simion, Jason Stanley, Lisa Miracchi Titus, Deb Tuerkheimer, Sarah Wright, two anonymous reviewers for Oxford University Press, and audience members at the Social Norms and Epistemology Conference at St. Louis University, the Epistemic Norms Conference in Leuven, Belgium, the Institut Jean Nicod, the Intellectual Humility and Public Deliberation Workshop at the University of Connecticut, Western Michigan University, the University of Groningen, Miami University, the 2017 Bled Epistemology Conference, the III International Conference on Analytical Epistemology and VIII Conference on Social Epistemology in Santa Maria, RS, Brazil, the 2018 Summer School in Philosophy at the University of Cologne, Northern Illinois University, the University of Rochester Humanities Center, the 2019 Southern Society for Philosophy and Psychology, the 2019 conference for the *Journal of Criminal Law and Criminology*, Texas Christian University, the 2019 Epistemology Seminar of the Instituto de Investigaciones Filosóficas at the Universidad Nacional Autónoma De México, Denison University, the 5th Penn Reasons and Foundations of Epistemology Conference, Calvin College, Howard University, the North American Association for Philosophy & Education, the Epistemic Injustice in the Aftermath of Collective Wrongdoing Conference in Bern, Switzerland, the University of Zurich, the Epistemic Injustice and Blame Workshop in Glasgow, Scotland, Hofstra University, the Royal Institute of Philosophy, Louisiana State University Ethics Institute, Fordham University, Texas A&M University, the University of Wyoming, the Barnes Philosophy Club, and the Social and Political Dimensions of Epistemic Risk Conference at the University of Seville.

I am also grateful to Andy Hull for his meticulous and efficient work on the index, helping me cross over the finish line with this project just when I needed it the most.

Invaluable support from the John Simon Guggenheim Memorial Foundation and the Alice Kaplan Institute for the Humanities gave me much-needed time during the 2021–2022 academic year to complete the research for this book. My sincere thanks to everyone who made these fellowships and, therefore, this book, possible.

Anthony Ehlers, who is not only an extraordinarily talented artist, but is also a journalist, activist, and full-time college student in the Northwestern Prison Education Program, painted the powerful image for the cover of this book. It depicts the inside of F house in Stateville Correctional Center in Crest Hill, IL, also known as the 'roundhouse,' which is a panopticon—a form of social control designed by English philosopher, Jeremy Bentham, in which a central observation tower is placed within a circle of prison cells. While the guard can see every cell and every incarcerated person from the tower, the incarcerated people cannot themselves see inside the tower and thus they never know whether they are being watched. Because of this, the theory is that they will be motivated to act as though they are being watched at all times, leading to a highly effective form of discipline and control. In reality, however, such an architectural design has been described as 'perfectly engineered to induce extreme aggravation, anxiety and stress among [incarcerated people]' who are said to 'universally despise the building.'[1] Anthony himself has spent countless hours living inside of this 'inhumane'[2] cell house, as have many of my other students in the Northwestern Prison Education Program, and it is a deeply meaningful and compelling image for a book that, at its core, is about the abuse of power and control. I am immeasurably grateful to Anthony for his vision, artistry, generosity, and kindness in creating this cover design.

My former graduate student, and current colleague and dear friend, Lauren Leydon-Hardy, has spent countless hours on the phone with me over the years discussing issues at the intersection of epistemic agency and injustice while we each walk our dogs in different states. Lauren not only finishes some of my sentences better than I can myself, she is also a constant reminder of how to do philosophy with unflinching integrity, zeal, and purpose.

From my earliest days at Brown, when he was my teacher and advisor, to the present day as my treasured friend, Ernie Sosa has always been my North Star, guiding me toward a life in philosophy that weaves together one's personal and professional values by doing so himself. He is a model of selflessness, wisdom, and grace, and it is doubtful that I would have been in a position to write this book had I not been gifted with Ernie's presence all of these years.

My brilliant and compassionate daughters, Isabella and Catherine Reed, enrich my life beyond words and inspire me every day with their unwavering commitment to a world that is more just, more truthful, and more hopeful. I am especially grateful to Isabella for her seemingly endless empathy, awe-inspiring levels of courage, and irrepressible joy; and to Catherine for her bold authenticity, depth of heart, and boundless creativity.

As with everything in my life, my greatest debt is to my husband, Baron Reed—my fiercest champion, most constructive critic, deepest intellectual companion, truest friend, and unrivaled love. When Baron and I met in graduate school, we would often be so engrossed talking with one another that we would be startled to hear birds chirping outside, realizing that we had stayed up all night lost in conversation. I may need more sleep now than I did then, but there is still no other person on Earth with whom I would rather create, exchange, and develop ideas. Baron invariably sees the best version of what you are grasping for and generously and patiently talks with you until you see it yourself. But even more importantly, Baron sees the best version of who you are and with

[1] https://www.injusticewatch.org/news/prisons-and-jails/2020/stateville-roundhouse-covid/.
[2] https://www.injusticewatch.org/news/prisons-and-jails/2020/stateville-roundhouse-covid/.

astonishing vision and steadiness, walks with you as you become that person. Neither the Northwestern Prison Education Program, nor this book, would have been possible without my soul-nurturing partnership with Baron, the 'greatest surprise of my life.'

Finally, the source of all of the love and hope and dreams that led me to launch the Northwestern Prison Education Program, which ultimately put me in contact with the extraordinary students who inspired this book, is my beloved mother, Janice Nora Lackey (1940–2012). One of the most indelible marks my mother left on me is a profound appreciation of the unparalleled power of education. Some of my earliest memories as a child are of spending long hours playing with my sister in the courtyard of our local community college while my mom sat through classes and took exams. She was a single mother, working multiple jobs and raising three children entirely on her own, yet she filled our kitchen with conversations about the works of Jane Austen and Sigmund Freud and Thomas Hardy. I was around 11 years old when she walked me through *Tess of the d'Urbervilles*, chapter by chapter, as she read it in one of her literature classes. I watched her give up sleep to obtain an associate and then a bachelor's degree, and I witnessed her navigate a world ill-equipped for and often hostile to single mothers, with superhero-levels of wisdom and courage. These early years burned into my mind a single fact about education—it is uniquely empowering. As I became an adult, I was determined to bring that power to others, and so I became an educator, first at Northwestern and now also at the Northwestern Prison Education Program. It has been 10 years since she passed away, and the cavern of grief at her loss is as deep as it was the morning she took her last breath. But I honor her memory every day by striving to love as she loved, and to live as she lived.

This book is dedicated to the remarkable students I have met in the Northwestern Prison Education Program at Stateville Correctional Center and at Logan Correctional Center. Each of you is a living, breathing realization of the audacious ambition of education. Over the years, I have watched you become poets and painters, visionaries and leaders, published authors and lovers of math and physics, policy writers and legal advocates, mentors and dreamers. I am humbled, and I am grateful, and I am in awe of who you all are. Thank you for sharing this journey with me.

Introduction

A number of years ago, I was teaching a philosophy course in a maximum-security men's prison when I met a student, Demetrius, who was serving a lengthy sentence for a crime he was convicted of committing when he was 15 years old. He had initially been brought to the police station as a witness so that he could view a lineup of suspects. But Demetrius was soon deliberately separated from his father, interrogated for 12 hours by multiple white police officers without the presence of counsel, and ultimately coerced into confessing that he had murdered an elderly woman in a carjacking. Once he was reunited with his father, Demetrius recanted his confession. Nevertheless, and despite the lack of physical evidence connecting him to the crimes, Demetrius was convicted of the carjacking and murder, and he was sentenced to 80 years in prison—almost entirely on the basis of the false confession that was extracted from him by his interrogators.

I am a social epistemologist—I examine questions and issues that lie at the intersection of knowledge and the social world. And yet, after hearing Demetrius's story, I was struck by the fact that the tools of contemporary epistemology had absolutely nothing to say about the distinctively epistemic way in which the treatment of his confession by the criminal legal system wronged him. In particular, Demetrius's confession was not only extracted from him using interrogation techniques that are manipulative, deceptive, and coercive, he was then regarded as a truthteller or a giver of knowledge regarding the question of his guilt only under such conditions, despite his immediate and continued recantation. Moreover, what happened to Demetrius is neither anomalous nor unique to confessions. Indeed, at many layers of the criminal legal system in the United States, testimony is extracted from individuals through processes that compromise their epistemic agency and is then unreasonably regarded as representing the testifiers' truest or most reliable selves.

In this book, I aim to fill the gap in the current literature by identifying, naming, and developing the distinctively epistemic wrong perpetrated against Demetrius and so many others like him who are trapped in the United States criminal legal system. In particular, I show that a speaker is the victim of what I call *agential testimonial injustice* when testimony is *extracted* from him in a way that bypasses, exploits, or subverts his epistemic agency and is then given an unwarranted *excess* of credibility.

Epistemic agency is commonly understood as grounded in a subject's responsiveness to reasons or evidence. If you come to believe that the death penalty

Criminal Testimonial Injustice. Jennifer Lackey, Oxford University Press. © Jennifer Lackey 2023.
DOI: 10.1093/oso/9780192864109.003.0001

should be abolished because I present compelling arguments on behalf of this conclusion that you appreciate, then I have respected your epistemic agency in bringing about this result. In contrast, if I hack into your social media accounts and inundate your feeds with anti-death penalty propaganda to elicit this belief, then I have bypassed or subverted your epistemic agency. I am not engaging with you as a rational agent who can recognize and respond to the force of reasons, but rather, I am treating you as a puppet whose psychology can be shaped and molded according to my aims.

While talk of epistemic agency in relation to beliefs is not new, what I show in this book is that similar considerations can be extended to speech, especially to testimony offered in the criminal legal system. In particular, epistemic agency is exercised with respect to a person's *testimony* when it is responsive to reasons or evidence. If you admit guilt for harming a person because I present reasons that you find persuasive about the power of restorative justice, then I have appealed to your epistemic agency to elicit this speech. In contrast, if I get you to admit guilt for a harm that you didn't inflict through threats of incarceration and separation from your children, then I have exploited or undermined your epistemic agency. I am treating you as a mere epistemic means to my desired end rather than as an epistemic end in yourself. I want you to say certain words, perhaps to acquire evidence to press charges or to affirm a conviction at a parole hearing, and you're not regarded as a knower whose autonomy and dignity deserve to be respected, but as a source of epistemic outputs that I can exploit and use.[1]

I should say at the outset, however, that I will talk about the epistemic wrongs identified in this book being the result of brute state power but will not be here engaging in the further task of analyzing the underlying aims or interests of this power, such as the carceral state being a vehicle for the preservation of white supremacy and racial oppression. My intervention is more limited in scope: as a social epistemologist, I will focus specifically on the development and application of agential testimonial injustice within the criminal legal system, and while I frequently talk about prejudices and biases fueling particular instances of extracted speech, readers are encouraged to consult the vast body of literature by scholars who have provided powerful general analyses of the history and racist politics of mass incarceration in the United States.

Philosophers have devoted a considerable amount of attention in recent years to a form of testimonial injustice that is quite different from the one at issue in this book. According to this view,[2] a speaker is a victim of testimonial injustice when she is afforded a deficit of credibility in virtue of a hearer's bias or prejudice that targets her social identity. For instance, if a police officer rejects a woman's

[1] While I will focus in this book on speech that has been extracted, similar considerations apply to silence, such as when a victim's silence about the domestic violence she suffers is extracted by threats from her abuser. I will discuss this further in Chapter 5.

[2] See Fricker (2007).

report of sexual assault because his sexism leads to him discrediting her, this would be a clear instance of testimonial injustice. In particular, the police officer's sexist beliefs manifest as a prejudice that targets the victim's gender identity in a way that results in her testimony being regarded as less credible than the evidence supports. When a speaker is the victim of this sort of *prejudicial testimonial injustice*, she is said to be epistemically wronged in being unfairly denied what she is owed as a knower.

There is, however, a deep and important sense in which prejudicial testimonial injustice is understood as fundamentally involving an absence, one that is often marked by passivity or neglect. It is a failure to not believe that someone is as credible as she in fact is, which is driven, at least in most cases, by epistemic inaction. And speakers are passive victims in the testimonial exchanges in question, with no role—not even of unjust complicity—in the perpetration of testimonial injustice.

In the chapters that follow, I show that there is a radically different kind of testimonial injustice, one that is fundamentally agential in nature and is marked by overt action on both sides—a deceptive ploy by the police about incriminating evidence, for instance, and a signed false confession by the suspect, or a coercive threat by the State and a misidentification by the eyewitness. Within the criminal legal system specifically, I argue that agential testimonial injustice of this sort is the result of brute State power targeting the epistemic agency of its citizens, extracting false testimony that is often life-shattering, and, in so doing, rendering the victims in question complicit in their own undoing. Through a detailed analysis that draws on work across philosophy, the law, and social psychology, I argue that the State treats the accounts given by these testifiers under conditions devoid of, or with diminished, epistemic agency as representing their truest selves, even when the very same testifiers deny those accounts in non-extracted statements. Thus, despite the fact that these various kinds of testimony play distinct roles in the legal system, I show that they are all susceptible to a single fundamental problem: our failure to properly recognize and then respect the agential capacities of the persons whose testimony is drawn into the workings of the criminal legal system. By the end, it will be clear that this distinctive epistemic wrong is not only perpetrated across the United States criminal legal system from the very beginning of the process in interrogation rooms to its final stages in front of parole boards, but also that it is done in ways that are widespread, alarming, and pernicious. Hence the title of this book—*criminal* testimonial injustice.

Another dimension of prejudicial testimonial injustice is that an excess of credibility cannot give rise to this epistemic wrong. If a speaker is regarded as more credible than the evidence supports, she is said to be unfairly burdened with epistemic labor, or may become arrogant or close-minded, but these are long-term or downstream effects. Being regarded as more reliable, truth-giving, or knowledgeable than you in fact are does not by itself wrong you as an epistemic agent.

In contrast, I show in this book that there are multiple ways in which an unwarranted excess of credibility systematically results in agential testimonial injustice. It is, for instance, not just that false confessions are coerced out of suspects or that misidentifications are manipulated out of witnesses—it is also that such testimony then plays a massively oversized evidential role in criminal proceedings, grounding convictions even in the face of powerful counterevidence. Moreover, recantations offered by these very same speakers under conditions where their epistemic agency is *not* compromised are met with incredulity and derision. The excess of credibility afforded to this extracted testimony, then, results in a distinctive kind of epistemic wrong.

This extraction of testimony and excess of credibility afforded to it also undermine what is arguably one of the central aims of the criminal legal system itself: the truth. Ronald J. Allen and Alex Stein, for instance, note the 'simple... observation' that '[t]he coin of the legal realm is truth. Factfinders (judges or jurors) operating in that realm... try to get to the truth itself' (2013, p. 567). In a similar spirit, Thomas Weigend maintains that 'the criminal process is about truth' (2011, p. 389) and Kenneth S. Klein talks about the 'truth-finding function of trial courts.' This is repeatedly found in case law as well. In *Nix v. Whiteside*, the 'very nature of a trial' is said to be 'a search for truth' (*Nix v. Whiteside*, 475 U.S. 157, 166 (1986)) and according to *Tehan v. Scott*, 'the basic purpose of a trial is the determination of truth' (*Tehan v. Shott*, 382 U.S. 406, 416 (1966)). Indeed, even when other aims of the criminal legal system are taken to be more fundamental, such as conflict resolution or the restoration of peace, truth is still of central importance. As Weigend notes, 'To reach any of its goals, the [criminal legal] process must reflect an honest effort to determine what "really happened".... [A] successful restoration of "social peace"... [for instance] presupposes that the relevant facts have plausibly been established; society cannot close the file on a disturbing incident unless convincing factual findings have been made by an agency with authority to do so' (2011, p. 390).

What we will see in the coming chapters, however, is that *extracted testimony is unreliable testimony*. Backed into a corner, threatened with the death penalty, more time in prison, or the loss of one's children, desperate and terrified, people will say just about anything. Suspects will falsely confess to even the most violent actions, eyewitnesses will confidently point to someone whom they know did not pull the trigger, innocent defendants will plead guilty to unimaginable crimes, victims will recant reports of life-altering assaults and violations, and those who are convicted will express profound remorse for things they simply did not do and apologize to victims they did not victimize. Even if the criminal legal system disregards concerns about subverting the epistemic agency, autonomy, and dignity of its citizens, and the colossal injustices that thereby follow, the fact that the manipulative, deceptive, and coercive tactics being employed are systematically leading courts away from the ultimate aim of truth should be profoundly alarming.

In addition, we will see that the epistemic problems do not end with extraction. The excess of credibility that is afforded to false testimony not only causes a host of further attacks on epistemic agency, but also leads to a deeper entrenchment of distance from the truth. Recantations from those who have falsely confessed, or misidentified defendants, or pleaded guilty are met with wholesale rejection, which leads to ignoring exculpatory evidence, a failure to investigate other suspects, and the perpetuation of wrongful convictions. Accurate reports of assault are ignored in favor of false retractions that are often elicited by the abusers themselves, resulting in the erroneous vilification and even prosecution of victims. Shorter sentences and parole are granted to those who express remorse and apologize to victims, even when they are in fact entirely innocent themselves, which in turn bolsters misguided confidence in the track record of the criminal legal system. If one of the central goals of the criminal legal system is truth, then we should care about eradicating agential testimonial injustice.

Nevertheless, while I frequently focus on cases of innocence in this book, it is important to note that agential testimonial injustice can also be perpetrated against those whose testimony is true. Bypassing or undermining a person's epistemic agency, and then regarding him as a truthteller only under such conditions, fails to respect the epistemic autonomy and dignity that all persons—regardless of guilt—deserve. Even if a defendant in fact pulled the trigger, for instance, unfairly threatening to arrest his wife or take his children away unless he confesses is still to fail to treat him epistemically as he ought to be. Of course, extracting false speech may involve a greater violation than happens with extracted true speech, and it certainly often brings with it a host of additional horrific injustices, such as wrongful convictions and years of incarceration. But what I show in this book is that agential testimonial injustice is a distinct, and previously unrecognized, epistemic wrong perpetrated across the criminal legal system against the innocent and the guilty alike. For this reason, even though I will highlight various relevant unjust outcomes, such as being wrongfully convicted because of a coerced false confession, my main focus will be the attack on epistemic agency itself.

The book is divided into six chapters and a conclusion. One of the core components of the concept of agential testimonial injustice is that speakers are given an excess of credibility, so it is helpful to have a sense of what a sufficient amount of credibility involves. I begin, then, in Chapter 1, with a discussion of how to best understand proper assessments of credibility. I raise several objections to the standard norm of credibility assessments operative in the philosophical literature, arguing that testimonial injustice can involve both distributive and normative dimensions. In particular, I show that credibility assessments must be both relational—including not only the speaker in question but also the other members of the relevant conversational contexts—and temporally non-local—taking into account not only evidence that hearers have but also evidence that they should have. While these conclusions will be broadly relevant to the arguments in the remaining five chapters of this book—and I will flag when the material here applies to the phenomena in the criminal legal system—one of the main functions of this is to show that even when the standard conception of testimonial injustice is significantly expanded and revised in these ways, there is a fundamentally distinct notion left entirely unexplained. This will provide the theoretical motivation for the introduction of the concept of agential testimonial injustice, which will be developed in the remaining chapters.[3] Specifically, I offer a close, interdisciplinary analysis of a broad range of phenomena in the criminal legal system where the perpetration of agential testimonial injustice is most vivid: confessions, eyewitness testimony, guilty pleas, recantations from sexual assault and domestic violence survivors, and admissions of guilt and expressions of remorse at sentencing hearings and to parole boards. I argue that work in criminal law and social psychology on these issues makes clear the importance of radically expanding the discussion of testimonial injustice in philosophy to include an entirely new kind that focuses on epistemic agency. At the same time, I show that this expanded philosophical framework makes a valuable contribution to criminal law and social psychology by providing essential normative tools for understanding some of the distinctive epistemic wrongs at work in criminal proceedings in the United States.

I then turn, in Chapter 2, to confessions, which have long been regarded in the criminal legal system as the 'gold standard' in evidence. Despite this, interrogators in the United States systematically use tactics that are manipulative, deceptive, and coercive, leaving suspects desperate, confused, vulnerable, and ultimately willing to falsely confess to even the most unimaginable crimes. While there are many obvious wrongs suffered by those who falsely confess, I show in this book that they also face the unique and previously unrecognized epistemic wrong of agential testimonial injustice. In particular, after false confessions are extracted from innocent suspects and defendants, they play a massively oversized role evidentially in the criminal proceedings that follow. Indeed, 'the introduction of a confession makes the other aspects of a trial in court superfluous, and the real trial, for all practical purposes, occurs when the confession is obtained' (*Colorado v. Connelly*, 479 U.S. 157, 182 (1986)). For instance, unlike a fingerprint or a shell casing, a confession often leads the police to regard a case as solved, thereby closing the investigation and increasing the likelihood of overlooking exculpatory evidence. Recantations from innocent suspects and defendants are met with incredulity and dismissal, further exacerbating not only an attack on their agency, but also the unwarranted excess of credibility afforded to their original confessions. I ultimately show that there is an instructive parallel between practices in ancient Athens and Rome and our own criminal legal system: just as Athenian and Roman courts regarded the testimony of enslaved persons as reliable only when obtained via torture—and thereby offered under conditions devoid of epistemic agency—so, too, do our courts privilege the testimony of confessing

[3] This first chapter engages in some detail with the philosophical analysis of the concept of testimonial injustice and can be skipped for those who are more interested in the development of agential testimonial injustice and its application to the United States criminal legal system.

selves, even when confessions are extracted through interrogation techniques that compromise or undermine their epistemic agency.

Eyewitness testimony is a powerful form of evidence, and this is especially true in the United States criminal legal system. At the same time, eyewitness misidentification is the greatest contributing factor to wrongful convictions proven by DNA testing. In Chapter 3, I offer a close examination of this tension between the enormous epistemic weight that eyewitness testimony is afforded in criminal proceedings and the fact that there are important questions about its reliability as a source of evidence. I argue that lineups and interrogations often function by way of extracting testimony from an eyewitness through practices that are manipulative, deceptive, or coercive. I then show that this extracted testimony is systematically afforded an unwarranted excess of credibility that leads to not only life-altering wrongs perpetrated against suspects and defendants, but also to the eyewitnesses themselves being victims of agential testimonial injustice. I conclude that since much of the testimony of eyewitnesses is both extracted and given an excess of credibility, there is a fairly widespread form of epistemic injustice being inflicted upon testifiers in the United States criminal legal system. This calls for reforms along both dimensions—the use of lineups and interrogations should respect a witness's epistemic agency, rather than bypassing, exploiting, or undermining it, and the weight of the resulting testimony should be viewed in the broader context of its significant fallibility.

In Chapter 4, I turn to plea deals. Despite the powerful and lasting images of the courtroom in the criminal legal system, the reality is that convictions in the United States are rarely the result of trial by jury, with 97.4% of federal felony convictions obtained through guilty pleas[4] and the rate of state felony convictions not far behind.[5] The aim of this chapter is to take a close look at the normative status of plea deals in the criminal legal system, with particular attention paid to the plea-bargaining process. I begin with the widely cited criticism that plea deals are coercive. Despite the frequency with which this worry is expressed, it is rare to see it situated within a deeper understanding of what makes a process coercive in the first place, and so I start with how to best understand coercion. After raising objections to existing accounts, I develop and defend a new view according to which coercion involves an unfair offer or threat that closes a person out of a reasonable decision-making space. I then apply this notion to the practices in the American criminal legal system, showing that plea bargaining very often involves the extraction of guilty pleas that are not only coercive but also manipulative and deceptive. Indeed, guilty pleas are usually not the result of anything that can rightly be called a 'deal,' but are instead the product of the wielding of state power

[4] United States Sentencing Commission, 2019 Sourcebook of Federal Sentencing Statistics, https://www.ussc.gov/research/sourcebook-2019.

[5] See Rakoff (2014).

that leaves defendants cornered, desperate, and in the dark, leading even innocent people to accept plea deals rather than face the alternatives. American plea bargaining thus involves a form of systemic testimonial injustice perpetrated against its citizens, often with life-altering consequences, that not only takes place on a massive scale, but is also state-sanctioned.

In Chapter 5, I take a close look at the way biases, prejudices, and myths about race and gender cause, fuel, and exacerbate agential testimonial injustice, leading to a multi-directional attack on the credibility of some of the most vulnerable defendants, witnesses, and victims in the American criminal legal system. According to this 'multi-directional model,' credibility assessments wrong testifiers in a multitude of directions and a variety of ways, all of which can be magnified by other factors at both the intrapersonal and interpersonal levels, such as myths and prejudices that target social identities, other biases, and the content of the testimony in question. For instance, the epistemic status of testimony is inflated when suspects confess to a crime and when eyewitnesses identify a suspect but deflated when they recant. Conversely, the credibility of statements of victims of sexual violence is discounted when they report being sexually assaulted, but elevated when they recant. These excesses and deficits are magnified, redirected, or even turned on their heads as social identities are added. The excess of credibility afforded to a confession or an eyewitness identification, for instance, can be even greater when the confessor or suspect is Black, and greater still when the victim is white. The discounting of the testimony of victims of sexual violence can be even greater when the victim is a Black woman but can be entirely redirected into a massive excess of credibility when the victim is white and the suspect is a Black man. Moreover, when deeply entrenched racist and sexist myths and prejudices are operative in the assessments of credibility, then conditions are ideal for confirmation bias and tunnel vision to be operative. What we have, then, is not a linear regression of deficits leading to ever-increasing discounting of credibility, but a multi-directional attack that twists and turns and, in so doing, maximizes the epistemic wrongs perpetrated within the criminal legal system, especially against the most vulnerable suspects, defendants, witnesses, and victims.

In Chapter 6, I turn to the final stages of the criminal legal process and show how admissions of guilt and expressions of remorse are extracted from those who are innocent at sentencing hearings and in front of parole boards.

The right of allocution, which permits a criminal defendant to speak at his own sentencing hearing prior to the sentencing itself, may be thought to provide defendants with a robust role to play in their own destinies. But the reality is that defendants are told not only what *not* to say at such hearings, but also what *to* say and *how* to say it, and failure to comply with these expectations will result in more time behind bars. In particular, courts do not want to hear allocution stories of innocence presented as a mitigating factor, even when defendants are in fact innocent, and defendants are expected to follow a script in which they admit guilt, apologize to the victim, and display an understanding of the seriousness of the crime, all while expressing an appropriate amount of remorse. Given how high the stakes are, especially in light of the dehumanizing conditions of American prisons, even innocent defendants can be backed into a corner in which the only real option seems to be admitting guilt for a crime they did not commit in order to avoid additional years of imprisonment. Moreover, once admissions of guilt, expressions of remorse, and apologies are extracted from defendants, they then play a normatively oversized role in sentencing. Indeed, the uttering of a string of words that are false, feigned, and coerced frequently result in a shorter sentence while a true insistence of innocence leads to a lengthier one.

Similar issues arise at parole hearings, where assertions of innocence and the failure to admit guilt and express remorse are significant barriers to being granted parole. Indeed, those who are innocent are often left with no path toward freedom except for taking responsibility for a crime that they didn't commit and apologizing to a victim and community whom they didn't harm. This reveals two sides of the same credibility coin, so to speak. Given that assertions of innocence at parole hearings are so undermining of the aim to be released, they should be given far more weight as evidence of actual innocence than they in fact are. The flip side of this deficit of credibility afforded to declarations of innocence is an excess of credibility given to admissions of guilt and remorse. When such an admission is bestowed with the power to be the sole factor standing between incarceration and freedom, its normative status is massively inflated, both epistemically and morally. In particular, despite professing innocence countless times, often for decades, including at the original trial, one admission of guilt—in the context of knowing full well that this is a quid pro quo for release—is taken to finally reflect the person's true, authentic self and to repair the fractured relationships in the community.

I conclude the book by showing that an attack on epistemic agency is therewith an attack on autonomy, dignity, and ultimately on personhood. Suspects, defendants, witnesses, and victims who find their words, actions, and even feelings subjugated to the will of the State are not only wronged as epistemic agents, they are significantly violated as persons.

We are living in a moment that is suffused with a growing recognition of the pain of historical injustices and a national reckoning with their present-day manifestations. It is a time when outrage, despair, and hope are mixed in uncertain proportions, as we struggle toward a better, more just world. Progress will come only if we are able to see, name, and grasp the full scope of the wrongs being inflicted upon one another, especially when they are targeting those who are most vulnerable. In uncovering one of the central epistemic pathologies ravaging innocent victims in the United States criminal legal system, I hope to make progress toward understanding what it would mean to form and cultivate a community in which the epistemic agency of all members is able to truly flourish.

1
Credibility and Testimonial Injustice

When someone tells us something, it might involve matters as mundane as how to get to a grocery store or that they own a cat and as urgent as whether they were assaulted or committed the murder in question. Whether we believe what we are told depends, in large part, on how credible we take the speaker to be. Assessing people's credibility is found in just about every corner of our existence, from navigating the world to making decisions that are quite literally the difference between life and death.

One of the central components of the concept of agential testimonial injustice is that speakers are given an excess of credibility. Given this, we might ask at the outset how to best understand proper assessments of credibility. Otherwise put, what is the norm governing our evaluations of the credibility of others?

I will devote the remainder of this chapter to exploring this question in some detail, especially in the context of the conception of prejudicial testimonial injustice. The reason for this is twofold. First, it will be helpful to have a deeper understanding of what a *proper* assessment of a speaker's credibility requires in order to grasp what it means for there to be an *improper* one. More precisely, if agential testimonial injustice entails affording a speaker an excess of credibility, then we ought to have a sense of what a sufficient amount of credibility involves. Second, I will raise several objections in what follows to the standard norm of credibility assessments operative in the philosophical literature. While this will be broadly relevant to the arguments in the remaining five chapters of this book—and I will flag when the material here applies to the phenomena in the criminal legal system—one of the central functions of this is to show that even when the standard view is significantly expanded and revised, there is a fundamentally distinct notion of testimonial injustice left entirely unexplained. This will provide the theoretical motivation for the introduction of the concept of agential testimonial injustice, which will then be applied to the criminal legal system in Chapters 2–6.

1. Credibility

With these points in mind, let's begin with Miranda Fricker's view, according to which 'there is no puzzle about the fair distribution of credibility, for credibility is a concept that wears its proper distribution on its sleeve. Epistemological nuance aside, the hearer's obligation is obvious: she must match the level of credibility she

Criminal Testimonial Injustice. Jennifer Lackey, Oxford University Press. © Jennifer Lackey 2023.
DOI: 10.1093/oso/9780192864109.003.0002

attributes to her interlocutor to the evidence that he is offering the truth' (2007, p. 19). On Fricker's view, a broadly evidentialist norm governs our assessments of the credibility of others[1] and, moreover, she closely links failure to satisfy this norm with the widely discussed notion of testimonial injustice: '[a] speaker sustains... testimonial injustice if and only if she receives a credibility deficit owing to identity prejudice in the hearer; so the central case of testimonial injustice is identity-prejudicial credibility deficit' (2007, p. 28).[2] A speaker suffers a credibility deficit when the credibility that she is given by a hearer is less than the evidence that she is offering the truth warrants, and a hearer has the relevant kind of identity prejudice when she has a prejudice against the speaker in virtue of the latter's membership in a social group. Prejudice here is being understood in terms of not being properly responsive to evidence. A prejudicial stereotype, for instance, is a generalization about a social group that fails to be sufficiently sensitive to relevant evidence. Where this prejudice 'tracks' the subject through different dimensions of social activity—economic, educational, professional, and so on—it is systematic, and the type of prejudice that tracks people in this way is related to social identity, such as racial and gender identity. Fricker argues, then, that when a hearer violates the evidentialist norm by giving a speaker a credibility deficit in virtue of, say, her race, the speaker is wronged 'in her capacity as a knower,' and is thereby the victim of testimonial injustice. What this means is that a speaker is also in the epistemic clear when she satisfies the evidentialist norm of credibility, at least with respect to committing an act of, and a hearer suffering an instance of, testimonial injustice.

There are, however, at least two different readings of this evidentialist norm that should be distinguished. On the one hand, it might be understood *categorically*: for every speaker and hearer, the hearer should match the credibility judgment of the speaker to the evidence that she is offering the truth. According to this categorical reading, hearers are required not only to have their credibility judgments of speakers track the available evidence, but also to make such judgments in the first place. The problem, though, is that this demands too much, as there are many instances in which hearers need not have any beliefs at all about the credibility of speakers. As I walk down the street, I have no obligation—epistemic or moral—to judge the credibility of all of the random passersby that I overhear, nor am I required to form beliefs about the reliability of every source on the internet that comes across my computer screen. This is even clearer when one's attention is better focused on activities of greater epistemic and moral value. A surgeon, for instance, need not assess the credibility of nurses talking about the

[1] For different answers to this question, though ones unlike that defended in this chapter, see Jones (2002) and Maitra (2010).

[2] I should mention that Fricker goes on in her (2007) to develop a more broadly virtue-theoretic epistemological framework.

weather while she is removing her patient's appendix. In all of these cases, hearers aren't failing in any of their truth-related aims, nor are they harming speakers by their actions. This shows that an entirely categorical reading of the norm of credibility is untenable.

Given this, perhaps it is best to understand the norm *conditionally* in the following way: for every speaker and hearer, if a hearer makes a credibility assessment of a speaker, then the hearer should match the credibility judgment of the speaker to the evidence that she is offering the truth. Unlike the categorical reading, this version requires that credibility assessments of speakers track the available evidence only when hearers form the relevant beliefs, thereby permitting the complete absence of such assessments in the first place. Otherwise put, it is only when one forms a belief about the reliability of a speaker that one is required to have it match the available evidence. This clearly avoids the objection facing the categorical norm that it requires too much of hearers. The problem here, however, is that this conditional version of the norm demands too little, as there are many cases in which hearers fail to form beliefs about the credibility of speakers when they ought to—epistemically and/or morally. For instance, suppose that a group of scientists is collaborating on a research project, but the men don't form any beliefs at all about the reliability of their women co-workers because they have no intention of relying on their testimony. This is due to a deep-rooted though unconscious sexism to which all of the men subscribe. As a result, they not only miss out on crucial data that would dramatically alter their beliefs about the scientific results, they also harm the women by unjustly blocking their participation in the research. Here it is clear that the men have failed to fulfill both epistemic and moral obligations, despite their satisfaction of the conditional norm. In particular, they do not consider evidence that they should have—namely, the testimony of the women scientists—and they fail to regard their co-workers as even possible contributors to the domain of inquiry, which clearly wrongs the women in their capacity as knowers.

Indeed, it is arguable that the most pernicious forms of testimonial injustice result from failures to make credibility assessments in the first place. Suppose that members of a despised racial group are regarded by some as being so outside the realm of personhood and agency that they are not even appropriate candidates for such assessments. The problem here is not that they are afforded credibility deficits, even massive ones, but that they are regarded as lying outside the realm of knowers altogether. This shows that an entirely conditional reading of the norm of credibility is indefensible.

The upshot of these considerations is that concealed in the evidentialist norm of credibility are two distinct norms, both of which are important. For not only are there epistemic and moral wrongs that come with failing to match our credibility assessments of hearers to the evidence, so, too, are there such wrongs with failing to make such credibility assessments in the first place. This same point might be expressed in terms of the questions that need to be asked: not only do we need to ask what should ground our judgments of speakers' credibility when we make them, we also need to ask when we are required to make such judgments at all. Thus, a complete account of our obligations as consumers of testimony, and the corresponding injustices that follow with our flouting them, needs to flesh out both the categorical and the conditional readings of the norm of credibility.

Given the central scope of this book, however, I will restrict my attention to the conditional reading of the evidentialist norm, according to which hearers ought to make credibility judgments of speakers that match the available evidence, should they make such judgments.[3] Assuming that a hearer satisfies both dimensions of this norm, it is said to follow that (i) the hearer is not subject to epistemic criticism, (ii) the hearer is not wronging the speaker in her capacity as a knower, and (iii) the speaker thereby does not sustain testimonial injustice. In what follows, I will show that this is wrong in a number of different ways.

2. Hearer-Excess Testimonial Injustice

Consider, again, a group of scientists collaborating on a research project, though instead of the men failing to form any relevant beliefs about the reliability of their women co-workers, suppose they appropriately judge them in accordance with the evidence. Since the evidence indicates that all of the women are highly credible in the domain in question, the men form the corresponding beliefs that they are reliable sources.

Despite this, suppose that the men do not accept any of the testimony offered by their female co-workers. This is because while they take the women to be reliable with respect to what they are reporting, the men are sexists and, as a result, always illegitimately take themselves to be *more* reliable than women. More precisely, while the men give the women the right level of credibility—that is, the amount that they are due, given the evidence—they invariably give themselves a *credibility excess* relative to women, despite there being no evidence to support this. There are at least two different ways in which this credibility excess might affect the men's beliefs, despite their appropriate credibility judgments. First, while they might take the women to be reliable in the domain in question[4] and they might have no beliefs to the contrary, their inflated senses of self might make them regard it as outrageous that the women could know something that they don't. Second, the men might take the women to be reliable in the domain in

[3] I will drop 'conditional' in what follows. Since this will not be my focus, I will also assume that the hearers in question are making judgments of speakers' credibility when they should be.

[4] Of course, reliability is not the same as infallibility, so it is possible to regard someone as reliable even in a very narrow domain and yet still consistently reject even a number of her reports.

question, but they might be antecedently committed for no good reason to a belief that conflicts with what the women report. Given that the men are ignoring relevant evidence in the formation of their beliefs, they clearly are violating an epistemic norm. Moreover, since the women are not believed when offering testimony because of the men's sexist attitudes, they are wronged by the men in their capacity as knowers and are thereby the victims of testimonial injustice. While the men undeniably satisfy the evidentialist norm of credibility, then, (i)–(iii) are nonetheless false. This shows that the satisfaction of this norm is clearly inadequate at rendering hearers in the epistemic clear when it comes to testimonial injustice.

It is worth pausing here to reflect on the notion of credibility excess in greater detail, especially as it relates to testimonial injustice. It is standard to think of injustices targeting groups as always grounded in certain kinds of unwarranted dispositions or beliefs about the *deficiencies* of their members. Indeed, this is at the very heart of Fricker's notion of testimonial injustice, which she understands as necessarily involving 'a credibility *deficit* owing to identity prejudice in the hearer' (2007, p. 28, emphasis added). But what we have seen is that there can be testimonial injustices when, rather than the speaker suffering a deficit, the hearer receives an illegitimate *excess* relative to the speaker. For the sake of ease of expression, let's call these two different forms of testimonial injustice *speaker-deficit* and *hearer-excess*, respectively. Though I have never seen a discussion of the latter phenomenon in this context, it has important consequences, not only for our understanding of the norms governing credibility assessments, but also for the epistemic impact of violating them.[5]

To see this, notice that, typically, when we judge someone to be reliable on a topic, we are inclined to believe her testimony on this topic. This is most likely why discussions of testimonial injustice have focused exclusively on the assessment of speakers: if I judge you to be a reliable epistemic source based on the available evidence, then the appropriate belief should simply come along for the ride. Hearer-excess testimonial injustice, however, provides a clear way to drive a wedge between such a judgment and the corresponding acceptance of testimony. Indeed, in the case described above, the sexist scientists invariably regard themselves as more reliable than women, and hence the disconnect between their credibility judgments of the women and the corresponding acceptance of their testimony is *systematic*. That this is not only a case of testimonial injustice but paradigmatically so should be clear, as a failure to be believed, even if given the proper degree of credibility, surely harms speakers epistemically, especially when

[5] José Medina (2011) has insightful and compelling work on credibility excesses, but he does not discuss them specifically in relation to hearers themselves, which I regard as one of the most important forms of such excesses. Davis (2016) also discusses how credibility excesses can lead to testimonial injustice, but she focuses on phenomena such as typecasting and compulsory representation.

it is systematic. In fact, it is arguable that a credibility deficit with testimonial acceptance is, in many ways, less harmful than an appropriate credibility assessment without testimonial acceptance. This is even clearer as the stakes go up: if you are not believed when you report that you're suicidal, or have been raped, or are innocent of the crime in question, then the harms that may come to you are many and severe, no matter my satisfaction of the norm of credibility. This omission from the norm governing testimonial acceptance and, therewith, from the account of testimonial injustice is, then, no small oversight.

Notice, too, that it won't do for the norm of credibility to require not only the proper credibility assessment of speakers, but also the corresponding attitudes. In particular, it is not enough to modify the evidentialist norm as follows: for every speaker and hearer, if a hearer makes a credibility assessment of a speaker, then the hearer should match the credibility judgment of the speaker to the evidence that she is offering the truth and believe, disbelieve, or withhold accordingly. The reason that this norm is inadequate is because there are two separate epistemic wrongs in cases of hearer-excess testimonial injustice—the lack of acceptance with respect to the speaker's testimony and also the very credibility excess that the hearer gives to himself, especially in relation to the speaker—and yet this norm captures only the former. For instance, while the sexist male scientists discussed above violate this revised norm of credibility by virtue of failing to form beliefs on the basis of the testimony offered by their female co-workers, such a norm leaves open the possibility that it can be satisfied even when they continue to illegitimately give themselves a credibility excess.

One reason the focus in the philosophical literature might have been solely on speaker-deficit testimonial injustice is because many people are aware of implicit bias[6] and its effects. We know, for instance, that we have relatively unconscious attitudes toward members of underrepresented groups and we know that these attitudes impact our other attitudes and actions. Thus, when we reflect upon our assessments of speakers, it is natural to wonder whether implicit bias is affecting the amount of credibility we assign. But work in cognitive psychology has also drawn increased attention to our unwarranted *assessments of ourselves*. For instance, the Dunning-Kruger effect is a cognitive bias in which incompetent individuals incorrectly rate their abilities much higher than they are. This bias is attributed to a metacognitive inability of the incompetent to recognize their own incompetence—that is, a metaignorance or ignorance of ignorance.[7] This overconfidence that we have in ourselves is not only widespread and prevalent—hence the title of Dunning's piece in *Pacific Standard*, 'We Are All Confident Idiots'[8]—it is also potentially harmful in both global and local ways. According to Daniel Kahnemann, it is the bias that 'leads governments to believe that wars are quickly

[6] See, for instance, Greenwald and Krieger (2006).
[7] See Dunning and Kruger (1999).
[8] https://psmag.com/we-are-all-confident-idiots-56a60eb7febc#.s4dkyy2lr.

winnable and capital projects will come in on budget despite statistics predicting exactly the opposite,'[9] and thus, it is the one he says he would most like to eliminate if he 'had a magic wand.' But it is not difficult to see that such overconfidence is also likely to lead to hearer-excess testimonial injustice, for it is precisely a bias in favor of ourselves that lies at the heart of such a phenomenon. The Dunning-Kruger effect, then, makes clear both how prone we are to committing acts of hearer-excess testimonial injustice and how harmful such acts can be.

While Fricker doesn't consider cases of hearers giving themselves a credibility excess, she does discuss their doing so with respect to speakers and explicitly rejects that it can result in testimonial injustice, at least in the paradigmatic sense that is of interest to her. She writes:

> On the face of it, one might think that both credibility deficit and credibility excess are cases of testimonial injustice. Certainly there is a sense of 'injustice' that might naturally and quite properly be applied to cases of credibility excess, as when one might complain at the injustice of someone receiving unduly high credibility in what he said just because he spoke with a certain accent. At a stretch, this could be cast as a case of injustice as distributive unfairness—someone has got more than his fair share of a good—but that would be straining the idiom, for credibility is not a good that belongs with the distributive model of justice…those goods best suited to the distributive model are so suited principally because they are finite and at least potentially in short supply….Such goods are those for which there is, or may soon be, a certain competition, and that is what gives rise to the ethical puzzle about the justice of this or that particular distribution. By contrast, credibility is not generally finite in this way, and so there is no analogous competitive demand to invite the distributive treatment. (Fricker 2007, pp. 19–20)

Fricker grounds her denial that credibility excesses can lead to testimonial injustice in her rejection of a distributive model of credibility.[10] In particular, she argues that credibility is not finite in a way that lends itself to a distributive

[9] https://www.theguardian.com/books/2015/jul/18/daniel-kahneman-books-interview.

[10] José Medina agrees: 'Credibility is indeed not a finite good that can be in danger of becoming scarce in the same way that food and water can…' (Medina 2011, p. 19). Similarly, he writes, 'The credibility excess assigned to some can be correlated to the credibility deficits assigned to others not because credibility is a scarce good (as the distributive model wrongly assumes), but because credibility is a comparative and contrastive quality, and an excessive attribution of it involves the privileged epistemic treatment of some (the members of the comparison class, i.e., those like the recipient) and the underprivileged epistemic treatment of others (the members of the contrast class, i.e., those unlike the recipient). An excessive attribution of credibility indirectly affects others who are, implicitly, unfairly treated as enjoying comparatively less epistemic trust. In my view, this is due to a disproportion in credibility and authority assigned to members of different groups. Credibility is not a scarce good that should be distributed with equal shares, but excesses and deficits are to be assessed by comparison with what is deemed a normal epistemic subject' (Medina 2011, p. 20).

treatment. Consider, for instance, finite goods, such as wealth, land, or food. Not everyone can own 20 acres because there is only a limited amount of land to go around. For some to have a lot of it necessitates that others have a little, or none at all. But other goods don't limit one another in this way. To give moral praise to one person need not be to deny it to another. We can say equally of Abraham Lincoln, Ida B. Wells, and Martin Luther King Jr. that they are exceptional moral agents. In this way, there is an important sense in which moral praise is an infinite good: there is often enough of it to go around.

Credibility, according to Fricker, is like moral praise rather than like land: it is an infinite good. If two friends tell me about their vacations this summer, believing that one of them snorkeled in Thailand need not impact my trusting that the other went hiking in Peru. I can give them both as much credibility as I like since not only is there plenty to go around, but giving some of it to one need not take any away from the other. Because of this, it seems it isn't unjust to give someone more credibility than is owed since this doesn't deprive someone else of a good that is deserved.

This conclusion should be resisted in two different ways. The first can be seen by focusing on social identity prejudices that lead to what we might call *content-based credibility excesses*. Standard stereotypes often involve a variety of beliefs:[11] Black people are regarded as disproportionately prone to violent crime,[12] Muslims in America are feared for potential connections with terrorism,[13] and so on. Each of these stereotypes can, and often does, lead to credibility excesses that wrong speakers. According to Fricker, however, 'credibility deficit can constitute...a wrong [as a knower], but while credibility excess may (unusually) be disadvantageous in various ways, it does not undermine, insult, or otherwise withhold a proper respect for the speaker *qua* subject of knowledge; so in itself it does her no epistemic injustice, and *a fortiori* no testimonial injustice' (2007, p. 20). If a Black man is taken to be highly knowledgeable about criminal behavior because he is a Black man, then he has been wronged as a knower just as much as if he is taken to be less reliable than he ought to be about, say, the stock market. Being regarded as highly knowledgeable about domains that are stigmatized or devalued can be insulting to a speaker *qua* knower, regardless of any long-term disadvantages that might be accrued, leading to what we might call *content-based testimonial injustice*. We can, for instance, imagine the Black man who is turned to as the expert about criminal behavior reacting with horror or indignation at being regarded as knowledgeable about such a topic. This is not merely because he is worried about, say, being passed over for professional opportunities in the future because of this credibility excess, but also because he rightly finds it disrespectful with respect to his epistemic identity. Specifically, being regarded as knowledgeable in

[11] I will discuss this in far greater detail in Chapter 5.
[12] Johnson (1996) and Rand (2000).
[13] Sides and Gross (2013).

stigmatized domains can be an affront to one's epistemic dignity—it says, 'you are the sort of person who should know about *x*, where *x* is, for instance, shameful or disgraceful.' Such a credibility excess clearly undermines or withholds a proper respect for the speaker *qua* subject of knowledge.

The second way in which the conclusion that only credibility deficits lead to immediate epistemic wrongs is to be resisted is through the phenomenon of hearer-excess testimonial injustice. Let's return to the case from above: when the male scientists give themselves a credibility excess relative to the women, despite there being no evidence to support this, they are wronging the women as knowers in two immediate ways: first, they fail to give the women the epistemic standing in the community that they deserve and, second, they fail to believe the women's testimony, despite giving them the proper amount of credibility. Both of these are wrongs in themselves, even if they do not beget further long-term negative consequences for the women down the road. Let's begin with the former: even though the women get their due relative to the evidence, they do not get their due in relation to their colleagues, and one's standing in a community can be even more important to one's identity as a knower than is receiving exactly the right amount of credibility. Suppose, for instance, that the male scientists give the women a slight credibility deficit but give themselves an even greater deficit. Surely, this is less insulting or undermining to the women as knowers than is receiving their due, but always being regarded as nonetheless unworthy of belief in their community. This brings us to the latter point: not being believed can, in and of itself, be immediately and profoundly disrespectful and undermining. Indeed, following Bernard Williams and Edward Craig, many regard the very purpose of knowledge attributions to be to 'flag reliable informants,' where an informant is one who 'gives information to another.'[14] Thus, when one fails to give information to others through the total absence of testimonial acceptance, there is a deep and important sense in which one is not regarded as a knower at all. And when this failure is illegitimate, it clearly wrongs one as a knower.

3. Distributive Testimonial Injustice

While hearer-excess testimonial injustice is worth highlighting in its own right, especially as it relates to the Dunning-Kruger effect, it is in fact an instance of a broader phenomenon, which we might call *distributive testimonial injustice*.

To see this, notice that the evidentialist norms discussed earlier focus exclusively on our judgment *of a single speaker*, but leave out our evaluations not only

[14] See, for instance, Williams (1973), Craig (1990), Neta (2006), and Greco (2007). I should note that I reject this view as a general account of knowledge attributions in Lackey (2012), but I can still grant that *one* of the purposes of some knowledge attributions is to 'flag reliable informants.'

of ourselves, *but also of the other members of the conversational context or community in question*. Even if the sexist scientists we've been considering appropriately judge a female colleague's credibility and have the corresponding attitudes about her, they might still be subject to epistemic criticism if they give a credibility excess to others in virtue of their sexism. The initial epistemic failure is obvious: the scientists' beliefs about, say, their male colleagues are wildly out of sync with the evidence. So even if their beliefs about the female scientists match the evidence, their credibility assessments about the male ones do not. Moreover, this has an obvious impact on the epistemic status of their other relevant beliefs. For instance, given their credibility assessments, they almost certainly regard the male scientists as more reliable than the female ones, believe that their female colleagues are less capable than the male ones, and so on. So this initial epistemic failure begets further epistemic failures.

Moreover, even if you appropriately judge me on the basis of the available evidence and believe accordingly, if you illegitimately regard everyone else as better than I am, I am still the victim of an injustice. Indeed, if others receive a credibility excess, then a credibility deficit to me and an appropriate assessment of my credibility might be functionally equivalent. If this ungrounded asymmetrical treatment pertains specifically to our reports, then I am the victim of testimonial injustice in particular. In addition, this initial wrong leads to further wrongs. If you regard my colleague as more reliable than I am, then you will listen to him over me when we disagree, offer him rather than me professional opportunities, and so on. To distinguish this form of distributive testimonial injustice from the hearer-excess kind identified earlier, let us call this *peer-excess* testimonial injustice.

In addition, there is a further kind of distributive testimonial injustice that is worth discussing, as it is importantly different from either hearer-excess or peer-excess. I will call this type of testimonial injustice *expert-excess*.

We typically think of any extra weight that an expert's testimony might be afforded, especially in relation to a novice's, as epistemically warranted. Indeed, a certain kind or amount of epistemic deference on the part of novices might be built directly into the very notion of being regarded as an expert.[15] However, I want to suggest that there are also cases where distributive testimonial injustice arises because experts are given an unwarranted credibility excess in virtue of the very fact that they are taken to be experts. As a powerful illustration, it is worth quoting at length a passage from Deborah Tuerkheimer's (2014) book on flawed convictions resulting from 'Shaken Baby Syndrome':

> In their standard formulation, Shaken Baby Syndrome (SBS) prosecutions rested entirely on the claims of science—which meant, as a practical matter, that they

[15] See, for instance, Zagzebski (2012) and Grundmann (2021). For an opposing view, see Lackey (2018*c*).

> depended on the testimony of medical experts. Doctors came to court and explained that, notwithstanding the absence of any other signs of abuse, shaking could be proved by three neurological symptoms: bleeding beneath the outer layer of membranes surrounding the brain, bleeding in the retina, and brain swelling. The relationship between these three symptoms—'the triad'—and shaking was described as pathognomonic, meaning that shaking was the only causal explanation possible. The science could also rule out an accidental jostle, given how forceful the shaking must have been to generate these injuries. The science could even identify a perpetrator—the caregiver last with the lucid baby—since the infant's loss of consciousness would necessarily have been immediate. Remarkably, the state could present the testimony of doctors and use it alone to establish the guilt of the accused.
>
> SBS was a prosecution paradigm, a category of cases involving functionally similar facts. [Audrey] Edmunds's case fell squarely within this paradigm. Her trial took place in 1996, when SBS-changes were becoming increasingly common. The caregiver consistently maintained her innocence. No witness purported to have seen her shake the baby. There were no apparent indicia of trauma. Yet solely on the basis of expert testimony regarding the triad, Edmunds, a mother of young children, was found guilty of reckless homicide. The triad convicted her, and she was sentenced to eighteen years in prison.
>
> (Tuerkheimer 2014, pp. xi–xii)

Tuerkheimer goes on to detail how challenges to the view that the triad could be caused only by SBS first emerged in 2001, with research that shows that these three symptoms can result from non-traumatic origins, such as infection or an illness like sickle-cell anemia. In addition, doctors learned that there can be a delay of days or even hours between the time of an injury and the point at which the baby loses consciousness, thereby undermining the legitimacy of identifying a perpetrator of abuse merely by locating the lucid baby's last caregiver. Nevertheless, the criminal legal system has failed to track these developments, with previous convictions on the basis of the triad not being revisited and new cases still being prosecuted based on the debunked science.

What I want to do here, though, is highlight how SBS cases provide a powerful example of expert-excess testimonial injustice. First, it is clear that there are SBS cases where the experts are given an unwarranted credibility excess. Indeed, no matter how much evidence is stacked on the side of the defense—the defendant may consistently and steadfastly maintain her innocence, she may have years of working with children with no history of negligence or violence, there may be a multitude of character witnesses, no signs of trauma on the purportedly shaken baby, and so on—it is utterly *overwhelmed* by the testimony of a single 'expert.' Indeed, the 'expert's' testimony is taken to be so decisive that the defense mounted by the defendant's team seems doomed at the outset. In such a case, beliefs about the scientist's expertise and, therewith, about her credibility are not only insensitive to relevant evidence, they are *epistemically resilient* in the strongest sense. Short of a massive paradigm shift involving the debunking of the science, there is no amount of counterevidence that the defense could produce that would show the defendant to be innocent in the face of the triad.[16] Of course, this is not to say that expert testimony ought not be weighed heavily; instead, problems arise when such testimony screens off all other evidence and produces tunnel vision[17] where one, and only one, option is singlemindedly pursued without proper regard to the overall body of evidence.

Second, it is also likely that many of the unwarranted credibility excesses in SBS cases are the result of the social identity of the testifying scientists.[18] *Qua* experts, they are immediately afforded a massive amount of credibility, no matter how much evidence conflicts with what they report. Otherwise put, if, say, 20 pieces of exculpatory evidence are outweighed by a single piece of expert testimony, what is doing the work at least in many of the cases? The fact that the testimony is made by a purported expert. Change this feature of the cases, and have the same testimony be offered by a non-expert—even one with the same degree of reliability as the 'expert' has with respect to the proposition in question—and there almost certainly would be different verdicts. This provides reason for thinking that unwarranted credibility excesses are entirely at issue in at least some cases of SBS convictions.[19]

While I focus here on scientists, there are many different kinds of experts, and similar considerations arise in the case of authorities. For instance, unwarranted credibility excesses are often afforded to police officers and prosecutors over suspects and defendants,[20] not necessarily because of any sort of expertise, but simply in virtue of their social status as authority figures.

What distributive testimonial injustice reveals is that there is a deep and important social dimension to the norm at issue here. In particular, it cannot be applied only to my assessment of you, completely independent of other members of the relevant context, including myself. This is because it matters epistemically not only how I judge you, but also how I judge you in relation to myself and other members of your community. To think that a subject can satisfy such a norm, and

[16] I'm excluding evidence ruling out that the defendant was the last person with the lucid baby.

[17] Tunnel vision is discussed in greater detail in Chapters 2 and 5.

[18] I should make clear that my conception of social identity here is broader than Fricker's, including features like expertise in addition to race, gender, and so on. Given this, she might deny that this is an instance of testimonial injustice in her sense. Since my central purpose in this chapter is to expand the notion of testimonial injustice, rather than to specifically argue that Fricker's view is inadequate, I am less interested in showing that Fricker is wrong about having such a narrow conception of social identity and more focused on developing notions of testimonial injustice that have clear epistemological significance.

[19] There are similarly vivid cases of expertise-excess testimonial injustice involving arson. See, for instance, http://www.newyorker.com/magazine/2009/09/07/trial-by-fire.

[20] See Warren (2018) and Trivedi and Van Cleve (2020).

thereby be immune to epistemic criticism, simply by giving a single speaker an appropriate credibility rating—in isolation from the assessment of, say, her peers—is quite implausible. We are social creatures, and how we are judged in relation to others has clear epistemic significance.[21] Thus, the only way to avoid the credibility excess problem is to understand the norm governing such assessments as applying to a subject both in her assessment of herself and of other members of her community.

Distributive testimonial injustice, then, occurs, when credibility is improperly distributed among members of a conversational context or community due to prejudice. If we want to retain Fricker's emphasis on the importance of social identity, we could follow her and say that the unfair distribution has to be the result specifically of identity prejudice. I commit an act of such injustice, then, if, for instance, I give the men in my department a credibility excess because they're men, even if I give the women their due. I am the victim of distributive testimonial injustice if, for instance, all of the men in my department are given a credibility excess because they're men, even if I get my due. At the heart of this notion of testimonial injustice is that credibility assessments need to be understood *relationally*: whether my credibility assessment of you is epistemically just can only be characterized in relation to my assessments of other members of the relevant conversational context or community.

As may be recalled, Fricker flatly rejects there being a sense of testimonial injustice that can be understood along distributive lines. This is because credibility is a concept that 'wears its proper distribution on its sleeve'—which involves matching credibility assessments to the evidence—and is not finite in a way that lends itself to a distributive treatment. I have already argued against the first of these reasons, as hearer-excess testimonial injustice makes clear that simply matching assessments of speakers to the evidence is not enough. So let's consider the second reason.

Suppose, for instance, that it is somehow an objective fact that each U.S. citizen is owed a $10,000 tax break, and while Black Americans receive such a break, whites get a $20,000 one simply because of their race. Even if Black Americans are somehow getting their due in terms of tax breaks, they are still being treated unjustly as citizens by virtue of how whites are being treated. Justice requires that we look not just at what people are due narrowly, but also at the distribution of goods within the broader social structure of which they are a part. This is true of goods like tax breaks, but also with epistemic ones like credibility. Moreover, as mentioned above, when some members get more than their due of certain goods, this often begets downstream injustices. Just as whites will have greater purchasing power because of the larger tax break, so, too, men will have greater epistemic

[21] Medina (2011) makes a similar point in defending his 'proportional view of testimonial injustice,' though he arrives at this conclusion through quite different arguments.

power because of the excess in credibility. If, for instance, there is disagreement between a woman and a man, the latter will systematically be believed over the former, and so women will ultimately fail to get what they are owed in terms of credibility—it will just be via a more circuitous route.

Another area where the finitude of credibility is clearest is with respect to expertise. If everyone were an expert, the concept would lose its force, for it is only against the backdrop of there being novices or laypersons that expertise gets a foothold. Otherwise put, not everyone can be an expert, and so for some to be credited with this epistemic status is for others not to be. For instance, suppose that in the scenario we've been envisaging, only five of the scientists are to be regarded as experts on the question of their research. Given the credibility excess that the men are given, it is likely that they will also be regarded as the five experts, while the women scientists will be denied this status despite getting their 'due' with respect to the evidence. Thus, if credibility is tied to expertise, then there is only a limited amount of the former to go around, as there is only a limited amount of the latter to go around. Once again, then, any reasons stemming from the finitude of credibility for rejecting the distributive conception of testimonial injustice introduced here are misguided.

4. Normative Testimonial Injustice

I have thus far argued that the evidentialist norm of credibility assessments faces a number of problems posed by distributive testimonial injustice, where hearer-excess, peer-excess, and expert-excess testimonial injustice are particular instances of it. There is a further concern I would like to raise about this norm before turning to the criminal legal system.

To begin, notice that, according to the evidentialist norm, subjects satisfy their credibility-assessment obligations by virtue of matching their relevant beliefs to the evidence they *have in their possession*. Crucially, however, we are evaluated not only with respect to the evidence that we do have, but also in terms of the evidence that we *should have*. If my daughter tells me that she inadvertently left our cat outside overnight in the winter and appeals to the fact that she didn't know he was there to justify her actions, this ignorance alone does not get her off the epistemic hook. For instance, if it is her responsibility to make sure that he is in every night, and she simply failed to check where he was because she was texting her friends, then her belief that he was in the house last night is surely not epistemically justified. Were it to be, then we could end up with all sorts of justified beliefs simply by dramatically limiting the evidence to which we are exposed.

This concept of evidence that we should have is at the heart of the notion of what I have elsewhere called a *normative defeater*, which can be either *rebutting* or *undercutting*.[22] A normative defeater is a doubt or belief that a person ought to have that indicates that her belief is either false (i.e., rebutting) or unreliably formed or sustained (i.e., undercutting). Thus, if I believe that the animal in my backyard is a bobcat by seeing one there, I might get powerful evidence that such a belief is false by your telling me that bobcats have never lived in my state, or that my basis is a poor one by my optometrist reporting to me how much my vision has deteriorated. Even if I reject the testimony in both cases, I am still on the hook for this counterevidence if I do so for no good reason at all. Why? Because it is evidence that I should have. The justification that my bobcat-belief might have initially enjoyed, then, has been normatively defeated.

It should further be clear that some of the greatest epistemic failings come about from beliefs formed on the basis of insufficient evidence, where such a basis is the result of colossal irresponsibility. Racists, sexists, and bigots often believe in accordance with the evidence that they have in their possession precisely because they surround themselves with likeminded people and news sources that support everything they already want to believe. This limiting of the available evidence has the result that important considerations that challenge or undermine one's beliefs are deliberately excluded from one's evidential base. Surely, however, one's beliefs are not justified via this intentional ignorance, and the reason for this is that we are epistemically evaluated in terms of evidence both that we do, and that we should, have.

It might be objected that the evidentialist can accommodate these sorts of cases by arguing that the subjects in fact have relevant evidence that can capture the epistemic deficiencies in question. In particular, they have *evidence that there is evidence* that should have been gathered, and this provides them with a defeater for the target beliefs without needing to invoke the concept of normative defeat. For instance, it might be said that the reason my daughter is still on the epistemic hook in the above case is that she has evidence that there is evidence that she should have acquired; namely, despite the fact that she believes that our cat is in the house, she knows that it is her responsibility to check that he is, and yet she didn't. Thus, she has evidence that she should have had more evidence concerning the cat's specific location.[23]

By way of response, notice, first, that it isn't obvious that this response works even in the case of my daughter and the cat, which is arguably the sort of scenario for which it is best suited. Sure, if my daughter believes that the cat is in the house

[22] For discussions involving what I call normative defeaters, see BonJour (1980) and (1985), Goldman (1986), Fricker (1987) and (1994), Chisholm (1989), Burge (1993) and (1997), McDowell (1994), Audi (1997) and (1998), Williams (1999), BonJour and Sosa (2003), Hawthorne (2004), Reed (2006), Lackey (1999 and 2008) and (2020*b*), and Goldberg (2017). What all of these discussions have in common is simply the idea that evidence can defeat knowledge (justification) even when the subject does not form any corresponding doubts or beliefs from the evidence in question.

[23] I'm grateful to Kevin McCain for pressing this objection.

and also believes that she didn't check on him last night, then she clearly has evidence that there is relevant evidence that bears on her belief. But we can also imagine a case in which my daughter believes that the cat is the house and she is too distracted with her texting to remember that she failed to check on him. In such a case, the absence of the relevant memorial belief means that my daughter doesn't have evidence that there is evidence that she failed to gather. Nevertheless, her belief is nonetheless epistemically unjustified because there is *evidence that she should have.*

This point is even clearer in cases where people make life choices that severely restrict the evidence in their possession but aren't aware of all of the relevant consequences that follow from their choices. When white nationalists are surrounded by only sources that support their preferred racist views, they might be so insulated that they are unaware that there is in fact specific evidence that they have failed to gather. Of course, in a broad sense they might be aware that there is evidence 'out there' that conflicts with their beliefs. But surely this isn't sufficient for their having evidence that there is evidence that they should have since this is arguably true of each one of us. I know right now that there is evidence 'out there' that conflicts with many of my beliefs, yet this by itself doesn't prevent them from being justified. If it did, there would be very little knowledge of any kind. What we think is the problem with the racist beliefs of the white nationalists is that there is evidence they *should* gather, regardless of whether they are aware that it exists. When the white nationalist says, 'I had no idea that there was evidence that challenged my beliefs of white nationalism,' this might mean that he lacked the higher-order evidence, but it does not render his beliefs free from normative defeat. This is why evidence that one should have cannot be fully captured by evidence that one in fact has, even when higher-order evidence of the sort considered here is factored in.

Let us say, then, that *normative testimonial injustice* occurs when credibility is improperly assigned due to ignoring evidence that should be taken into account, and the ignoring of this evidence is the result of prejudice (perhaps specifically of identity prejudice, if we wish to follow Fricker). So, for instance, I commit an act of normative testimonial injustice if I give the women in my department a credibility deficit because my sexism leads me to culpably fail to possess evidence that they are just as reliable as the men. Perhaps I refuse to read their work, or engage them in conversation, or listen to positive recommendations about them. I am the victim of normative testimonial injustice if, for instance, I am given a credibility deficit because my being a woman leads a hearer to reject relevant evidence that speaks to my reliability.

Now, it might be tempting to think that ruling out normative testimonial injustice involves a simple modification to evidentialism, one that leaves the view intact in spirit, even if not in letter. But I think this is mistaken. Evidentialism is a paradigmatic instance of what Sarah Moss calls 'time-slice epistemology,' where the core thesis of such a view is that 'what is rationally permissible or obligatory for you at some time is entirely determined by what mental states you are in at that time. This supervenience claim governs facts about the rationality of your actions, as well as the rationality of your full beliefs and your degreed belief states' (Moss 2015, p. 172). Normative defeaters fly in the face of time-slice epistemology by virtue of making epistemic justification a matter, not only of one's mental states at a given time, but also of the mental states one should have at a time. Moreover, according to Moss, there is an important connection between time-slice epistemology and the view that 'all fundamental norms of rationality are temporally local' (Moss 2015, p. 172). Thus, the evidentialist clearly endorses a *temporally local* version of the norm of credibility, according to which one's obligations concerning credibility assessments are exhausted by temporally local facts. In contrast, the view that I am defending here is *temporally non-local*, understanding the obligations in question as involving facts that go beyond the evidence that is represented in the hearer's present psychology.

5. Wide Norm of Credibility

We have seen that straight evidentialist norms of credibility are fundamentally incapable of ruling out both distributive and normative testimonial injustice.[24] We have also seen that our credibility assessments must be both relational—including not only the speaker in question but also the other members of the relevant conversational context or community—and temporally non-local—taking into account not only evidence that hearers have but also evidence that they should have. For the sake of ease of expression, I will say that both of these features are subsumed by the norm being *wide*. In contrast, the evidentialist norms are *narrow*, being attuned to only one speaker and taking into account only the evidence that is represented in the hearer's present psychology.

More precisely, the following *wide norm of credibility* avoids the problems that have been identified facing the standard evidentialist norm: for every speaker and hearer, if a hearer makes credibility assessments of the relevant members of a conversational context or community, the hearer should match those assessments to the evidence she not only has but should have that those speakers are offering the truth, and the hearer should believe, disbelieve, or withhold accordingly. As should be clear, satisfaction of this wide norm is incompatible with content-based and distributive testimonial injustice, as this norm requires that credibility assessments not only match the evidence, but also include all of the relevant members of the conversational context or community in question, including ourselves.

[24] This is not to say that these are the only forms of testimonial injustice that fail to be appropriately handled by the evidentialist norm. See, for instance, Dotson (2011), Peet (2015), and Munroe (2016).

Thus, even if I give a speaker her due in light of the evidence, I am failing in my epistemic obligations if I also illegitimately give others or myself a credibility excess. Credibility is a good, and its proper distribution matters in our normative assessments.

The wide norm also rules out normative testimonial injustice by virtue of making evidence that both is, and should be, in a hearer's possession relevant to her corresponding credibility assessments. In this way, hearers cannot get off the normative hook by simply avoiding exposing themselves to evidence that conflicts with, say, their otherwise racist or sexist beliefs.

In terms of understanding which conversational context or community, and which members in it, are relevant to the assessment of a speaker's credibility in the wide norm, the answer will depend on the content of the testimony in question. If you are a scientist testifying about your recent finding in the lab, then the relevant community will include your fellow scientists rather than, say, your family members and neighbors. If, on the other hand, your testimony is about a childhood trauma, then the relevant community will include those family members and friends around at the time of the event. The parameters of the relevant contexts and speakers, and which ones bear on which assessments, will necessarily be imprecise, but this is a topic that has been widely discussed with respect to other topics and I will not add to it here.[25]

One significant consequence of the wide norm is that we need to be attentive not just to our attitudes toward individual speakers, but also to the broader social environments in which we find ourselves. Our credibility assessments of individual speakers often reverberate throughout our communities, bringing about direct and indirect consequences for many others in their wake. This is especially true in cases of disagreement or in attributions of expertise, where credibility is finite and its proper distribution is of critical importance. Imagine a court of law: the evidence being presented from the prosecution is often in direct opposition to that offered by the defense. To side with one is necessarily to side against the other. To regard one witness as an expert is often to find the other a crank or puppet of the opposing side.

To see this vividly, consider the case of Lara McLeod, a woman who was raped by her older sister's fiancé, Joaquin Rams.[26] After reluctantly reporting it to law enforcement, she was arrested and charged with making a false report, while her sister was charged with obstructing justice for 'aiding Lara's alleged deceit.' The charges were ultimately dropped against the sisters and, with the gift of hindsight, the police now admit that mistakes were made. But what I want to point out here is the way in which attributions of credibility led to the charges in the first place.

[25] See, for instance, Stalnaker (2014).

[26] For an extended discussion of this case, see http://www.buzzfeed.com/katiejmbaker/the-police-told-her-to-report-her-rape-then-arrested-her-for#.avG329Yj8.

There is no doubt that a credibility deficit was at work with regard to the testimony of both Lara and her sister, Hera. For instance, while 'the chief of police admitted the department bungled aspects of the investigation . . . he stressed that women do lie about rape, so it was important for officers not to be too credulous. . . . "It is not uncommon for people to make false, malicious, salacious allegations of sexual assault," he said. "That does happen." '[27] There is, however, also no doubt that a credibility excess was operative in the evaluation of Joaquin's reports and the evidence he provided. Indeed, it was this very excess that led the police to go on the offensive and bring charges against Lara and Hera, for it is only their accepting Joaquin's version of events that explains how both Lara and Hera could be accused of lies and deception. This is supported by what the chief of police now says about the case: 'One of the shortcomings in this case is the fact that they didn't do further investigation on the specific charge against you,' he said to Hera. 'To leap to the conclusion that you needed to be charged at the time you did I thought was cut short.'

This case makes clear the sense in which credibility can be finite: between Lara, Hera, and Joaquin, there is only so much of it to go around. Somebody is telling the truth and somebody is lying, and where the truth is said to fall is *ipso facto* to point the finger of falsehood at the other. Hence, the very credibility that the police gave to Joaquin's testimony by virtue of accepting his version of events justified the charges of lies and deception brought against Lara and Hera. Otherwise put, the unjustified credibility excess given to Joaquin provided the very basis for the credibility deficit suffered by Lara and Hera.

So far I have focused on the benefits of the relational component of the wide norm, but such a norm also makes clear that we are obligated to assess speakers in terms of both the evidence that we do have and the evidence that we should have. Given this, it is to our advantage epistemically to pay close attention to our social environment. In particular, since much of the evidence that might be functioning as normative defeaters is socially disseminated, our epistemic status will be directly impacted by the information that is 'out there.' For instance, the sort of work that has been done by feminists conceptualizing sexual harassment and silencing has expanded the scope of testimonial injustice. Questions about whether our words are sexually harassing or silencing others are ones that cannot be evaded, no matter how much we try. Similarly, we now have specific knowledge from psychologists about phenomena like implicit bias and the Dunning-Kruger effect, and this makes it inappropriate for us to ignore the possibility that these sorts of features are shaping our current beliefs.

It is also worth noting that work in psychology supports the central theses in this chapter. Greenwald and Pettigrew (2014), for instance, argue that prejudice is

[27] https://www.buzzfeednews.com/article/katiejmbaker/the-police-told-her-to-report-her-rape-then-arrested-her-for.

best understood in *differential* terms, which favors viewing credibility assessments relationally rather than individually. Moreover, there is substantial empirical work showing 'that discrimination occurs more often as differential favoring [of ingroup members] than as differential harming [of outgroup members]' (Greenwald and Pettigrew 2014, p. 670). For instance, in Hodson et al.'s (2002) study, white subjects evaluated two presumed college applicants, one white and one Black. While the two applicants were otherwise matched, one applicant had higher high school grades and the other had higher scores on a standardized aptitude test. Thus, the two applicants deserved to be treated as roughly equally qualified. Hodson et al. found, however, that in comparing the white and Black applicants, 'subjects who scored relatively high on a measure of prejudice attributed greater predictive weight to the measure on which' the white applicant was superior (Greenwald and Pettigrew 2014, p. 675). This is just one of many, 'well-established empirical paradigms, including laboratory studies of minimal group and similarity-attraction paradigms, field experiments using unobtrusive observations of helping behavior, and field audit studies of police profiling and of treatment accorded to potential job seekers, apartment renters, and home buyers,' all of which support the conclusion that ingroup favoritism is more significant as a basis for discrimination in the United States than is outgroup-directed hostility (Greenwald and Pettigrew 2014, p. 679). Moreover, it is important to note that ingroup favoritism is conceptually and causally distinct from outgroup hostility: one does not cause or include the other.[28] This makes clear not only the role of credibility excesses in interpersonal interactions, but also how prevalent and harmful they are in terms of discriminatory behavior. In particular, if favoring ingroups—such as giving fellow whites an excess of credibility—is a more powerful and prevalent cause of discrimination in the United States than is hostility toward outgroups—such as giving Black people a deficit of credibility, then distributive testimonial injustice identified in this chapter ought to be a central focus of future discussions.

6. Moving Beyond the Standard Conception of Testimonial Injustice

Credibility is a good, one that grounds and shapes our identities, is integral to relationships and successes, and can be necessary for our literal survival. But contrary to what is widely thought, it is not a limitless good. When some get too much of it, others often get too little. Justice demands, then, that we look at its proper distribution not just individually, but relationally as well. Moreover, our

[28] See Brewer (1999).

obligations with respect to credibility assessments are not exhausted by our current psychological states but, rather, involve facts that are temporally non-local. In both of these ways, standard evidentialist norms fail.

The wide norm of credibility is sensitive to these relational and normative dimensions of our credibility assessments and because of this, its satisfaction is incompatible with both distributive and normative testimonial injustice. In this way, that we are social creatures whose obligations depend in part on the members of our communities and features of our broader social environment is recognized and appreciated.

While this represents a significant improvement over the standard view, there is a deep and important sense in which even with all of these modifications, testimonial injustice is understood as fundamentally involving an absence or failure, one that is marked by inaction and passivity. Not believing in accordance with the evidence, even in relational terms, and neglecting to gather evidence one should have, are both failures. They are driven, at least in most cases, by epistemic inaction. And hearers are passive victims in the testimonial exchanges in question, with no role, not even of unjust complicity, in the perpetration of testimonial injustice.

In the chapters that follow, I will show that there is a radically different kind of testimonial injustice, one that is fundamentally agential in nature and is marked by overt action on both sides—a deceptive ploy by the police about incriminating evidence, for instance, and a signed false confession by the suspect, or a coercive threat by the State and a misidentification by the eyewitness. Within the criminal legal system specifically, I will show that agential testimonial injustice of this sort is the result of brute State power targeting the epistemic agency of its citizens, extracting false testimony that is often life-shattering, and, in so doing, rendering the victims in question complicit in their own undoing.

2

False Confessions and Agential Testimonial Injustice

In the criminal legal system,[1] confessions have long been considered the 'gold standard' in evidence.[2] Indeed, the United States Supreme Court regards a confession as arguably the most compelling evidence of guilt admissible in court,[3] so powerful that 'the introduction of a confession makes the other aspects of a trial in court superfluous, and the real trial, for all practical purposes, occurs when the confession is obtained' (*Colorado v. Connelly*, 479 U.S. 157, 182 (1986)).[4] An immediate problem arises for this gold standard, however, when the prevalence of false confessions is taken into account. 'A false confession is an admission to a criminal act—usually accompanied by a narrative of how and why the crime occurred—that the confessor did not commit' (Kassin et al. 2010, p. 5).[5] Since 1989, there have been 375 post-conviction DNA exonerations in the United States, and 29% of these involved false confessions.[6] Moreover, false confessions involve everything from minor infractions to detailed accounts of violent crimes. In the largest sample ever studied, Drizin and Leo (2004) analyzed 125 cases of

[1] Unless otherwise noted, I will be focusing on the criminal legal system in the United Stated in this book.

[2] Portions of this chapter were first published as Jennifer Lackey, 'False Confessions and Testimonial Injustice,' *Journal of Criminal Law & Criminology*, vol. 110, no. 1, pp. 43–68 (2020).

[3] Kassin et al. (2010, p. 9), citing *Miranda v. Arizona* (1966).

[4] See also 'A defendant's confession is like no other evidence. It is probably the most probative and damaging evidence that can be admitted against him....' (*Arizona v. Fulminante*, 499 U.S. 279, 280 (1991)).

[5] 'Confessions may be deemed false when: (1) it is later discovered that no crime was committed (e.g., the presumed murder victim is found alive, the autopsy on a "shaken baby" reveals a natural cause of death); (2) additional evidence shows it was physically impossible for the confessor to have committed the crime (e.g., he or she was demonstrably elsewhere at the time or too young to have produced the semen found on the victim); (3) the real perpetrator, having no connection to the defendant, is apprehended and linked to the crime (e.g., by intimate knowledge of nonpublic crime details, ballistics, or physical evidence); or (4) scientific evidence affirmatively establishes the confessor's innocence (e.g., he or she is excluded by DNA test results on semen, blood, hair, or saliva)' (Kassin et al. 2010, p. 5).

[6] https://innocenceproject.org/dna-exonerations-in-the-united-states/. As Kassin et al. note, however, 'because this sample does not include those false confessions that are disproved before trial, many that result in guilty pleas, those in which DNA evidence is not available, those given to minor crimes that receive no post-conviction scrutiny, and those in juvenile proceedings that contain confidentiality provisions, the cases that are discovered most surely represent the tip of an iceberg' (2010, p. 3).

Criminal Testimonial Injustice. Jennifer Lackey, Oxford University Press. © Jennifer Lackey 2023.
DOI: 10.1093/oso/9780192864109.003.0003

proven false confessions in the United States between 1971 and 2002 and found that 81% occurred in murder cases, followed by rape (9%) and arson (3%).

In this chapter, I take a close look at false confessions in connection with the phenomenon of testimonial injustice. I show that false confessions provide a unique and compelling challenge to the current conceptual tools used to understand this epistemic wrong. In particular, I argue that we cannot make sense of the unjust ways in which false confessions function in our criminal legal system by focusing exclusively on speakers getting *less credibility* than they deserve. I conclude that the way we conceive of testimonial injustice requires a significant expansion to include what I call *agential testimonial injustice*, which occurs when testimony is *extracted* from speakers in a way that bypasses, exploits, or subverts their epistemic agency[7] and is then given an unwarranted *excess* of credibility. At the same time, I show that work by legal scholars and social scientists can benefit by viewing the practices that produce confessions through the lens of this expanded notion, and hence that epistemological tools can shed light on issues with enormous moral and practical consequences.

1. False Confessions

It will be helpful to situate the extraction of confessions within a slightly broader historical context, beginning with the details of the case that led to one of the most important Supreme Court decisions regarding confession evidence.

On March 30, 1934, Raymond Stuart, a white planter, was murdered in Kemper County, Mississippi. Shortly thereafter, on April 4, 1934, three Black tenant farmers—Arthur Ellington, Ed Brown, and Henry Shields—were indicted and arraigned, with their trial beginning the next morning and lasting just two days. On April 6, 1934, all three defendants were found guilty of Stuart's murder and sentenced to death based 'solely upon confessions' (*Brown v. Mississippi*, 297 U.S. 278, 279 (1936)). However, there is also 'no dispute' that these confessions were extracted through acts of 'extreme brutality' by state authorities. For instance, on the night of March 30th, a deputy sheriff, Dial, went to the home of Ellington with others and requested that he accompany them to the home of the deceased. When they arrived at the Stuart residence, a number of white men had gathered there and accused Ellington of the crime. When he denied any involvement in the murder, 'they seized him, and with the participation of the deputy they hanged him by a rope to the limb of a tree, and having let him down, they hung him again, and when he was let down the second time, and he still protested his innocence, he was tied to a tree and whipped, and still declining to accede to

[7] The first appearance of the concept of 'epistemic agency' in the philosophical literature is in Reed (2001).

the demands that he confess, he was finally released and he returned with some difficulty to his home, suffering intense pain and agony' (*Brown v. Mississippi*, 297 U.S. 278, 281 (1936)). Moreover, the record shows that there were clearly visible signs at the trial of the rope having been on Ellington's neck. A day or two later, Dial returned to Ellington's home and arrested him, but took a route to the jail that led into Alabama, stopping in that state to again severely whip Ellington, 'declaring that he would continue the whipping until he confessed, and the defendant then agreed to confess to such a statement as the deputy would dictate, and he did so, after which he was delivered to jail' (*Brown v. Mississippi*, 297 U.S. 278, 281–82 (1936)).

Brown and Shields were also arrested and taken to the same jail as Ellington. On the night of April 1st, Dial, accompanied by the jailer and a number of white men, one of whom was also an officer, went to the jail and ordered Brown and Shields to strip, after which 'they were laid over chairs and their backs were cut to pieces with a leather strap with buckles on it, and they were likewise made by the said deputy definitely to understand that the whipping would be continued unless and until they confessed, and not only confessed, but confessed in every matter of detail as demanded by those present; and in this manner the defendants confessed the crime, and as the whippings progressed and were repeated, they changed or adjusted their confession in all particulars of detail so as to conform to the demands of their torturers' (*Brown v. Mississippi*, 297 U.S. 278, 282 (1936)).

It is also undeniable that race played a central role in the extraction of the defendants' testimony in this case. When Dial was put on the stand, for instance, he readily acknowledged the whippings he inflicted and, in reference to Ellington in particular, stated that it was '[n]ot too much for a negro; not as much as I would have done if it were left to me' (*Brown v. Mississippi*, 297 U.S. 278, 284 (1936)). Despite this, the trial judge not only admitted the confessions into evidence, the defendants were found guilty and sentenced to death solely on this basis, with the Mississippi Supreme Court later holding that the defendants had received due process of law and affirming their convictions and death sentences.[8]

In response to this case, the United State Supreme Court ruled in *Brown v. Mississippi* (297 U.S. 278 (1936)) that a confession that is extracted via police violence, and is thereby involuntary, violates the Due Process Clause of the Fourteenth Amendment and thus cannot be entered as evidence. While this represented a significant development in the status confession evidence is afforded in the courts, confessions obtained via police torture persist, but are now shrouded in lies and deception. In addition, extracted confessions continue to result from practices driven by racism that disproportionately target people of color. For instance, between 1972 and 1991, over 120 people, predominantly Black, were

[8] See Cloud (1996, p. 1213).

tortured under the command of notorious Chicago Police Department Commander Jon Burge.[9] Unlike Dial, who readily admitted whipping Ellington, Burge was convicted of obstruction of justice and perjury for lying about engaging in the physical abuse and torture of suspects in custody at Chicago Police Department's Area Two.[10] However, evidence showed that 'Burge abused multiple victims in Area Two, suffocating them with plastic bags; shocking them with electrical devices; and placing a loaded gun to their heads.'[11] Indeed, the torture was so widespread that in May of 2015, Chicago became the first city in the United States to provide reparations for racially-motivated police violence when the Chicago City Council unanimously passed the Reparations Ordinance.[12] While Chicago has been known as both the 'torture capital of the world'[13] and, not unrelatedly, the 'false confessions capital,'[14] it is not entirely unique in these regards, as 'confession law is replete with cases of Black defendants who were physically coerced into confessions and whom juries convicted despite uncontradicted evidence of such coercion' (Johnson 1996, p. 269).

Moreover, false confessions can be effectively extracted from suspects and defendants even when physical violence is not used, and this fact is especially relevant for our purposes. Indeed, 'psychologically oriented interrogation techniques are just as capable of eliciting... false confessions as are physical ones' (Leo 2009, p. 338).[15] Kassin and Wrightsman (1985) first identified three different kinds of false confessions, which they call 'voluntary'—offered 'in the absence of elicitation,' 'coerced-compliant'—offered when 'the suspect publicly professes guilt in response to extreme methods of interrogation, despite knowing privately that he or she is truly innocent,' and 'coerced-internalized'—offered when the suspect 'through the fatigue, pressures, and suggestiveness of the interrogation process... actually comes to believe that he or she committed the offense' (pp. 76–78). Leo and Ofshe (1997) expanded this taxonomy to include five distinct types of false confessions—voluntary, stress-compliant, coerced compliant, coerced-persuaded, and noncoerced-persuaded—which are often classified as simply voluntary, compliant, and persuaded false confessions. Since the focus in this chapter is on false confessions that have been extracted, I will turn my attention to compliant and persuaded false confessions.

9 https://chicagotorturejustice.org/about-us/history/.

10 https://www.justice.gov/opa/pr/former-chicago-police-officer-jon-burge-sentenced-lying-about-police-torture.

11 https://www.justice.gov/opa/pr/former-chicago-police-officer-jon-burge-sentenced-lying-about-police-torture.

12 https://www.chicago.gov/content/dam/city/depts/dol/supp_info/Burge-Reparations-Information-Center/BurgeRESOLUTION.pdf.

13 https://www.yesmagazine.org/social-justice/2015/05/15/chicago-is-the-first-city-to-offer-reparations-for-victims-of-police-violence-now-they-want-to-make-sure-no-one-forgets.

14 https://www.cbsnews.com/news/chicago-the-false-confession-capital/.

15 Leo (2009) is here focusing specifically on compliant false confessions, which will be identified in what follows.

'A compliant false confession is one given in response to police coercion, stress, or pressure to achieve some instrumental benefit—typically either to terminate and thus escape from an aversive interrogation process, to take advantage of a perceived suggestion or promise of leniency, or to avoid an anticipated harsh punishment' (Leo 2009, p. 338). One of the most distinctive features of compliant false confessions is that guilt is admitted while the confessor fully knows that he is innocent and that what he is saying is false.[16] Because of this, compliant false confessions are often recanted[17] shortly after the interrogation is over.[18] Psychological coercion is the central source of compliant false confession,[19] with classically coercive influence techniques, such as threats and promises, being the underlying cause of most present day compliant false confessions.[20]

A persuaded false confession is one that occurs when 'police interrogation tactics cause an innocent suspect to doubt his memory and he becomes temporarily persuaded that it is more likely than not that he committed the crime, despite having no memory of committing it' (Leo 2009, p. 339). Typically, persuaded false confessions unfold in three sequential steps, with the first involving the interrogator causing the suspect to doubt his own innocence. This is often the result of a lengthy, accusatorial, and deceptive interrogation where the interrogator repeatedly accuses the suspect of committing the crime, attacks the suspect's denials, and presents the suspect with fabricated evidence of his guilt.[21] The second step is to provide a reason to the suspect that explains how he could have committed the crime in question without remembering it, which often involves a version of a 'repressed' memory theory, such as an 'alcohol- or drug-induced blackout, a "dry" blackout, a multiple personality disorder, a momentary lapse in consciousness,... posttraumatic stress disorder, or, perhaps most commonly, that the suspect simply repressed his memory of committing the crime because it was a traumatic experience for him' (Leo 2009, p. 339). The third and final step is the creation of a postadmission narrative, which is often replete with errors and offered in hypothetical, tentative, and speculative terms since the false confessor is reasoning from inference rather than knowledge.[22]

Broadly speaking, there are two different kinds of factors that can significantly impact the likelihood of false confessions occurring. First, there are *dispositional factors*. The two most commonly-cited dispositional factors are juvenile status and mental impairment, including developmental disabilities and mental illness.[23] Both of these groups are wildly overrepresented in the population of proven false confessions. For instance, of the first 200 DNA exonerations in the

[16] Leo (2009, p. 338).

[17] A recantation 'denotes a formal, intentional renunciation by a witness of her former testimony' (Repka 1986, p. 1434).

[18] Leo (2009, p. 338). [19] Leo (2009, p. 338). [20] Leo and Ofshe (1997).

[21] Leo (2009, p. 339). [22] Gudjonsson (2003).

[23] Kassin (2005) and Kassin et al. (2010).

United States, 35% of the false confessors were 18 years or younger and/or had a developmental disability.[24] In their sample of wrongful convictions, Gross et al. (2005) found that 44% of exonerated juveniles and 69% of exonerated persons with mental disabilities were wrongly convicted because of false confessions. There are a number of considerations that are explanatorily relevant here. In both groups, for instance, there can be impairments in adjudicative competence, such as the ability to assist in one's own defense. There can also be a diminished capacity to grasp legal terms, such as *Miranda* rights.[25]

Second, there are *situational factors*. Because of the 'consistency in which they appear in cases involving proven false confessions' (Kassin et al. 2010, p. 16), the length of the interrogation and the interrogation tactics used to elicit confessions are often highlighted, especially minimization and maximization. Regarding length, guidelines outlined by Inbau et al. (2001) advise that single interrogation sessions not exceed four hours. Yet Drizin and Leo (2004) found that in cases in which interrogation time was recorded, 34% lasted 6–12 hours, 39% lasted 12–24 hours, and the mean was 16.3 hours. Moreover, lengthy interrogations are often accompanied by other factors that can increase the likelihood of false confessions, such as isolation from significant others, which 'constitutes a form of deprivation that can heighten a suspect's distress and incentive to remove himself or herself from the situation,'[26] and sleep deprivation, which 'strongly impairs human functioning.'[27]

Perhaps most relevant for our purposes are minimization and maximization tactics, which research has shown can lead to false confessions.[28] Minimization is a 'soft-sell' approach in which the interrogator 'tries to lull' the suspect into a 'false sense of security by offering sympathy, tolerance, face saving excuses, and even moral justification' (Kassin and McNall 1991, p. 235). Such techniques come in three different forms: 'those that minimize the moral consequences of confessing, those that minimize the psychological consequences of confessing, and those that minimize the legal consequences of confessing' (Kassin et al., 2010, p. 12). For instance, the interrogator may offer sympathy and understanding to normalize the crime, saying, for instance, 'I would have done the same thing;' the interrogator might offer minimizing explanations of the crime, such as raising the possibility that the murder was spontaneous or accidental; and the interrogator might communicate promises that the suspect will be punished less severely if he or she confesses. Promises of leniency, which have been shown to be 'particularly coercive in interrogations' (Joselow 2019, p. 1641), heighten the risk of false confessions by leading a suspect to believe that the only way to reduce or escape

[24] Kassin et al. (2010, p. 19).
[25] Regarding juveniles, see Saywitz, Nathanson, and Snyder (1993) and Grisso et al. (2003).
[26] Kassin et al. (2010).
[27] Pilcher and Huffcut (1996).
[28] Klaver, Lee, and Rose (2008).

punishment is to confess.[29] Among the promises that have been made to a suspect in exchange for a confession are that a lighter sentence will be recommended,[30] that lesser charges will be prosecuted,[31] that medical treatment will be received,[32] and that he will be treated better.[33] Calvin Ollins, for instance, was 14 years old and had mental limitations when he, along with three others, was wrongfully convicted of the 1986 rape and murder of Lori Roscetti in Chicago. After being interrogated for five hours, during which Ollins was threatened with violence and the death penalty, he finally admitted guilt when detectives promised to release him if he confessed.[34] As he says, 'They told me… "You just go ahead and cooperate, and we'll let you go home." I thought I was going home, but… I've been here ever since then' (Joselow (2019, p. 1641).

Maximization is a 'hard-sell' approach that involves the interrogator trying to scare or intimidate the suspect, exaggerating the seriousness of not cooperating, and offering false claims about the evidence. Christopher Ochoa, for instance, confessed to the 1988 murder of Nancy DePriest, despite being completely innocent, after being repeatedly threatened with the death penalty by officers and prosecutors. One of the interrogating officers even grabbed Ochoa's arm and tapped his vein, saying, 'This is where the needle is gonna go if you don't cooperate… and I'm gonna make sure I'm there to watch it.'[35] When faced with what seems like a certain death sentence at trial, confessing, even when innocent, can seem like the only available or rational option.

In addition to invoking threats of this sort, the Supreme Court made it permissible in *Frazier v. Cupp* (394 U.S. 731 (1969)) for interrogators to outright lie to suspects, a tactic often referred to as 'the false evidence ploy.'[36] As Saul Kassin says, '"The victim's blood was found on your pillow," "You failed the polygraph," "Your fingerprints were on the knife" and "Your friend said she wasn't with you like you said" are some common but brazen lies told. There is almost no limit to the type or magnitude of deception permitted—one lie or many; small lies and whoppers; lies aimed at adults or anxious and unwary teenagers.'[37] Indeed, the Reid Technique,[38] which is one of 'the most widely used police interrogation

[29] Joselow (2019, p. 1650). [30] Joselow (2019, p. 1650). [31] Marcus (2006, p. 623).
[32] Marcus (2006, p. 623). [33] Marcus (2006, p. 623). [34] Joselow (2019, p. 1642).
[35] https://guiltypleaproblem.org/?id=christopher_ochoa.
[36] See Leo and Ofshe (2008) and Wynbrandt (2016).
[37] https://www.nytimes.com/2021/01/29/opinion/false-confessions-police-interrogation.html.
[38] The nine steps of the Reid Technique are as follows:

1. **The positive confrontation.** The investigator verbalizes to the suspect that there is sufficient evidence that points to their guilt.
2. **In theme development**, the investigator will place moral blame on a fictitious person as to remove the suspect from the scenario and attempt to develop a sympathetic moral monologue.
3. **Handle denials.** Investigators should not permit a suspect to speak when they ask for permission to do so, because they are likely to deny the accusations. Innocent suspects are more apt to quickly deny an accusation rather than ask for permission to speak.

procedure in North America' (Moore, Cutler, and Shulman 2014, p. 34), encourages the ploy as it is 'clearly the most persuasive' interrogation tactic within 'the area of deception' (Inbau et al. 2013, p. 255).[39] Consider, for instance, the case of Marty Tankleff who, in 1989, was accused at the age of 17 of murdering his parents despite the complete absence of evidence against him. 'Tankleff vehemently denied the charges for several hours—until his interrogator told him that his hair was found within his mother's grasp, that a "humidity test" indicated he had showered (hence, the presence of only one spot of blood on his shoulder), and that his hospitalized father had emerged from his coma to say that Marty was his assailant—all of which were untrue (the father never regained consciousness and died shortly thereafter)' (Kassin et al. 2010, pp. 17–18). Following these lies, Tankleff became disoriented and confessed, saying that because his father never lied, perhaps he had blacked out and killed his mother.[40] Despite immediately recanting, Tankleff was convicted of murdering his parents solely on the basis of this confession and was sentenced to 50 years to life in prison.[41] Nineteen years later, his conviction was vacated and the charges were dismissed.[42] Importantly, the false evidence ploy has been 'implicated in the vast majority of documented police-induced false confessions' (Kassin et al. 2010, p. 12). Unwitting suspects who deny involvement in a crime can be met with purportedly decisive evidence of guilt by interrogators, which can lead to confusion, desperation, and resignation.

4. **Overcoming objections.** Suspects who are guilty typically offer claims of innocence and present objections to support those claims. Rather than argue with the suspect, the investigator should accept those claims as truthful statements.
5. **Procurement and retention of suspect's attention.** Here, the investigator will focus the suspect's attention on the themes presented by the investigator rather than on the punishment they could potentially receive.
6. **Handling the suspect's passive mood.** Themes presented by the investigator will be intensified and further concentrated on the motivation and justification of the suspect. The interviewer will continue to display sympathy while encouraging the suspect to tell the truth.
7. **Presenting an alternative question.** Investigators will present at least two questions that are phrased to illustrate a clear contrast between two opposite choices; for example 'Sarah, was this the first time you have been involved in something like this, or has this occurred on other occasions?'
8. **Having the suspect orally relate various details of the offense.** Once the suspect has accepted one side of the alternative and subsequently admits guilt, the investigator will provide a follow-up reinforcement of said omission and request additional details about the circumstances.
9. **Converting an oral confession to written confession.** The investigator will make sure that they are working within the scope of the law, reading Miranda warnings using the suspect's language, and focusing on developing the oral confession to a final written confession for record. (https://www.police1.com/police-products/interview-recording/articles/using-behavioral-analysis-interview-techniques-to-elicit-confessions-hnqZVx2g4adqiIaD/).

[39] It should be noted, however, that Wicklander-Zulawski & Associates, which is one of the largest private police training agencies in the world, issued a press release in 2017 announcing the discontinuation of teaching the Reid Technique after having taught it for more than 30 years. See Kozinski (2018).

[40] https://www.law.umich.edu/special/exoneration/Pages/casedetail.aspx?caseid=3675.

[41] https://www.law.umich.edu/special/exoneration/Pages/casedetail.aspx?caseid=3675.

[42] Firstman and Salpeter (2008).

That the presentation of false evidence contributes to such confessions is reinforced by self-report studies, where suspects say that the reason they confessed is that they took themselves to be trapped by the weight of the evidence against them.[43]

Finally, false confessions are often facilitated by the very innocence of the suspect. Awareness of one's own innocence leads people not only to waive their *Miranda* rights to silence and to counsel,[44] but also to be more open and forthcoming in their interactions with police.[45] If you have nothing to hide, you might wonder why you should remain silent and get an attorney. Consider the case of Peter Reilly, who at 18 years old confessed and internalized guilt for the 1973 murder of his mother.[46] Solely on the basis of his confession, Reilly was prosecuted, convicted, and incarcerated, only to be exonerated two years later following the discovery of exculpatory evidence.[47] When Reilly was asked years later why he didn't invoke his *Miranda* rights during his interrogation by police, he said, 'My state of mind was that I hadn't done anything wrong and I felt that only a criminal really needed an attorney, and this was all going to come out in the wash' (Connery 1996, p. 93). Yet it is not uncommon for the testimony of those who are innocent to be used against them, such as by calling into question their reliability or sincerity on the basis of minor inaccuracies. In addition, when a suspect confesses, this often leads the police to regard the case as solved, thereby closing the investigation and increasing the likelihood of overlooking exculpatory evidence.[48]

2. Testimonial Injustice

With these points in mind, let's now take a closer look at the phenomenon of testimonial injustice.

Recall from the previous chapter that testimonial injustice of the prejudicial sort involves a speaker being afforded a *credibility deficit* in virtue of a *prejudice* on the part of a hearer that targets her *social identity*.[49] A speaker is said to suffer such a credibility deficit when the credibility that she is afforded by a hearer is less than the evidence that she is offering the truth warrants, and a hearer has the relevant kind of identity prejudice when she has a prejudice against the speaker in virtue of the latter's membership in a social group.[50]

[43] Gudjonsson and Sigurdsson (1999) and Moston, Stephenson, and Williamson (1992).

[44] See Kassin and Norwick (2004). [45] Kassin (2005). [46] Kassin (2005).

[47] https://www.law.umich.edu/special/exoneration/Pages/casedetailpre1989.aspx?caseid=268.

[48] Leo and Ofshe (1998).

[49] According to Miranda Fricker, for example, '[a] speaker sustains... testimonial injustice if and only if she receives a credibility deficit owing to identity prejudice in the hearer; so the central case of testimonial injustice is identity-prejudicial credibility deficit' (2007, p. 28).

[50] Anderson (2012) identifies structural epistemic injustices that may have locally, non-prejudicial causes, and require structural remedies. I am convinced by Anderson's arguments, and hence I do not think that all instances of testimonial injustice require a local, prejudicial origin.

Prejudice here is understood in terms of not being properly responsive to evidence. A prejudicial stereotype, for instance, is a generalization about a social group that fails to be sufficiently sensitive to relevant evidence.[51] Where this prejudice 'tracks' the subject through different dimensions of social activity—economic, educational, professional, and so on—it is systematic, and the type that tracks people in this way is related to social identity, such as racial and gender identity. For instance, if a police officer rejects a woman's report of sexual assault merely because his sexism leads to him discrediting her, and despite evidence that supports her credibility, this would be a paradigmatic instance of testimonial injustice. In particular, the police officer's sexist beliefs manifest as a prejudice that targets the victim's gender identity in a way that results in her testimony being regarded as less credible than the evidence supports.[52] When a hearer gives a speaker a credibility deficit in virtue of her social identity, Fricker (2007) argues that the speaker is wronged 'in her capacity as a knower' and is thereby the victim of testimonial injustice.

As we saw earlier, Fricker flatly denies that an excess of credibility can result in a speaker suffering testimonial injustice. A speaker cannot be wronged as a knower, she argues, by getting more credibility than she deserves. In addition to grounding this claim in the rejection of a distributive model of credibility, whereby credibility is said to not be a finite good that lends itself to concerns about proper distribution, she writes, 'I do not think it would be right to characterize any of the individual moments of credibility excess that such a person receives as in itself an instance of testimonial injustice, since none of them wrongs him sufficiently in itself' (Fricker 2007, p. 21). The idea here is that the only sense in which a credibility excess can give rise to testimonial injustice is cumulatively. For instance, over time, someone who is given more credibility than he deserves is likely 'to develop such an epistemic arrogance that a range of epistemic virtues are put out of his reach, rendering him closed-minded, dogmatic, blithely

[51] Fricker elsewhere adds that the prejudicial stereotypes that are relevant to testimonial injustice are those that also (i) have a negative valence, and (ii) stem from an 'ethically noxious' motivation (Fricker 2007, p. 34). Points (i) and (ii) have been challenged on both empirical and philosophical grounds (see, for instance, Munroe (2016)), and so I will not focus on them in what follows.

[52] Drawing on work by Patricia Hill Collins, Kristie Dotson focuses on a phenomenon very similar to testimonial injustice that she calls 'testimonial quieting,' which 'occurs when an audience fails to identify a speaker as a knower. A speaker needs an audience to identify, or at least recognize, her as a knower in order to offer testimony. This kind of testimonial oppression has long been discussed in the work of women of color. Take as an example a popular analysis of black women's lack of credibility found in the work of Patricia Hill Collins. In her book, *Black Feminist Thought*..., she claims that by virtue of her being a U.S. black woman she will systematically be undervalued as a knower. This undervaluing is a way in which Collins and other black women's dependencies as speakers are not being met. To undervalue a black woman speaker is to take her status as a knower to be less than plausible. One of Collins's claims is that black women are less likely to be considered competent due to an audience's inability to discern the possession of credibility beyond "controlling images" that stigmatize black women as a group' (Dotson, 2011, p. 242). I will discuss testimonial quieting, as well as some other epistemic wrongs developed in the literature, later in this chapter.

impervious to criticism, and so on' (Fricker 2007, p. 20). But this long-term testimonial injustice is importantly different from what Fricker takes to be the immediate, 'in itself' wrong that comes with a credibility deficit. Even José Medina, who is otherwise critical of Fricker's views about credibility excess, seems to agree with this general point when he writes, 'The fact that no epistemic harm can be detected in this immediate [in itself] way only shows the short-sightedness of an analysis that focuses exclusively on the individual moments of testimonial exchanges among particular subjects' (2011, p. 16).

In Chapter 1, I challenged the claim that credibility excesses cannot result in testimonial injustice from a multitude of angles. A content-based credibility excess, for instance, wrongs a speaker by regarding him as especially knowledgeable in a stigmatized or shameful domain that is an affront to his epistemic dignity. And distributive testimonial injustice shows that an excess of credibility afforded to hearers, other members of the conversational context, or experts can epistemically wrong a speaker in a relational sense even when she is given her due. I also called into question whether it is sufficient to simply match credibility assessments with the evidence a speaker has in her possession, arguing that normative testimonial injustice shows that credibility assessments need to be sensitive to evidence that hearers both have and should have. But there is a deep and important sense in which even with all of these extensions and revisions, testimonial injustice is here marked by passivity, absences, and failures. Not believing in accordance with the evidence, even in relational terms, and neglecting to gather evidence one should have, are both failures. They are driven, at least in most cases, by epistemic inactivity. And hearers are passive victims of testimonial injustice with no active role to play in the testimonial exchanges in question. In looking closely at false confessions, however, I will argue that there is a distinctive kind of testimonial injustice marked by activity and epistemic agency on both the side of the hearer and the speaker—the hearer extracts testimony by employing tactics that are manipulative, deceptive, and coercive, and the speaker offers the desired testimony in question, often with a painful sense of complicity, despite the fact that his epistemic agency has been circumvented, exploited, or subverted.[53]

3. Extracted Testimony

In 1993, Juan Rivera was sentenced to life in prison for the rape and murder of an 11-year-old girl, Holly Staker, in Waukegan, IL almost entirely on the basis of his false confession, which he later recanted. At the time of his interrogation, Rivera was a 19-year-old former special education student who suffered from

[53] Given that testimonial exchanges themselves are marked by substantive epistemic roles for both the speaker and the hearer, this should not be surprising. See Lackey (2008).

depression, had a third-grade reading level, and tried committing suicide on two earlier occasions.[54] No physical evidence linked Rivera to the crimes and readings from an ankle monitor that he was wearing at the time because of a nonviolent burglary showed that he was at home and was nowhere near where Holly's body was found at the time of the crimes.[55] Rivera was interrogated for four consecutive days, with one session lasting 26 hours straight during which time he was offered only coffee and cigarettes.[56] On the third day, polygrapher Michael Masokas from John Reid and Associates, in what 'he conceded was a raised voice and aggressive, accusatory tone, reported to Rivera that "at this point in time the investigation indicated that he did, in fact, cause the death of Holly." '[57] The interrogation continued and shortly after midnight on the fourth day, Sergeant Charles Fagan, said, 'Juan, you were in that apartment with Holly Staker, weren't you?', after which Rivera 'broke down and started sobbing uncontrollably—so intensely that he soaked his clothes.... He did not respond verbally but nodded affirmatively.... As the questioning continued, Rivera said he would kill himself before he went back to a maximum security prison.'[58] The interrogation continued until 3:00 A.M., when investigators left to type a confession for Rivera to sign. Shortly thereafter, Rivera began beating his head against the wall of the interrogation room, his muscles tensed up, he fell into a fetal position on the floor, and he was hyperventilating. Rivera was moved to a padded cell used for suicide watch where a psychiatric nurse with a decade of experience determined that he was in an acute psychotic state and was 'not in touch with the reality of what was going on around him.'[59] Rivera was described as sweating, having flared nostrils, being non-responsive, and sounding like 'people who talk in tongues.'[60] Despite all of this, Sergeant Fagan entered the padded cell at 8:10 A.M. and had Rivera sign the typed confession that the investigators had prepared. 'The document, a narrative account of what the investigators claimed Rivera told them, was so riddled with incorrect and implausible information, that Lake County State's Attorney Michael Waller instructed investigators to resume the interrogation in an effort to clear up the inconsistencies. On October 30th, despite Rivera's obvious fragile mental condition, the interrogation resumed, resulting in a second signed confession, which contained a plausible account of the crime.'[61] Investigators admitted that they

[54] Caldwell and Klinger (2017). [55] Caldwell and Klinger (2017).

[56] https://wgntv.com/news/cover-story/inside-the-phenomena-of-false-confessions/.

[57] https://wwws.law.northwestern.edu/legalclinic/wrongfulconvictions/exonerations/documents/rivera_brief.pdf.

[58] https://wwws.law.northwestern.edu/legalclinic/wrongfulconvictions/exonerations/documents/rivera_brief.pdf.

[59] https://wwws.law.northwestern.edu/legalclinic/wrongfulconvictions/exonerations/documents/rivera_brief.pdf.

[60] https://wwws.law.northwestern.edu/legalclinic/wrongfulconvictions/exonerations/documents/rivera_brief.pdf.

[61] https://innocenceproject.org/cases/juan-rivera/.

'may have suggested answers to some questions'[62] while eliciting this new version of Rivera's confession.

Because of trial errors and post-conviction DNA testing, Rivera had three separate jury trials in 1998, 2001, and 2009 and was found guilty and sentenced to life in prison on all three occasions, even after DNA testing of semen at the scene excluded him in 2004. 'The state's theory of why DNA belonging to someone other than the defendant was found in the victim was that the young girl had prior consensual sex with an unknown male, after which time Rivera raped her, failed to ejaculate, and then killed her' (Appleby and Kassin 2016, p. 127). It wasn't until the Center on Wrongful Convictions became involved that the Illinois Appellate Court ruled in 2012 that Rivera's conviction was 'unjustified and cannot stand,' and thus that the state would dismiss all charges.[63] Rivera had served 20 years in prison.

What we see in this case, as well as in those discussed earlier, is the suspect's *epistemic agency* being bypassed, exploited, or subverted in the extraction of the confession in question. Epistemic agency is often understood as being grounded in a subject's responsiveness to reasons or evidence,[64] and so epistemic agency is exercised with respect to a subject's testimony when that testimony is responsive to reasons or evidence.[65] In the interpersonal case—where the testimony of one person is brought about by another[66]—*rational persuasion* is a paradigmatic example of obtaining testimony while going *through* a speaker's epistemic agency. If, say, I present compelling data on behalf of there being anthropogenic causes of climate change, and you come to say that this is so on the basis of the force of the proffered evidence, I have elicited testimony from you by appealing to your rational capacities. Rational capacities are those 'that enable agents to assess and revise their beliefs in accordance with the basic canons of logic; to evaluate their epistemic and practical options against criteria generated by their beliefs, values, and preference sets; to make adjustments to these beliefs, values, and preferences sets in light of new information; and to act in accordance with their judgments about what they have most reason to do' (Gorin 2014*b*, p. 52). Eliciting testimony by going through your rational capacities involves the straightforward exercising of your epistemic agency. In contrast, epistemic agency is bypassed, exploited, or

[62] https://wwws.law.northwestern.edu/legalclinic/wrongfulconvictions/exonerations/documents/rivera_brief.pdf.

[63] In 2015, Rivera settled with officials of the city of Waukegan and Lake Count for $20 million, which at the time was the largest-ever settlement for a wrongful conviction in U.S. history. (https://abc7chicago.com/juan-rivera-wrongful-conviction-settlement-largest-in-history/566716/)

[64] See, for instance, Reed (2001) and (2013), Hieronymi (2008), and McHugh (2013).

[65] Epistemic agency is typically understood in terms of a subject's *beliefs* being responsive to reasons, but as should be clear, I am extending this notion to the *offering of testimony*. For arguments that the 'epistemic' is not restricted to beliefs, see Lackey (2018*b*) and (2020*b*).

[66] I want to emphasize that I do not think interpersonal cases of extracted testimony are limited to individual persons. I also think, for instance, that institutions can extract testimony, as often happens with admissions of guilt via plea deals. See Burns (2018) and Chapter 4.

subverted when a subject's ability to be responsive to reasons is circumvented, abused, or undermined.

As I understand it, testimony is *extracted* when it has been obtained through an interpersonal interaction that bypasses, exploits, or subverts the testifier's epistemic agency.[67] *Manipulation*, *deception*, and *coercion* are the three central ways in which interpersonal processes can extract testimony from a speaker.

At a high level of generality, there are two ways to influence a person's decision-making: change the options available—the decision space—or change how the person understands these options—the internal decision-making process.[68] Rational persuasion can operate at either place, but what is key is that the persuader appeals to the person's capacity for rational deliberation and choice. When arguments and data are presented on behalf of anthropogenic causes of climate change, I may be changing your decision space—perhaps you thought only natural causes were even on the table—or the way that you understand these options—perhaps you previously thought that increased levels of greenhouse gases could be explained naturally. But in both cases, I am appealing to your epistemic agency.

In contrast, manipulation typically bypasses or circumvents epistemic agency and, in this sense, it is often understood as *arational influence*.[69] Susser et al. characterize manipulation as 'hidden influence—the covert subversion of another person's decision-making power' (2019, p. 3). Manipulation, they say, is 'subtle and sneaky,' and what is distinctive about it is that 'it undermines our sense of authorship over our decisions' (2019, pp. 17–18). In a similar spirit, Robert Goodin argues that 'One person manipulates another when he deceptively influences him, causing the other to act contrary to his putative will' (1980, p. 19). Alan Ware agrees, writing that in order for A to manipulate B, 'B either has no knowledge of, or does not understand, the ways in which A affects his choices' (1981, p. 165).

The covert or hidden nature of manipulation, however, may not be as clear as these authors suggest.[70] Placing sugary candy and drinks in the checkout lines, for instance, is paradigmatically regarded as manipulative behavior. For instance, when Assembly member Buffy Wicks (D-Oakland) introduced a bill in California

[67] For discussions of the phenomenon of extracted testimony, see Lackey (2016), McKinney (2016), and Lackey (2020*a*). McKinney (2016) provides a detailed account of what she calls 'extracted speech' and characterizes it (when it is unjust) as follows: 'Unjust Locutionary Extraction: At context C in community A, S experiences ULE=def (1) S's utterance U is elicited from S in C (e.g., via extraction); (2) either (a) U licenses wrongs against S in A; or (b) the process of (1) itself wrongs S' (McKinney 2016, p. 265). Unlike McKinney's view, the account of extracted testimony that I develop is distinctively epistemic in nature and is conceptually connected to epistemic agency. For discussions of extracted testimony specifically in the context of false confessions, see Lackey (2016) and (2020*a*).

[68] See Susser et al. (2019, p. 14).

[69] There is also a form of manipulation that involves *rational* influence that *exploits* epistemic agency, which I will discuss in Chapter 3.

[70] Noggle (1996), Barnhill (2014), and Gorin (2014*a*) all challenge whether it is necessary for manipulation to be covert or hidden, but from slightly different angles than what I argue here.

in 2019 that would prohibit stores from doing this, she wrote, 'My bill helps consumers stick to healthier choices by stopping the manipulative practice of putting sugar-sweetened beverages at the checkout line.'[71] Moreover, shoppers who buy candy and soda from the checkout line are often the very same people who deliberately ignore these items in the aisles in the store.[72] Now, if a grocery store openly acknowledges that they are keeping candy and soda in the checkout lines to influence shoppers' behavior, does this make the practice not manipulative? If I'm trying to convince you of the depravity of someone who murdered a child, and my arguments have thus far failed to convince you, I might resort to showing you extremely graphic photos of the crime scene. If, before I show you these, I make clear that I'm trying to influence your judgment through an emotional response you cannot control, does this make what I'm doing not manipulative?

Both seem manipulative precisely because I am trying to exert arational influence over you, even if I am out in the open about it. I am preying upon internal weaknesses of yours to bring about my desired aim. In considering whether there can be cases of overt manipulation, Susser et al. argue that 'either you cannot resist the influence and have therefore been coerced, or you can resist it and do not, in which case you have simply been moved by bad reasons' (2019, p. 21). But this set of options is too crude. Humans might generally find it enormously difficult to resist sugary drinks in the checkout line or to not be moved to judgment upon looking at graphic photos of murdered children. It doesn't follow that such decisions are coerced, but nor does it seem to simply amount to instances of acting for bad reasons. Instead, it seems that there is manipulation at work.

Here is one more case: suppose I know that your anger will overtake you if I mention your ex-girlfriend, and I want to sabotage your interview for a job so that you don't move out of state. Minutes before your interview, I bring up your ex-girlfriend, but I also make clear that I'm trying to ruin your interview to keep you in New York. Have you been coerced by your own anger? This sounds odd. It also doesn't seem that you have simply acted for bad reasons since you didn't act for reasons at all. Instead, it seems that I've manipulated you. As Susser et al. themselves say, '[m]anipulation…means taking hold of the controls.…It is to deprive [the one being manipulated] of authorship over their actions. That is what it means to feel like someone else's puppet:…when a person is manipulated that person feels *played*' (2019, pp. 16–17, original emphasis). In a similar spirit, Allen Wood says that '[t]he manipulative person "steers" the other as a driver steers an automobile. The automobile is already moving through its own internal combustion engine and momentum, but its direction is influenced by the one who steers it' (2014, pp. 33–34). All of this seems clearly true in this case. Upon bombing the

[71] https://a15.asmdc.org/press-releases/20190220-wicks-bill-would-whisk-sugary-drinks-out-checkout-aisles.

[72] See Miranda (2008).

interview because you had been thrown into a fit of rage, and then not being offered the job, you would quite plausibly feel played. You may correctly think that I steered you in precisely the direction I wanted, even if I was overt about it. Indeed, just as there are bald-faced lies,[73] we might think of this as *bald-faced manipulation*.

In this way, manipulation can be understood as intentional, arational influence[74]—the circumvention of another person's rational decision-making power for the manipulator's desired end.[75]

Deception and manipulation need not, but frequently do, go hand-in-hand in that people are often manipulated by being fed false information. To deceive is, roughly, to aim to bring about a false belief in another person.[76] I deceive you if I tell you that I am currently out of town, aiming for you to believe this, when in fact I am typing this from my house. While the category of 'deception' subsumes deceiving, it is a broader phenomenon, including, for instance, concealing information.[77] According to Thomas Carson, '[t]o conceal information is to do things to hide information from someone—to prevent someone from discovering it. Often, concealing information constitutes deception or attempted deception' (2010, p. 57). Concealing information can be understood widely here, so that it subsumes, among other phenomena, concealing evidence. Moreover, notice that concealing information is importantly different from withholding information. To withhold information is to fail to provide it, rather than to hide or keep it secret. If I am trying to find a home for my challenging puppy, I withhold information about her lack of being housebroken if you don't ask me anything about it and I don't mention it. But if I frantically discard all of the training pads lying throughout my house before you come over, then I am concealing the information that she is not trained.[78]

[73] See Sorensen (2007) and Lackey (2013).

[74] I will complicate this view of manipulation in Chapter 3, but this account is sufficient for present purposes.

[75] This is very similar to Wood's characterization of manipulation: 'What is characteristic of manipulative behavior is that it influences people's choices in ways that circumvent or subvert their rational decision-making processes, and that undermine or disrupt the ways of choosing that they themselves would critically endorse if they considered the matter in a way that is lucid and free of error' (2014, p. 35). Cass Sunstein also focuses on the bypassing of rational capacities: 'I suggest that an effort to influence people's choices counts as manipulative to the extent that it does not sufficiently engage or appeal to their capacity for reflection and deliberation' (2015, p. 216).

[76] Chisholm and Feehan provide a comprehensive definition that includes the many ways of deceiving: 'To deceive $=_{df}$ to cause another person to acquire a false belief, or to continue to have a false belief, or to cease to have a true belief, or be prevented from acquiring a true belief, or to allow another person to acquire a false belief, or to continue to have a false belief, or to cease to have a true belief, or be prevented from acquiring a true belief' (Chisholm and Feehan 1977, p. 145).

[77] See Lackey (2013).

[78] Cohen (2018) argues that 'deception is restricted to cases where a falsehood is communicated *and* it is the direct cause of the false belief; other cases are manipulations. This will constitute an explication of the idea of deception…as convincing the other of a falsehood. Manipulations that cause false beliefs fail this condition' (2018, p. 488). In my own work (e.g., Lackey 2013), I have distinguished between deceiving and deception, where the former is similar to how Cohen understands deception

Like rational persuasion, manipulation and deception can target both ways of influencing a speaker's decision-making: the decision space and the internal decision-making process. Stores can manipulate the options available to you by having only sugary drinks available at checkout lines, or they can manipulate the way in which you understand these options by having only sugary drinks at eye level, or in aesthetically pleasing display cases, and so on. You can be deceived by being told that your only options are to purchase the deluxe internet package or none at all, and you may be deceived with respect to how you see your options by being shown the incredible internet speed using a server that is not the company's in question.

In contrast, coercion is said to be different in that it precisely targets the decision space or the available options. Joel Rudinow argues that to coerce another person is to offer 'irresistible incentives' (1978, p. 341) and Allen Wood claims that coercing someone means eliminating all of the 'acceptable alternatives' (2014, pp. 21–23). When I say, 'give me your money or I'll shoot you,' there is really only one acceptable option here, and that is to comply with my demand for your money.[79]

Unlike manipulation, however, coercion is said to depend on the rationality of the person being coerced. Christian Coons and Michael Weber write that 'the instruments of coercion (threats, incarceration, and other penalties) are attempts to alter the context of choice, making it rational for you to comply. In this way, the coercer typically treats the coerced as rational. In fact, coercion depends on the target's being rational' (2014, p. 15). In other words, while coercion robs someone of choice, it does not affect that person's ability to engage in rational decision-making. Indeed, coercion is effective only insofar as the one being coerced is rational enough to appreciate that there is really only one acceptable alternative between turning over money and being shot. As Susser et al. write, 'Coercing someone forces them to act the way the coercer wants, not by undermining or circumventing their decision-making faculties, but by making the coercer's way the only acceptable one' (2019, pp. 15–16).

With these views in mind, let's return to the confessions discussed earlier, all of which are extracted in ways that fail to go through the epistemic agency of the suspects. The interrogation processes themselves are highly *manipulative*—instead of going through the rational faculties of the suspects, the interrogators *bypass* or *circumvent* them. In the case of Juan Rivera, for instance, conditions

and the latter to his conception of manipulation. For the purposes of this chapter, it is not necessary that these differences be settled since I will be relying on examples that are clearly manipulation and deception, no matter how these concepts are defined.

[79] While this standard view of coercion is sufficient for the aims of this chapter, I discuss coercion in far more detail in Chapter 4 where I offer a new account and apply it to plea bargaining in the criminal legal system. The view of coercion developed in Chapter 4 can quite straightforwardly be applied to the tactics identified in this chapter that are used to extract confessions from suspects.

were created to influence his ability to withstand pressure, such as isolation, sleep deprivation, extremely lengthy interrogations, and a lack of food. While it was noted earlier that situational factors of this sort significantly increase the likelihood of eliciting false confessions, what should be emphasized here is that the creation of these conditions is itself an explicit tactic used by interrogators to wear suspects down[80] so as to achieve the desired end.

Moreover, police interrogations of suspects are themselves inherently manipulative. As Kassin et al. maintain, '[t]oday's interrogators seek to manipulate a suspect into thinking that it is in his or her best interest to confess. To achieve this change in perceptions of subjective utilities, they use a variety of techniques, referred to broadly as "maximization" and "minimization"' (2010, p. 12). In a similar spirit, Greenspan and Driscoll note that '[p]olice interrogations are...manipulative, in that a detective is attempting to use various ploys—including deceptive statements—to persuade someone to do something he is initially reluctant to do, namely admit to having committed a criminal act' (2016, p. 23). Feigning sympathy or understanding, diminishing the moral seriousness of the crime, lying about the evidence or about the potential consequences of not confessing, threatening a suspect with the death penalty—these are all tactics and ploys used by interrogators to influence a suspect into doing something that is against his own self interests. Certainly, confessing to a crime one didn't commit that is likely to result not only in a lengthy prison sentence, but also in the loss of much of what one holds dear, is not in one's best interest. But even for those who are not innocent, confessing to a crime after an intense interrogation without the presence of counsel can often result in far worse consequences than would have obtained had one not cooperated with authorities. Given this, interrogators know that they need to create a situation in which suspects come to believe something that is patently false; namely, that it is in fact better for them to capitulate and give the interrogators what they want. Suspects thus need to be lulled into a false sense of security, or to be made to feel trapped and desperate, or to be driven to the breaking point, or to come to believe the narrative they are fed, all of which require that the interrogators steer suspects in this direction without in fact presenting epistemically compelling considerations on its behalf. Thus, they engage in paradigmatically manipulative behavior, which circumvents the epistemic agency of the suspects.

In addition to being manipulative, some of these tactics are overtly *deceptive*, where deception *exploits* rather than bypasses epistemic agency. Telling Marty Tankleff that his hair was found within his mother's grasp and that his hospitalized father had emerged from his coma to say that Tankleff was his assailant are lies that investigators knew would not only have a powerful psychological impact

[80] See Gudjonsson (2003).

on a 17-year-old child whose parents had just been murdered but would also appeal directly to his rational faculties. And, indeed, these deceptive tactics did just this, as Tankleff reasoned that because the investigators and his father wouldn't be dishonest, he must be involved in the murder of his parents, despite having no memory of it. As he reported in a 2009 interview, 'I was brought up [to believe] that cops don't lie. When the cops turned around and said, "Your father said you did it," I started to doubt myself because I knew my father would never lie.'[81] The interrogators are here exploiting Tankleff's epistemic agency, counting on him to reason precisely as he did. Similar considerations apply when investigators told Juan Rivera that 'the investigation indicated that he did, in fact, cause the death of Holly [Staker].' Given that there was no compelling evidence linking Rivera to the crime, this is an overtly deceptive practice aimed at making him feel trapped by the weight of the case against him.[82]

Finally, some of the interrogation tactics used to elicit confessions are *coercive* and thereby *subvert* the epistemic agency of the suspects. When Christopher Ochoa, for instance, was threatened with execution, he saw only one acceptable option and that was to cooperate with the authorities. In many respects, the threat of the death penalty, made particularly vivid by the officer pointing to the vein where the needle would go for lethal injection, functioned very similarly to the threat of a bullet in the classic case of coercion, 'Give me your money or I'll shoot.' Just as there is really only one acceptable option here, and that is to comply with my demand for money, Ochoa had only one path forward when facing execution, and that was to give investigators the confession they were seeking. Moreover, police interrogations in general, and the Reid technique in particular, have themselves been described as 'inherently coercive' (Kassin 2005, p. 218). Consider, for instance, step 7 of the Reid Technique, where investigators are advised to present two questions, both of which assume guilt, but where one offers a better justification of the crime, such as 'did you plan this out or did you just snap?' By presenting only two options, the suspect can easily come to believe that he has to choose one even when he is innocent and both involve admitting guilt. As Alan Hirsch, who has testified in roughly 30 cases about the Reid technique, notes, 'It's an interrogation method designed to create anxiety, stress and eventually desperation. The suspect concludes that confessing is the best or even the only way

[81] https://www.oprah.com/oprahshow/marty-tankleffs-wrongful-conviction/all.

[82] In addition to deception of this sort, police officers literally fabricated evidence against Rivera: 'What made Juan Rivera's wrongful conviction all the more horrifying [were] the deceitful efforts police officers made to falsely substantiate the coerced false confession. Before trial, the prosecution trumpeted a slam-dunk piece of evidence: a pair of sneakers, supposedly belonging to Rivera, stained with Holly Staker's blood. Oddly, the prosecution never introduced this seemingly pivotal piece of evidence at trial. The reason for this omission was eventually discovered, after the DNA exoneration: it turns out that the shoes were not actually sold in the U.S. until after the murder. This means that the blood was planted' (https://loevy.com/blog/juan-riveras-coerced-false-confession/).

out… It breaks down innocent people as well as guilty people. It's too effective.'[83] The presentation of just two options is often accompanied with the suggestion of either positive or negative consequences, depending on which is chosen. Indeed, the 'suggestion of reward, or in the alternative, punishment, is one of the most persuasive techniques that police use in interrogating suspects. Police often limit the options open to the suspect to two: (1) you did it and if you do not confess I cannot help you so you are going to be punished harshly, or (2) you did it and if you do confess, you are a good person and I can help you' (Drizin and Colgan 2004, p. 136).

To the extent that coercion involves eliminating acceptable alternatives so that only one remains, it is clear that the suspect is coerced into choosing the least incriminating admission of guilt in step 7 of the Reid Technique. As Leo writes, 'The suspect may perceive that he has no choice but to comply with the detectives' wishes, because he is fatigued, worn down, or simply sees no other way to escape an intolerably stressful experience. Some suspects come to believe that the only way they will be able to leave is if they do what the detectives say. Others comply because they are led to believe that it is the only way to avoid a feared outcome (e.g.,… rape in prison). When a suspect perceives that he has no choice but to comply, his resultant compliance and confession are, by definition, involuntary and the product of coercion' (2009, p. 335). In such cases, the epistemic agency of suspects is neither bypassed nor exploited but subverted. By virtue of leaving no reasonable options left in the suspect's decision-making space but compliance, his ability to exercise his epistemic agency is undermined at its core.

It is helpful to take a step back here and note the value of testimony that is offered *through* the exercise of epistemic agency. Interestingly, in establishing the classic contours of the right to remain silent in *Miranda v. Arizona*, the Court was primarily concerned with the expressive or testimonial liberty of suspects and defendants.[84] For instance, in discussing the aim of *Miranda* warnings, the Court notes that they enable 'the defendant under otherwise compelling circumstances to tell his story without fear, effectively, and in a way that eliminates the evils in the interrogation process' (*Miranda v. Arizona*, 384 U.S. 436, 466 (1966)). Some of these 'evils' include lengthy and frequent interrogations, especially of suspects who are cognitively impaired, whereby 'an… environment is created for no purpose other than to subjugate the individual to the will of his examiner' and where an atmosphere of intimidation is created that is 'equally destructive of human dignity' as physical intimidation is (*Miranda v. Arizona*, 384 U.S. 436, 457 (1966)).

The Court is here clearly interested in ensuring that suspects are able to freely offer testimony that has not been brought under the sway of an interrogator.

[83] https://www.theguardian.com/film/2019/oct/15/when-they-see-us-ava-duvernay-netflix-lawsuit-reid.

[84] Natapoff (2005, p. 1477).

Indeed, there is an important sense in which *Miranda* warnings are less about, say, the right to remain silent and more about protecting a defendant's right to 'speak in the unfettered exercise of his own will' (*Miranda v. Arizona*, 384 U.S. 436, 460 (1966)). As Natapoff notes, the privilege against self-incrimination is '[a]t bottom... not about silence but expressive choice' (2005, p. 1478).

For our purposes, it is important to note that the Court is taking steps to ensure that defendant speech is the result of the proper exercise of epistemic agency. Speech that is the product of the unfettered exercise of one's own will and is not subjugated to that of another just is testimony that is able to be responsive to reasons rather than merely to the influences, pressures, and aims of outside forces. Respecting and engaging with the rational capacities of defendants thus lies at the heart of not only our sense of the proper treatment of persons as epistemic and moral agents, but also the Court's commitment to the importance of testimonial liberty.

4. Credibility Excess

I began this chapter by highlighting that the United States Supreme Court regards confession evidence as possibly the most powerful evidence of guilt admissible in court. At the same time, we have seen that false confessions are often acquired through manipulation, deception, and coercion. What I now want to show is that when the extracted testimony of a confessing self is epistemically privileged over a recanting self, this results in an unwarranted excess of credibility being afforded to the confessor.

The first point to note is that confession evidence is *weighed too heavily*, which is made clear by the fact that confessions in the criminal legal system are standardly regarded as virtually decisive evidence of guilt. Leo makes this point powerfully when he writes:

> This chain reaction starts with the police. Once they obtain a confession, they typically close their investigation, clear the case as solved, and make no effort to pursue any exculpatory evidence or other possible leads, even if the confession is internally inconsistent, contradicted by external evidence, or the result of coercive interrogation. Even when other case evidence subsequently emerges suggesting or demonstrating that the suspect's confession is false, police almost always continue to believe in the suspect's guilt and the underlying accuracy of the confession. (2009, pp. 340–41)

Rather than viewing a confession as a piece of evidence in need of corroboration—as, for instance, a fingerprint would be—it is often regarded as conclusive evidence of guilt. Once a suspect admits he did it, or nods in agreement, or signs a confession, the investigation is closed and the investigators turn to building a case for the prosecution. Given that many confessions are extracted from suspects who are dispositionally likely to falsely confess, and that interrogations involve situational factors that increase the likelihood of eliciting a false confession, there is no plausible justification for the massively elevated evidential status afforded to confession evidence in the criminal legal system. Indeed, against the background of the manipulative, deceptive, and coercive tactics used by interrogators, it is even clearer that confessions ought to be treated as a highly fallible piece of evidence, in need of substantial additional support, rather than as definitive of guilt.

This is even more vivid when it is noted that the totality of the evidence against a given confession is often substantial, while the evidence in its favor is remarkably thin. Returning to the case of Juan Rivera, there was a significant amount of evidence revealing that he was an unreliable confessor under the conditions in question, including that he was aggressively interrogated for four consecutive days, was deprived of sleep and food during this time, was sobbing uncontrollably, was beating his head against the wall of the interrogation room, fell into a fetal position on the floor, was hyperventilating, was on suicide watch, was determined to be in an acute psychotic state and 'not in touch with the reality of what was going on around him,' was sweating, had flared nostrils, was non-responsive, and sounded like 'people who talk in tongues.' In addition, there was a massive amount of evidence that revealed that his confession was false, including the complete absence of physical evidence linking him to the crimes, the DNA that excluded him, the fact that his ankle monitor showed him to be at home during the timeframe of the crimes, and the inaccuracies and incoherencies in his original confession. It is astonishing that despite all of this evidence pointing to the unreliability of his confession, Rivera was found guilty of Holly Staker's rape and murder at three separate jury trials. Yet, it is precisely this unwarranted epistemic grip that confessions exert at every stage of the criminal legal process that explains how this appalling miscarriage of justice could possibly happen.

That confessions are weighed too heavily is further supported by looking at the sheer number of instances of testimony that often need to be discounted in order to retain belief in the correctness of a corresponding conviction. Consider, for analogy, how the testimony of victims of sexual assault is often rejected or discounted,[85] but how numbers can sometimes add up to tip the balance.[86] So, for instance, a handful of girls and women accusing Larry Nassar of sexual harassment or assault wasn't enough for many to believe them, but when over 300 women came forward, the public started to side with their word over his

[85] See, for instance, Tuerkheimer (2017).

[86] It is instructive to compare this point to Charles Mills's discussion of the testimony of Black people: 'At one point in German South-West Africa, white settlers demanded "that in court only the testimony of seven African witnesses could outweigh evidence presented by a single white person"' (Mills 2007, p. 32).

denials.[87] We saw something similar in the case of Bill Cosby, where 60 women reported being victimized at the hands of the once respected comedian and actor.[88] Now while this involves the addition of new testifiers, we can see a structurally similar problem at work in false confessions. A confessing self often reports guilt only once—under conditions of manipulation, deception, and coercion—while a recanting self reports innocence hundreds, even thousands of times, often over a period of years. And yet despite this, the one report of guilt utterly overwhelms the thousands of reports of innocence, with no justification for this radical asymmetry in treatment of confession versus recantations. This provides another lens through which we can see that false confessions receive a massive excess of credibility.

In addition to being weighed too heavily, confessions *block or screen off the gathering and proper interpretation of additional evidence*, which is often fueled by a number of biases. Many investigators, for instance, enter the interrogation room with a bias against the innocence of the suspect in question. Such *interviewer bias* can lead police to 'attempt to gather only confirmatory evidence and to avoid all avenues that may produce negative or inconsistent evidence' (Bruck et al. 1998, p. 140). Indeed, once a confession is regarded as conclusive of guilt, there is no point in pursuing other suspects, theories, and avenues. Instead, all efforts are directed at making the case against the confessing suspect as airtight as possible. *Confirmation bias*, which involves the 'seeking or interpreting of evidence in ways that are partial to existing beliefs, expectations, or a hypothesis in hand' (Nickerson 1998, p. 175), impacts both the gathering and understanding of confessions and evidence that would otherwise be taken to be exculpatory. Rather than seeing the foreign DNA in Holly Staker as straightforward evidence of Rivera's innocence, for example, prosecutors interpreted it as indicating that Rivera failed to ejaculate when he raped Staker. Similarly, *tunnel vision* is a 'compendium of common heuristics and logical fallacies' (Martin 2002, p. 848) whereby 'investigators, prosecutors, judges, and defense lawyers alike... focus on a particular conclusion and then filter all evidence in a case through the lens provided by that conclusion. Through that filter, all information supporting the adopted conclusion is elevated in significance, viewed as consistent with the other evidence, and deemed relevant and probative. Evidence inconsistent with the chosen theory is easily overlooked or dismissed as irrelevant, incredible, or unreliable' (Findley and Scott 2006, p. 292). Quite clearly, confessions are elevated in epistemic significance, viewed as consistent with evidence that is powerfully undermining, and regarded as probative when they shouldn't be. Again, Rivera's confession was regarded as so powerful that it epistemically overwhelmed

[87] https://www.chicagotribune.com/sports/college/ct-spt-michigan-state-larry-nassar-settlement-20180516-story.html.

[88] https://www.usatoday.com/story/life/people/2018/04/27/bill-cosby-full-list-accusers/555144002/.

evidence that would otherwise be interpreted as incontrovertibly revealing his innocence.

Relatedly, confessions are *highly resistant to counterevidence*. To see this, notice that knowledge is taken to be incompatible with the presence of defeaters, with can be either *doxastic* or *normative*, and either *rebutting* or *undercutting*.[89] A doxastic defeater is a doubt or belief that you have that indicates that one of your beliefs is either false (i.e., rebutting) or unreliably formed or sustained (i.e., undercutting). A normative defeater is similar, except it concerns doubts or beliefs that you *should have*, given the evidence available to you. So, for example, if I believe that the animal in my backyard is a bobcat by seeing one there, I might get powerful evidence that such a belief is false by you telling me that bobcats have never lived in my state, or that my basis is a poor one by my optometrist reporting to me how much my vision has deteriorated. If I accept both instances of testimony, then I have doxastic defeaters, rebutting in the first case, undercutting in the second. But even if I reject the testimony in question, I am still on the hook for this counterevidence if I do so for no good reason at all. Why? Because it is evidence that I *should have*. The justification that my bobcat belief might have initially enjoyed, then, has been normatively defeated.

These tools can help us see the extent to which Rivera's false confession was resistant to counterevidence over the course of decades and by people at every stage of the criminal legal process—including police officers, prosecutors, and jurors. Given all of the research discussed above, Rivera was, first and foremost, a prime candidate for providing a false confession: he was a special education student, had endured four days of aggressive interrogation, was hungry, sleep-deprived, and was shown to be in the middle of a psychotic episode. Moreover, Rivera's original confession was riddled with inaccuracies and implausible information. All of this, by itself, should challenge the reliability of Rivera as a source of information about his own guilt. In other words, those accepting Rivera's confession had undercutting defeaters (whether doxastic or normative), since they had evidence that clearly showed that their beliefs that Rivera raped and murdered Holly Staker were unreliably formed or sustained. In particular, they had evidence that the source of their beliefs about Rivera's guilt—namely, Rivera himself—was not reliable under the interrogation conditions in question. But they also had doxastic rebutting defeaters since the DNA evidence excluded him as a source of the semen at the scene of the crime, and his ankle monitor showed

[89] Normative defeaters were discussed briefly in the previous chapter. For various views of both doxastic and normative defeaters, approached in a number of different ways, see BonJour (1980) and (1985), Nozick (1981), Goldman (1986), Pollock (1986), Fricker (1987) and (1994), Chisholm (1989), Burge (1993) and (1997), Plantinga (1993), McDowell (1994), Audi (1997) and (1998), Bergmann (1997), Williams (1999), BonJour and Sosa (2003), Hawthorne (2004), Reed (2006), Lackey (1999 and 2008) and (2020*b*), and Goldberg (2017).

that he was at home during the time of the crimes, thereby calling into question the truth of their beliefs that he was guilty.

When one has a defeater of any kind, the only way in which the target belief can be rationally retained is if one has a *defeater-defeater*—that is, a further belief or evidence that defeats the original belief or evidence. So, for instance, the rebutting defeater for my bobcat belief might itself be defeated if I come to learn that a bobcat recently escaped from the local zoo. Or the undercutting defeater might be defeated if I discover that my optometrist consulted the wrong chart when concluding that my vision is unreliable. But notice: there is simply no way in which the State's incredible theory in which the 11-year-old child was sexually active with some unknown male, and Rivera didn't ejaculate despite raping her, successfully works as a defeater-defeater here. Similarly, the prosecution suggested that Rivera's ankle monitor might have malfunctioned or that he may have somehow slipped out of it to commit the crimes in question. However, there was no evidence at all to support these claims and Rivera's electronic bracelet had functioned properly shortly before and shortly after Holly Staker's rape and murder.[90] Thus, there is simply no interpretation of the available evidence that makes the State's theories *more plausible* than the alternative one: namely, that Rivera falsely confessed under duress to a crime he didn't commit.

Finally, confessions *distort* other evidence. Despite awareness of the reality and prevalence of false confessions, as well as their causes and effects, outrageous theories of the prosecution are often taken to be more plausible than the possibility that a suspect falsely confessed. This occurs even when there is powerful evidence on behalf of a defendant's innocence. Consider, again, the State's explanation of why another person's DNA was found in Holly Staker. The fact that Rivera was convicted of the child's murder shows that the State's bizarre theory was regarded as more credible than the possibility that he confessed to a crime he didn't commit—in other words, a single confession trumped evidence that would otherwise be taken to be decisively exculpatory.[91]

[90] https://www.law.northwestern.edu/legalclinic/wrongfulconvictions/exonerations/il/juan-rivera.html.

[91] Here is another, equally outrageous, example: In '[t]he 2004 case of South Carolina against Billy Wayne Cope... Cope woke up one morning to find his 12-year-old daughter strangled to death in her bed. Police identified Cope as the perpetrator and interrogated him for several stressful hours during which time they told him that he failed a lie detector test and used other interrogation tactics that put innocent people at risk (see Kassin et al., 2010 for a review). After 2.5 days, Cope eventually confessed in a statement that was filled with contradictions and factual errors. Shortly thereafter, it was revealed that Cope's daughter was also sexually assaulted. Subsequent DNA tests revealed that the semen and saliva found on the girl's body did not match Cope, but it did match James Sanders, a serial sex offender who had broken into other homes in the area as well. One would think from this series of events that Cope would have been released from jail, freed, and compensated. Instead, however, the prosecutor—armed with a police-induced confession that did not match the facts of the crime and with no evidence of a link between the two men—charged Cope with conspiracy and theorized that he had pimped his daughter out to Sanders. On the basis of this theory, the jury convicted both Cope and Sanders. Cope's conviction was recently affirmed at the state level; in 2014, the U.S. Supreme

Unfortunately, this is not an isolated or unusual move on the part of the State. As Jacqueline McMurtrie notes, 'The unnamed-lover theory is used so often by prosecutors that it has its own moniker: "the unindicted co-ejaculator"' (2015, p. 855). Similarly, in a widely ridiculed interview on an episode of *60 Minutes*, 'Chicago: The False Confessions Capital,'[92] then-State's Attorney Anita Alvarez discussed the case of the 'Dixmoor Five' in which DNA evidence ruled out five defendants who had falsely confessed to the rape and murder of 14-year-old Cateresa Matthews. After serving a total of 95 years behind bars, all five were exonerated in 2011, and the Illinois State Police settled in 2013 a civil rights case brought on their behalf for a record $40 million.[93] Moreover, the semen found inside Matthews matched Willie Randolph, who had previously been convicted of rape and had 39 arrests. Despite all of this, when asked about this case in a 2012 interview, Alvarez still said that it was possible that the five defendants raped and murdered the girl, and that Randolph wandered past the field where her body was and committed an act of necrophilia.[94] The most plausible explanation for the prevalence of these logic-defying theories of the prosecution and the powerful role they play in securing convictions is that the false confessions distort the other evidence question because they receive a massive, unwarranted excess of credibility.

Thus, confessions are weighed too heavily: confession evidence is regarded as virtually definitive of guilt. Confessions block or screen off the gathering and proper interpretation of additional evidence: interviewer bias, confirmation bias, and tunnel vision lead to a single-minded commitment to the guilt of the confessing suspect. Confessions are resistant to counterevidence: exculpatory evidence, inconsistencies in confessions, and evidence of the unreliability of the suspect when offering the confession are all dismissed. And confessions distort other evidence: outrageous theories of the prosecution are taken to be more plausible than the possibility that a suspect falsely confessed.

In light of these features of false confessions, we can also see how, contrary to what Fricker (2007) argues, *credibility can be finite, and thus how its proper distribution is crucial* for assessing whether a speaker is the victim of testimonial injustice.[95] Typically, when we talk about distributing credibility, we have in mind doing so across different people. If a woman says she was assaulted and the

Court refused to grant Cope's request for an appeal' (Appleby and Kassin 2016, p. 129). Moreover, in 2010, the Center on Wrongful Convictions 'identified 19 cases in which confessors to rape and/or murder were tried and convicted despite having been excluded by DNA tests of key biological materials' (Appleby and Kassin 2016, p. 128).

[92] https://www.cbsnews.com/news/chicago-the-false-confession-capital/.

[93] https://www.law.northwestern.edu/legalclinic/wrongfulconvictions/exonerations/il/the-dixmoor-five.html.

[94] http://blogs.chicagotribune.com/news_columnists_ezorn/2012/12/cook-county-states-attorney-alvarez-humiliates-herself-on-national-tv.html.

[95] See Chapter 1 for a discussion of Fricker's rejection of a distributive conception of credibility.

accused assailant denies this, then the question is: which person do we believe? But in cases of false confessions, we are talking about distributing credibility across different times in the life of the same person. There is the earlier, confessing self and the later, recanting self. The question then becomes, which self do we believe: the earlier or the later one?

Of course, the mere fact that two people disagree, even about matters of fact, does not by itself require that credibility be finite between them. I may tell you that a local restaurant is open while someone else tells you it's not. That we offer competing reports here does not require that only one of us be deemed worthy of trust or belief: you can be credible, even if wrong on a particular occasion, and I can lack credibility, even if right in a one-off case. Many disagreements are the product of innocent mistakes or a lack of information, and so there can still be enough credibility to go around.

But not all disagreements are like this. It's precisely when someone's credibility itself is on the line that its finitude rears its head. False confessions provide the clearest case here: when someone confesses to murder and then recants shortly thereafter, there are no errors or gaps in evidence to explain the disagreement away. To give credibility to the confessing self is *ipso facto* to deny it to the recanting self. Credibility becomes scarce.[96] What this shows is that false confessions uniquely pit one against oneself and reveal how an excess of credibility can lead to an egregious kind of testimonial injustice.[97]

5. Agential Testimonial Injustice

We are now in a position to identify an importantly different kind of testimonial injustice: a speaker is the victim of *agential testimonial injustice* when testimony is *extracted* from her in a way that bypasses, exploits, or subverts her epistemic agency and is then given an unwarranted *excess* of credibility.[98]

There are two different wrongs involved in agential testimonial injustice that are distinctively epistemic in nature, each of which will be explored in detail. The first kind results from the very act of *extracting* testimony from a speaker in a way that compromises or subverts her epistemic agency. This can happen in different

[96] I develop this in greater detail in Lackey (2020*a*). I also make this point in https://blog.apaonline.org/2016/04/21/pitted-against-yourself-credibility-and-false-confessions/.

[97] While I have here focused on earlier-self credibility excesses, it should be clear that similar considerations apply to later selves. Suppose, for instance, that a false 'memory' of abuse is coercively extracted by people in power to serve their purposes, and the testimony of this 'later self' is then given an unwarranted excess of credibility. This would be an example of a later-self credibility excess, with a corresponding form of testimonial injustice.

[98] Medina (2011), Davis (2016), and Lackey (2018*a*) all discuss the relationship between credibility excesses and testimonial injustice, but none do so in connection with epistemic agency, which is distinctive of the approach taken in this book.

ways. The clearest and most extreme case is where the extraction, such as the interrogation process, leads subjects to believe in the truth of their own reports, either wholly or partially, as found in what Kassin and Wrightsman (1985) call coerced-internalized false confessions and Leo and Ofshe (1997) call persuaded false confessions. In cases of coerced-internalized false confessions, both one's testimony and one's psychological and doxastic states have come under the sway of the will of another. By virtue of employing techniques that are manipulative, deceptive, and coercive, interrogators are able to alienate a suspect from her own epistemic resources regarding not only what she says, but also with respect to what she believes and remembers.

This can be powerfully seen in the case of Michael Crowe, who was 14 years old when his 12-year-old sister, Stephanie, was stabbed to death in her bedroom in Escondido, California at some point between the evening of January 21st and the morning of January 22nd of 1998. Michael was interviewed on three separate occasions by police, beginning the day Stephanie was found murdered. During this first interrogation, he reported that he woke up at 4:30 A.M. on the 22nd with a headache and walked down the hallway adjoining Stephanie's bedroom to get a Tylenol from the kitchen. Rather than being returned to his parents after this interview, Michael and his older sister were sent to a shelter for abused and neglected children. The following day, Michael was taken back to police headquarters, where he repeated the version of events he had earlier told police and expressed his anguish over his sister's death and his separation from his family.[99] This second interrogation grew increasingly aggressive, with the police suggesting to Michael that hair that had been found in Stephanie's hand would prove to be his and outright lying to him when they declared both 'that there was a mounting pile of physical and scientific evidence that would prove that he was Stephanie's killer' (Drizin and Colgan 2004, p. 135) and that they knew he was lying about walking to the kitchen because it would have been impossible to do so without seeing Stephanie's body. During the third and final interview with Michael, police continued to use the false evidence ploy, telling him that they knew the murderer was someone living in the house because all of the windows and doors had been closed and locked. In fact, a sliding glass door to the backyard had been left unlocked. In addition, Michael was subjected to a Computer Voice Stress Analyzer test, which is of 'questionable accuracy,' after which the police told him that the tests revealed that he was lying. When Michael began to 'sob uncontrollably' (Drizin and Colgan 2004, p. 135), the police suggested to him that he might be blocking out the fact that he murdered Stephanie. They went on to propose to him that there were 'two Michaels'—one who is good and another who is bad, and it was the bad Michael who killed Stephanie:

99 Drizin and Colgan (2004, p. 134).

MR. CROWE: If that's true, then the other Michael has taken over because I don't know what's going on because I don't remember.

DETECTIVE WRISLEY: You know what, that's possible.

MR. CROWE: It's the most horrible thing in the world. (Drizin and Colgan 2004, p. 139)

As the interrogation continued, Michael began to accept the police's narrative that 'bad Michael' had killed Stephanie and that 'good Michael' had blocked out what happened. 'He stated, "I'm not sure how I did it. All I know is that I did it." Although Michael, at that point in time, apparently believed that he had committed the murder, he was still unable to provide police with any details of the crime' (Drizin and Colgan 2004, pp. 141–42). The charges against Crowe were later dropped when a 'drifter in the neighborhood that night was found with Stephanie's blood on his clothing' (Kassin et al. 2010, p. 15).

Cases of coerced-internalized false confessions, such as Michael Crowe's, quite straightforwardly involve this first kind of epistemic wrong. To see this, recall that epistemic agency is commonly understood as involving a subject's responsiveness to reasons or evidence. On a strong reading of this, I exercise my epistemic agency with respect to my belief when it is responsive to reasons. When interrogators are able to manipulate not only the testimony of suspects, but their psychological and doxastic states as well, they are quite clearly interfering with the reasons-responsiveness of the suspects' beliefs. As Michael Crowe said in a 2008 interview, '[The police] strip away all your support systems, and once they've taken your family away from you and your friends, they start chipping away at your own beliefs and memory.'[100] This erosion of one's trust in one's own faculties—not through reasons, but through manipulation, deception, and coercion—results in a clear and overt attack on epistemic agency.

But even when subjects don't internalize their own guilt, and thus continue to believe in their innocence despite saying otherwise, there is an important sense in which their epistemic agency is compromised *in the extraction of their testimony*. To make this clear, let's look at a couple of cases where a speaker reports what she herself does not believe but in a way that does not at all interfere with her epistemic agency.

Consider, first, lying—where a speaker offers a statement, believes that it is false, and offers the statement with the intention to be deceptive.[101] Even though a liar aims to be deceptive in her reports, this does not at all interfere with her *ability* to be responsive to reasons in her beliefs or her testimony. Indeed, a liar might even be a *responsible* epistemic agent regarding her belief states, despite the fact that her statements aim away from the truth. Consider, next, cases of *selfless*

[100] https://www.oprah.com/oprahshow/wrongfully-accused_1/all.

[101] See Lackey (2013).

assertion,[102] where there are three components to this phenomenon: first, a subject, for purely non-epistemic reasons, does not believe the proposition in question; second, despite this lack of belief, the subject is aware that the proposition is very well supported by all of the available evidence; and, third, because of this, the subject asserts the proposition without believing it. A classic case of a selfless assertion is where a Creationist teacher correctly reports that *Homo Sapiens* evolved from *Homo erectus* to her students, even though she doesn't believe this herself. Here, the reported belief in question is resistant to counterevidence, and so the belief itself is at least not properly responsive to reasons. Nevertheless, the reporting of the selfless assertion does not in any way violate the speaker's epistemic agency and, in fact, is grounded in it. In particular, the speaker in such cases fails to report what she herself believes, but she does so for straightforwardly epistemic reasons. In this way, she is appropriately sensitive to reasons, not with respect to her own beliefs, but with respect to her testimony. On my view, then, selfless assertions straightforwardly reflect epistemic agency.

Let's now turn to the case of compliant false confessions, which, it may be recalled, are 'those in which suspects are induced through interrogation to confess to a crime they did not commit. In those cases, the suspect acquiesces to the demand for a confession to escape a stressful situation, avoid punishment, or gain a promised or implied reward' (Kassin et al. 2010, p. 14). Here, even if the beliefs of the suspects are responsive to reasons, this is utterly disconnected from the obtaining of their testimony. Unlike in the case of selfless assertions, for instance, where the offering of the reports is precisely what is grounded in the responsiveness to reasons, the tactics used to extract the confessions subvert the epistemic agency of the suspects. In so doing, such speakers are the victim of this first kind of epistemic wrong involved in agential testimonial injustice.

One of the particularly pernicious dimensions of the extraction dimension of agential testimonial injustice is how victims end up being cornered and powerless in the eliciting of their testimony yet also simultaneously rendered actively complicit in their own undoing. In this sense, agential testimonial injustice bears important similarities to other nearby phenomena, including torture, gaslighting, and predatory grooming. According to David Sussman, for instance, 'the wrong of torture' is not 'just disregarding, thwarting or undermining the victim's capacities for rational self-governance. Instead... torture forces a victim into the position of colluding against himself through his own affects and emotions, so that he experiences himself as simultaneously powerless and yet actively complicit in his own violation' (2005, p. 4). In a similar spirit, Kate Abramson maintains that 'because of the particular ways in which gaslighting works through manipulation, the destruction of the target's independent perspective is brought about, after a

102 See Lackey (2007) and (2008).

fashion, through her own complicity. If I'm manipulated into going along with something by a simple act of deception, I may feel embarrassed for having believed that person, but I won't typically feel I've been complicit in having been so duped. Gaslighting, in contrast, is accomplished through manipulative means that leave its target sensing (rightly so) that she has been turned against herself.... in this respect, gaslighting is closer to torture than any more ordinary form of manipulation' (forthcoming, p. 106 of manuscript). And Lauren Leydon-Hardy discusses how victims of predatory grooming are 'exposed to sustained patterns of behavior aimed at rendering them acquiescent to—or even complicit in—conduct which, outside of the context of a grooming relationship, might otherwise have been readily recognized as harmful or exploitative' (2021, p. 119). In all of these cases, the agency of victims is both compromised and exercised, resulting in a paradoxical state of both powerlessness and complicity. The gaslighting victim, for instance, is systematically manipulated so that she comes to no longer trust her own perceptions, emotional responses, memories, and beliefs. While the manipulator is an external force impinging on her agency, she is also complicit in her own untethering from reality by giving way to the destruction of her self-trust. In this way, gaslighting both erodes, and yet depends on, the victim's agency.

In many respects, both the powerlessness and the victim's complicity are even starker in cases of agential testimonial injustice. Consider, again, false confessions. Interrogating a suspect for days, presenting false evidence of guilt that seems overwhelming, and threatening to seek a lengthy sentence or the death penalty can leave a suspect feeling trapped, desperate, and helpless. According to Jim Trainum, a former Washington, D.C. police detective, 'The way the interrogation process is set up in this country is that it's designed not to get information from you, but to get a confession .... Basically, we create a situation where you are faced with what you perceive to be an inevitable consequence.'[103] At the same time, the only real path forward presented by interrogators is one of cooperation—including confessing to a crime that the suspect didn't commit—which involves active participation. Placing himself in the position of the suspect, Trainum continues his characterization of police interrogations: 'He's telling me, "I have all this evidence and they have these witnesses." He's telling me I'm going to be found guilty no matter what. I'm screwed. But he's also telling me that if I confess he's going to help me. I can go home. That this will go away. I just need to tell him what he wants to hear.'[104] Telling the interrogator 'what he wants to hear' requires action. Indeed, the suspect needs to actually utter the words, or sign the confession, or nod in agreement to the version of events outlined in order to cooperate. This combination of one's powerlessness at the inevitability of the outcome, and yet one's active participation in bringing it about, adds a further layer in which

[103] https://www.theatlantic.com/news/archive/2016/06/davontae-sanford/486290/.
[104] https://www.theatlantic.com/news/archive/2016/06/davontae-sanford/486290/.

the suspect is wronged. By virtue of orchestrating a situation in which the only option is for the suspect to literally point the finger at himself, the interrogator has turned the suspect's agency against himself and has thereby rendered him complicit in his own undoing. When the suspect finally gives the interrogator what he wants—a confession—he doesn't end up 'going home' but, instead, finds himself in a jail cell facing the horrors of being separated from loved ones, a lengthy prison sentence, and even the possibility of execution. Having one's agency, which is fundamental to being a person, co-opted in this way for the service of one's own demise is a violation at the deepest of levels.

This violation can be compounded in various ways. As we saw in the case of Michael Crowe, the impact of the interrogators can encroach on both one's actions as well as on one's perceptions, memories, and beliefs. This can, in turn, lead to the implication of not only oneself, but also of others. Amanda Knox, who was wrongfully convicted of the 2007 rape and murder of her British roommate, Meredith Kercher, while studying abroad in Perugia, Italy,[105] powerfully describes this process:

> [My interrogators] engaged in a relentless campaign of lies & gaslighting. They isolated me and made me vulnerable . . . . They kept me overnight. They told me I had amnesia, that I was so traumatized by events I'd witnessed, that I'd repressed them. They shouted at me to remember, REMEMBER! They slapped me . . . . They made me feel insane. Like I couldn't trust my own thoughts, my own memories. I started to believe them that I had amnesia, that I'd witnessed something horrific. . . . They wrote a statement for me, a confused and contradictory statement, that implicated my boss, Patrick, and placed me at the scene of the crime. Shaking and tired and gaslit into submission, I signed it.[106]

When the external forces at work by interrogators co-opt both a suspect's actions and her mind, leaving her so unmoored from her own cognitive faculties that she can't trust their deliverances, she can become a virtual stranger to herself. This can even lead to a suspect coming to believe that she committed a crime she didn't, as we saw with Michael Crowe, and to the implication of other innocent suspects, as Knox does with her boss. Once again, there is a paradoxical sense of both powerlessness and complicity in a suspect's own undoing here, often causing enormous guilt and shame. Knox expresses this consequence when she writes, '[My interrogators] twisted all available evidence to fit the incoherent statement they had coerced me into signing. That "false admission" was crucial in both my

[105] http://www.amandaknox.com.
[106] https://twitter.com/amandaknox/status/1355332022139408384.

guilty convictions... & for years, I blamed myself for what happened that night.'[107] Moreover, the blame doesn't end with the victim in such cases, as studies show that exonerees who falsely confessed are stigmatized more harshly than exonerees who have been convicted on other grounds, such as through eyewitness misidentification, precisely because they are perceived as being responsible for, or having otherwise contributed to, their wrongful conviction.[108] Thus, this sense of complicity in one's own unraveling—whether it is actual or merely perceived[109]—can give rise to a host of additional wrongs, including the formation of false memories and beliefs, the implication of other innocent suspects, misplaced guilt and shame, and unwarranted attributions of responsibility and blame.

The second kind of epistemic wrong involved in agential testimonial injustice specifically involves the *excess of credibility* given to the extracted testimony. Here, one is epistemically wronged by virtue of being regarded as a testifier—a giver of knowledge—only when one's testimony is extracted and is thus the product of a process that compromises one's epistemic agency. By virtue of the State saying that the reality described by the confessor in cases of false confessions—one that is reported only through manipulation, deception, and coercion—represents her truest states, *the confessor's status as a knower is reduced to what she reports only under conditions devoid of, or with diminished, epistemic agency*. This is especially problematic since the question of whether one is a murderer can literally be a matter of life and death. So, while it is true that the recanter—the later self who accurately, consistently, and steadfastly describes a different reality that is not extracted through manipulations, deception, or coercion—is wronged in being afforded a massive credibility deficit, there is a unique and powerful epistemic wrong done to the earlier self who receives a credibility excess. Indeed, the excess given in false confessions quite literally amounts to the State saying that confessors are knowers with respect to the testimony in question only insofar as they are *not* epistemic agents.

[107] https://twitter.com/amandaknox/status/1355332022139408384. In a similar spirit, one of the students in the Northwestern Prison Education Program, William Peeples, describes the shame that followed his coerced false confession: '[I]n the end I signed that typed confession, convinced that as the detective promised, I'd get a break since I cooperated, and I'd shown remorse and taken responsibility. To this very day I still kick myself for being so stupid, so weak!' (personal correspondence).

[108] See Clow and Leach (2015), Savage et al. (2018), and Faison and Smalarz (2020).

[109] Sukaina Hirji discusses the impact of perceived complicity in relation to double binds: '[P]art of what makes double binds so pernicious, and such an effective mechanism of oppressive structures, is that they co-opt an individual's agency while providing the illusion of freedom. It is not always obvious when one is in a double bind, and it is even less obvious what the choice structure is in such a bind. One consequence of this illusion of freedom is that it becomes easy to blame or criticize members of oppressed groups for acting in ways that reinforce their own oppression. Indeed, it is also easy for a member of an oppressed group to blame or criticize themselves for acting in ways that make them complicit in their own oppression. Without an understanding of the structure of double binds, it is tempting to locate responsibility at the level of individual agency, rather than at the level of the oppressive structures that make it impossible for an agent not to be complicit in their own oppression' (2021, p. 668).

There is an instructive parallel here: in ancient Athens, the testimony of enslaved persons, who were the property of their masters or the State, was typically inadmissible in judicial proceedings except under torture. As Michael Gagarin writes, 'One of the most criticized features of classical Athenian law is the bizarre institution of... "interrogation under torture." A well-known rule held that in most cases the testimony of slaves was only admissible in court if it had been taken under torture, and in the surviving forensic speeches the orators frequently... praise the practice as most effective' (Gagarin 1996, p. 1). This practice, as well as similar ones under the Roman Republic, was grounded in the view 'that the testimony of a slave freely given [is] so unreliable as to be altogether inadmissible' (Lowell 1897, p. 220). Thus, just as Athenian and Roman courts regarded the testimony of enslaved persons as reliable only when obtained via torture—and thereby offered under conditions devoid of epistemic agency—so, too, do our courts privilege the testimony of confessing selves, even when confessions are extracted through interrogation techniques that compromise or undermine epistemic agency.[110]

It is important to note that an excess of credibility can be afforded to a speaker in at least two different ways. The first is *belief driven*: a speaker is believed despite the fact that the evidence does not warrant belief or does not warrant belief to the degree in question. For instance, if a detective believes Juan Rivera's confession even though there is substantial evidence against its reliability, such as that he was in the middle of a psychotic episode when he offered a statement that was riddled with inconsistencies and inaccuracies after being coercively interrogated for four days, then he is afforded an unwarranted excess of credibility. Similarly, if there is relatively thin evidence that Rivera's confession is reliable, but a detective is certain of his guilt on its basis, then the detective's belief state outstripping the evidence can also result in a credibility excess in this first sense. The second way an excess of credibility can be afforded to a speaker is *action or function driven*: a speaker's testimony plays an epistemically oversized role that is unwarranted in the actions of others or the systems in which they are a part. For instance, suppose that those responsible for Rivera's conviction, such as the detectives and prosecutors, recognize that there are powerful reasons to question the truth and

[110] Similarly, Peters (1985) discusses the legal revolution that took place in Europe in the twelfth century that shaped European criminal jurisprudence until the end of the eighteenth century. One of the consequences of this legal revolution is that 'confession was elevated to the top of the hierarchy of proofs, so elevated, in fact, that jurists called confessions "the queen of proofs"' (1985, p. 41). Moreover, it is precisely because confessions were taken to be such compelling evidence of guilt, and torture was regarded as a reliable means of acquiring true confessions, that torture became so integrated into the European criminal legal system of this time. Peters writes: 'For all the uncertainties that attended the gathering and weighing of evidence, the testimony of witnesses, and the unpredictability of judges and juries, confession provided a remedy, and in some cases, chiefly capital ones, it came to be required. It is the importance of confession upon which hinges, if not the revival, then surely the spread and integration of torture into the legal systems of the thirteenth century' (1985, p. 44).

reliability of Rivera's confession, but nonetheless forge ahead with trying to prove his guilt of the rape and murder of Holly Staker. Even if they did not straightforwardly believe Rivera, his confession functioned within the criminal legal system in an unwarranted and oversized epistemic way and, in this sense, received an excess of credibility.[111]

What we have seen, then, is that there is an entirely different notion of testimonial injustice, one that is grounded in a violation of a person's epistemic agency. Indeed, agential testimonial injustice shares not a single feature with the prejudicial kind, but seems to be testimonial injustice nonetheless. For instance, while the excess of credibility afforded to confessing suspects may sometimes—even often—be grounded in racial prejudice targeting a person's social identity, it need not be. It can also be driven simply by practical features, such as a desire to close an investigation, to appease the public, or to build a compelling case for the prosecution. Moreover, since a confessing self's testimony may be given an excess of credibility while, at the same time, her recanting self receives a credibility deficit, prejudicial bias simply can't be telling the whole story because one person is given both an excess and a deficit of credibility regarding the very same question. In this way, the wrongness of agential testimonial injustice derives not from the wrongness of bias, and the speaker getting less credibility than she deserves because of this, but in her epistemic agency being bypassed, exploited, or undermined, and in then being regarded as a knower or truthteller only under these conditions.

Nevertheless, biases and prejudices that target a given suspect's social identify can certainly dramatically increase the likelihood that agential testimonial injustice will be perpetrated.[112] Andrew Taslitz (2006), for instance, provides a powerful description of what happens when the interrogation techniques we discussed earlier are fueled by racial discrimination:

> Now when we add race to the mix, the picture becomes clearer. Officers start with a presumption of the guilt of a young black male based upon one-sided and limited circumstantial evidence. The kid reacts with hostility and defensiveness. These reactions, combined with his powerless speech patterns, lead police to

[111] That there are these two ways to afford a speaker a credibility excess is mirrored on the side of credibility deficits. Consider, for instance, the case of Tom Robinson in *To Kill A Mockingbird*, which is discussed extensively by Fricker in her (2007). Robinson is a Black man accused in 1935 Alabama of raping Mayella Ewell, who is white. Despite the fact that Ewell sustained injuries on her face inflicted by a left-handed person, and Robinson's left arm is disabled, Robinson is found guilty of raping Ewell. This might be explained in two different ways. First, the racism of the jurors may have led them to ignore powerful evidence of his innocence in their belief states, resulting in them believing that he is guilty despite his claims of innocence. This is a belief-driven credibility deficit. Second, the racism of the jurors may have led them to vote that he is guilty of Ewell's rape, despite the fact that the evidence they have that she was attacked by a left-handed person prevents them from believing that this is the case. This is an action-driven credibility deficit.

[112] I will discuss this point in more detail in Chapter 5.

> believe he is lying. They close off alternative theories, heightening the pressure on the kid about whose guilt they are now convinced. They make real evidence sound more inculpatory than it is, they deceive him into believing there is still more inculpatory evidence against him, they appeal to his self-interest, and they hammer away at him for hours. Young, isolated, cut off from family and friends, fearful, and rightly seeing no way out, he confesses. Falsely.
>
> Should the youth take the stand at a suppression hearing, the judge, drawing on the same racially-stigmatizing images of black youth, won't believe him. The case goes to trial, and the jury likely sees a film just of his confession . . . the same defensiveness and linguistic barriers that made the kid seem to be a liar to the police prod the jury toward a similar conclusion. And the same stereotypes of black criminality and duplicity again favor jurors accepting the truthfulness of the confession rather than of its retraction. (Taslitz 2006, pp. 131–32)

Given that Black defendants are massively overrepresented in wrongful convictions, there is further reason to conclude that racism is a significant factor when looking at why confessing selves are given a credibility excess. For instance, Black defendants convicted of murder are 50% more likely to be innocent than other people convicted of murderer,[113] and 85% of juvenile exonerees who falsely confessed are Black.[114] Moreover, members of groups associated with delinquency, deviance, or moral deficiency, such as 'criminals' and 'prisoners,' are frequently the targets of systematic prejudice. A criminal record, for instance, presents a major barrier to employment,[115] the label of 'prisoner' or 'ex-con' is highly stigmatized,[116] and people who are incarcerated tend to be demonized as dangerous, dishonest, and disreputable.[117] Indeed, even 'suspect' can trigger bias. As Edwin Meese III famously said in 1985 while he was Attorney General of the United States, 'you don't have many suspects who are innocent of a crime. That's contradictory. If a person is innocent of a crime, then he is not a suspect.'[118] Thus, a plausible explanation in at least some cases is that a confession triggers these biases and prejudices, such as that the confessor is a 'criminal,' which enhances the excess of credibility afforded to the false confession in question.

While agential testimonial injustice is extraordinarily vivid in cases of false confessions that have been extracted, it should be noted that testimony obtained in ways that compromise or deny epistemic agency is not limited to such cases. Many abusive relationships, for instance, involve coercion of various degrees, including in testimonial contexts, and when what is reported under such

[113] Gross et al. (2017, p. 4). [114] Gross et al. (2005, p. 550). [115] See Pager (2007).
[116] See Harding (2003), LeBel (2008), and Hirschfield and Piquero (2010).
[117] See Gaubatz (1995) and Young (1999).
[118] https://www.washingtonpost.com/archive/politics/1985/10/11/meese-says-few-suspects-are-innocent-of-crime/272c4d16-f627-4ce4-896e-7faf8632a526/.

conditions is unjustifiably privileged, one is the victim of this kind of testimonial injustice. Imagine, for instance, a woman testifying that her partner has never been abusive while he is standing next to her, but she then retracts this once she is able to extricate herself from his control. If the former testimony is weighed far more heavily than the latter for no good reason, particularly when one is aware of the broader context of the abuse, this would be an instance of what I'm calling agential testimonial injustice.[119]

I have focused extensively on how the prejudicial conception of testimonial injustice cannot adequately explain the way in which those who falsely confess are epistemically wronged, but it is also worth briefly noting the way in which some of the other widely discussed kinds of epistemic wrongs in the literature fall short, too. *Testimonial smothering*, for instance is the 'truncating of one's own testimony' so that the testimony offered 'contains only content for which one's audience demonstrates testimonial competence' (Dotson 2011, p. 244). But the problem in the case of, say, Juan Rivera is not the silencing or smothering of his testimony, but the extraction of it—in this case, a confession—that is then weaponized through its elevated epistemic status. *Testimonial quieting* 'occurs when an audience fails to identify a speaker as a knower' (Dotson 2011, p. 244). The detectives conducting the interrogation, however, recognize Rivera as a knower, but only when he provides the testimony that they want to hear. Similarly, *epistemic oppression* 'refers to persistent epistemic exclusion that hinders one's contribution to knowledge production' (Dotson 2014, p. 115). Crucially, however, Rivera is not excluded from the epistemic community. Rather, he is included, but only when he offers testimony that is the result of manipulative, deceptive, and coercive tactics that compromise his epistemic agency. This is why the second component of agential testimonial injustice is so important to notice. It is not merely the extraction of the confession that is the problem, but also the recognition of the victim's status as a knower *only when* his agency has been bypassed, exploited, or subverted.

Relatedly, Leydon-Hardy identifies *epistemic infringement* as 'a category of epistemic misconduct that works through the systematic contravention of interpersonal social and epistemic norms in a manner that subverts the epistemic agency of targeted individuals' (2021, p. 122). While this may subsume the dimension of agential testimonial injustice involving extraction,[120] it does not capture the distinctive wrong inflicted on victims by recognizing them as a contributor to the epistemic community only under conditions devoid of, or with diminished, epistemic agency.

[119] Cases of this sort will be discussed in far more detail in Chapter 5.

[120] It should also be noted that extraction can involve the bypassing or exploiting of epistemic agency, rather than only its subversion.

Epistemic exploitation, according to Nora Berenstain, 'occurs when privileged persons compel marginalized persons to produce an education or explanation about the nature of the oppression they face' (2016, p. 570). This is clearly not what is happening with Rivera and others like him in the criminal legal system, as no one is compelling suspects and defendants to educate them about their oppression. Indeed, quite the contrary is the case, as when those who falsely confess recant and explain that their testimony was the result of, say, coercion, they are systematically silenced and regraded as liars. Emmalon Davis argues that *epistemic appropriation* should be understood as follows:

> Call th[e] first harm *epistemic detachment*. When epistemic detachment occurs, the intercommunal pool is expanded to incorporate new epistemic resources (e.g., concepts, interpretations, stories, and meanings), but the participatory role of marginalized contributors in the process of knowledge production is obscured. While epistemic detachment may occur independently from other epistemic harms, it is often compounded by a second harm, namely, *epistemic misdirection*. Epistemic misdirection occurs when epistemic resources developed within, but detached from, the margins are utilized in dominant discourses in ways that disproportionately benefit the powerful. That is to say, the benefits associated with the epistemic contributions of the marginalized are misdirected toward the comparatively privileged. Taken together, epistemic detachment and epistemic misdirection constitute what I am calling *epistemic appropriation*.
>
> (Davis 2018, p. 705)

A paradigmatic example of this phenomenon is the appropriation of a Black woman's words or story by white people in positions of power, which Davis argues is what happened to Sojourner Truth in Harriet Beecher Stowe's short article, 'Sojourner Truth, the Libyan Sibyl.'[121] While there is a broad sense in which the extracted confessions of suspects and defendants, who are often in marginalized positions, are used to benefit the powerful, such as through the convictions sought by prosecutors, it would be misleading to regard confessions as epistemic resources or contributions of the marginalized. Indeed, given that such testimony is obtained through the compromising of epistemic agency, it would be an affront to the epistemic dignity of suspects and defendants to regard this as their contribution in any normatively meaningful sense.

It is also worth noting that agential testimonial injustice can be fueled by, or interact with, some of the other forms of testimonial injustice developed in the previous chapter. Consider hearer-excess testimonial injustice, which involves a hearer giving himself an epistemic boost, especially relative to the amount of

[121] Davis (2018, p. 711).

credibility afforded to a speaker. Law enforcement professionals, for instance, are confident in their ability to accurately distinguish between truthful and deceptive statements made by suspects. Such confidence is the result of a combination of on-the-job experience and training programs that claim to reliably increase accuracy with judgments of this sort.[122] John E. Reid Associates, for example, claim that 'trained investigators can achieve an 85% level of accuracy through the use of various verbal cues (e.g., qualified or rehearsed responses), nonverbal cues (e.g., gaze aversion, frozen posture, slouching) and behavioral attitudes (e.g., lack of concern, anxiousness, and guardedness) presumably diagnostic of truth or deception' (Kassin et al. 2007, p. 382). Moreover, field research confirms that police officers are very confident in their skills, with some even believing that they have a 'sixth sense' (Kassin et al. 2007, p. 382). The problem is that research overwhelmingly indicates that this confidence is misplaced. Numerous studies over the years have shown that 'experts' perform only slightly better than ordinary people at detecting deception, that ordinary people perform no better than chance at doing so, and that training tends to produce only small and inconsistent changes in performance.[123]

What we see here, then, is hearer-excess testimonial injustice: investigators are massively overconfident in their ability to detect deception when interrogating suspects. This self-boost of credibility then provides optimal conditions for agential testimonial injustice. If a detective believes himself to be more reliable than he in fact is at distinguishing between truthful and deceptive statements, then he will falsely take himself to know when a suspect is lying even when he doesn't. When this suspect truly denies involvement in a murder he's investigating, then, he will feel confident in rejecting it and pressing forward with the employment of tactics to elicit a confession. Overconfidence in his own deception-detecting abilities thus gives rises to an extraction of a false confession. Moreover, this extracted confession will almost certainly be weighed too heavily in the criminal legal system, especially in relation to police testimony, which is systematically afforded an excess of credibility.[124] In this case, then, hearer-excess testimonial injustice begets both distributive testimonial injustice and agential testimonial injustice.

Here are two other examples: Black suspects are 'stereotyped as less honest and more criminal than the majority' (Johnson 1996, p. 316). Given this, an investigator is far more likely to believe that a Black suspect is guilty of a criminal act and lying when he asserts his innocence, thereby perpetrating an act of content-based testimonial injustice where the suspect is regarded as more knowledgeable in a stigmatized domain, such as criminal activity, because of his race. This can contribute to the detective pursuing the extraction of a confession with more zeal,

[122] Kassin et al. (2007, p. 382).
[123] Vrij (2000), Memon et al. (2003), and Granhag and Strömwall (2004).
[124] See Warren (2018) and Trivedi and Van Cleve (2020).

being poised to accept it, and then closing the investigation and building the case for the prosecution. Content-based testimonial injustice here works hand-in-hand with agential testimonial injustice.[125]

Relatedly, suppose that once the detective elicits the confession and closes the investigation, he fails to follow up on leads that he should pursue and thereby misses out on evidence that he should have that bolsters the credibility of the innocent suspect. Agential testimonial injustice here begets normative testimonial injustice, as once the confession is extracted and then given an excess of credibility, it leads to the failure to gather and examine additional evidence that the detective ought to have in his possession.

Agential testimonial injustice thus involves a testifier suffering two epistemic wrongs, both through the process by which the testimony is extracted and by virtue of the credibility excess it receives. I now want to briefly turn to why confessing selves might be given a credibility excess in the first place. And notice just how crucial it is to address this question. *For convictions based largely on false confessions can't be explained simply by pointing to the fact that recanting selves receive a credibility deficit.* In many cases, if you subtract the confession, you lose the conviction, too.[126] So, for instance, even if a defendant's testimony of innocence at a later time is rejected, what is often also needed to convince a jury of his guilt is the veracity of the original confession. Put bluntly, calling the recanter a liar isn't enough for a conviction—the confessor also needs to be regarded as a truthteller.

6. Why?

The first, and perhaps most obvious, reason why the testimony of confessors is privileged is that most of us find it very difficult to imagine ourselves confessing to something we didn't do, and so we conclude that the suspect must be guilty. This is especially compelling when a violent crime is at issue, such as murder or rape. The problem with this is that there is ample psychological research showing otherwise. For instance, in a well-known experiment by Kassin and Kiechel (1996), 69% of college students who were falsely accused of causing a computer to crash by pressing a key that they were told to avoid signed a confession. When false evidence is presented of guilt, this percentage is even higher, and it is not uncommon for suspects to even come to believe in their own guilt, either fully or partially. A different study by Nash and Wade (2009) used digital editing software

[125] I will discuss this in more detail in Chapter 5.

[126] Consider, again, the case of Tankleff discussed above: '*Solely on the basis of that confession, Tankleff was convicted*, only to have his conviction vacated and the charges dismissed 19 years later' (Kassin et al. 2010, p. 18, emphasis added).

to fabricate evidence of participants 'stealing' money from a 'bank' during a computerized gambling experiment. When presented with this evidence, *all* of the subjects signed the confession form, with 63% fully internalizing the act and 20% partially internalizing the act. The authors conclude, 'a combination of social demand, phoney evidence and false suggestion from a credible source can lead a substantial number of people to falsely confess and believe they committed an act they never did' (2009, p. 629).

Another reason we favor the confessor over the recanter is that false confessions affect the perceptions of others, including eyewitnesses, alibi witnesses, and forensic experts. In one study, 61% of those who had witnessed a staged theft changed their identifications after learning that certain lineup members had confessed.[127] In another study, only 45% of participants maintained their support of an alibi for a suspect after being told that she confessed to stealing money, a number that dropped to 20% when the experimenter suggested that their support might imply their complicity with the alibi.[128] What this data shows is that false confessions not only mislead in the first instance, *they also beget additional misleading evidence downstream*. When this is combined with how counterintuitive false confessions seem to many, including to judges and jurors, conditions become optimal for wrongful convictions.

Finally, the *practical interests* of those most responsible for securing justice often lead them, intentionally or unintentionally, to weigh confessions far too heavily, to disregard exculpatory evidence, and to rely on incredible theories to support their conclusions. This is often seen in the case of prosecutors, who can be blindly driven by a desire to 'win.' Recall, again, Anita Alvarez's logic-defying theory in the case of the exonerated 'Dixmoor Five,' according to which the five defendants raped and murdered Cateresa Matthews and that Willie Randolph, whose semen was found inside Matthews, wandered past the field where her body was and committed an act of necrophilia. Since the total evidence overwhelmingly tells against this outrageous theory, the most plausible explanation is that Alvarez was here motivated by her practical interests, which she thinks will be served by refusing to admit mistakes by her office.

7. Conclusion

In this chapter, I have argued that false confessions provide a unique, compelling, and practically urgent case in which an excess of credibility results in a distinctive kind of testimonial injustice. This reveals not only that credibility can, in fact, be finite, and that its proper distribution is often of critical importance—indeed, it

[127] See Kasel and Kassin (2009). [128] See Marion et al. (2016).

can literally be the difference between life and death—but also that in privileging earlier, confessing selves over later, recanting selves, the State often reduces the confessor to a knower only insofar as she is devoid of epistemic agency. In doing so, the State is quite straightforwardly saying to its citizens—you are worthy of being believed only when we undermine your epistemic agency and extract information from you through manipulative, deceptive, and coercive methods. That this is a particularly pernicious form of testimonial injustice, carried out by institutions in which we place our trust, cries out for a radical change in the epistemic lens through which we view confessions in the criminal legal system.

3
Eyewitness Testimony and Epistemic Agency

Eyewitness testimony is a powerful form of evidence, and this is especially true in the United States criminal legal system. A single witness picking out a suspect in a lineup can set in motion events leading to an arrest, and this same witness confidently pointing to the defendant in a courtroom can secure a conviction of guilt. As Justice William J. Brennan Jr. wrote in a 1981 dissent in *Watkins v. Sowders*, 'All the evidence points rather strikingly to the conclusion that there is almost nothing more convincing than a live human being who takes the stand, points a finger at the defendant, and says, "That's the one!"' (*Watkins v. Souders*, 449 U.S. 341, 352 (1982)).[1] At the same time, 'eyewitness misidentification is the greatest contributing factor to wrongful convictions proven by DNA testing, playing a role in more than 70% of [the 350] convictions overturned through DNA testing nationwide.'[2]

In this chapter, I offer a close examination of this tension between the enormous epistemic weight that eyewitness testimony is afforded in the United States criminal legal system and the fact that there are important questions about its reliability as a source of evidence. I first argue that lineups and interrogations often function by way of extracting testimony from an eyewitness through practices that are manipulative, deceptive, or coercive. I then show that when testimony that is extracted in these ways is given an unwarranted excess of credibility, the eyewitness in question is the victim of what I earlier called agential

[1] See also: 'An eyewitness who says "That is the person I saw pull the gun" is providing direct evidence of guilt in the sense that the criminal act and the defendant are directly linked. In contrast, physical evidence such as fingerprints indicate only that the suspect touched a given surface at some point in time, perhaps for reasons unrelated to the crime, and hence is circumstantial evidence' (Well et al. 1998, p. 604).

[2] https://www.innocenceproject.org/causes/eyewitness-misidentification/?gclid=EAIaIQobChMIotntz7qG6QIVY_rjBx2NQQCTEAAYASAAEgJGVfD_BwE. See also 'One of the principal reasons that eyewitness error is the leading cause of wrongful convictions is because it is one of the most powerful types of evidence that can be presented against a criminal defendant' (Wise et al. 2009, p. 441); 'There can be no reasonable doubt that inaccurate eyewitness testimony may be one of the most prejudicial features of a criminal trial. Juries, naturally desirous to punish a vicious crime, may well be unschooled in the effects that the subtle compound of suggestion, anxiety, and forgetfulness in the face of the need to recall often has on witnesses. Accordingly, doubts over the strength of the evidence of a defendant's guilt may be resolved on the basis of the eyewitness' seeming certainty when he points to the defendant and exclaims with the conviction that veils all doubt, "[T]hat's the man!"' (*Kampshoff v. Smith*, 698 F.2d 581, 585 (2d Cir. 1983)).

Criminal Testimonial Injustice. Jennifer Lackey, Oxford University Press. © Jennifer Lackey 2023.
DOI: 10.1093/oso/9780192864109.003.0004

testimonial injustice. The two epistemic wrongs of agential testimonial injustice arise from (i) the testifier's epistemic agency being circumvented, exploited, or subverted, and (ii) the testifier then being regarded as trustworthy or truthful only when she is not properly exercising her epistemic agency. I conclude that since much of the testimony of eyewitnesses is both extracted and given an excess of credibility, there is a fairly widespread form of epistemic injustice being inflicted upon testifiers in the United States criminal legal system. This calls for reforms along both dimensions—lineups and interrogations should go through a witness's epistemic agency, rather than bypassing, exploiting, or undermining it, and the weight of the resulting testimony should be viewed in the broader context of its significant susceptibility to influence and fallibility.

1. Eyewitness Testimony

There are many factors that contribute to eyewitness misidentification, but here I will focus on those that relate to the interpersonal aspects of the process by which the eyewitness makes the identification or offers the identifying testimony. In particular, there are two practices within the criminal legal system that are especially relevant for our purposes: *standard lineups of suspects* and *interrogation techniques used on eyewitnesses.*

In a standard lineup, the lineup administrator knows who the suspect is and is thus able to provide cues to the eyewitness that steer the selection toward the suspect, either intentionally or unintentionally. For instance, if an eyewitness picks out someone other than the suspect, the administrator may respond, 'Are you sure that's who you saw?' or 'Do you want to take another look?' Moreover, in both live and photo lineups, non-suspect 'fillers' often do not match the description provided by the eyewitness, which can cause the suspect to stand out to a witness. Indeed, '[r]esearch shows that placing an innocent suspect who fits the description of the offender in a lineup in which the fillers do not fit the description results in a high rate of mistaken identifications of that person, even when absolute similarity between the innocent person and the offender is only moderate' (Wixted and Wells 2017, p. 15). Still further, without instructions from the lineup administrator, the eyewitness often assumes that the perpetrator of the crime in question is in a standard lineup, which can lead to the selection of a person despite doubts.

To avoid biased lineups of this sort and resulting misidentifications, police have been advised to use 'double-blind' administration.[3] In particular, it is

[3] 'Double-blind lineup procedures are needed not only to prevent the investigator from unintentionally influencing which person the eyewitness picks, but also are needed to prevent the investigator from influencing the certainty of the eyewitness' (Wells 2006, p. 630). See also Lindsay and Wells (1985), Wells and Turtle (1986), Cutler and Penrod (1988), and Wells et al. (1998).

recommended that the lineup administrator not know which person is—or which photo depicts—the suspect and that the eyewitness is informed of the administrator's ignorance of this. A lineup should also consist of at least six members, five of whom are fillers unknown to the eyewitness and who match the eyewitness's description of the perpetrator. Moreover, the suspect's position in the lineup should be determined randomly, and the eyewitness should be advised that the perpetrator may or may not be among the members.

Police have also been advised to use a sequential presentation format for their lineup procedures.[4] People or photos should be presented one at a time, with a decision made before presenting the next, and eyewitnesses should not be allowed to go back over the sequence or to have people or photos placed next to one another. Sequential lineups of this sort have been shown to be superior in accuracy than simultaneous lineups, which can be explained by the fact that simultaneous lineups promote the use of relative judgments.[5] Relative judgments are those in which the witness chooses the lineup member who most resembles the witness's 'memory relative to other lineup members' (Wells 1984, p. 92). In contrast, sequential lineups promote absolute judgments in which witnesses compare faces 'directly to memory rather than to each other' (McAdoo and Gronlund 2016, p. 2). Consider, for instance, the impact of the lineup procedure on the wrongful conviction of Antonio Beaver. In 1996, a woman was attacked by a man with a screwdriver in St. Louis and described the attacker as a clean-shaven Black man who was wearing a baseball cap and had a gap between his teeth. About a week later, a detective arrested Antonio Beaver because he thought Beaver resembled the composite sketch. When Beaver was placed in a physical lineup with three other men, only Beaver and one other man were wearing baseball caps, and Beaver was the only one who had a gap in his teeth. The victim identified Beaver, he was convicted in 1997, and he was sentenced to 18 years in prison until DNA evidence exonerated him in 2007. As the Innocence Project writes, 'Since Beaver was placed in a lineup with only three other men, the odds that he would be chosen were already high. The fact that only two of the lineup members wore caps further increased the likelihood that he would be chosen. Finally, the gap in his teeth plus the presence of the cap made it almost certain that he would be chosen' (Innocence Project 2009, p. 11).

Sill further, an assessment of witness confidence should be taken at the time of the identification and before feedback from police or others.[6] This is important, as studies show that repeatedly questioning witnesses after an event can lead to an increase in confidence levels without any corresponding changes in accuracy levels. As John S. Shaw and Kimberly A. McClure note, 'Postevent questioning

[4] See, for instance, Lindsay and Wells (1985), Wells and Turtle (1986), Cutler and Penrod (1988), and Wells et al. (1998).

[5] Lindsay and Wells (1985).

[6] See Steblay and Loftus (2013, p. 150).

[leads] to significantly higher later confidence ratings for incorrect responses.... This finding is consistent with some anecdotal evidence from the legal arena that eyewitnesses often become more confident in their memories of a criminal episode as the time for testimony at trial draws near (and as the accumulated amount of postevent questioning increases)' (Shaw and McClure 1996, p. 630).[7] For instance, Malcolm Alexander was convicted of raping a white woman in 1979 who first 'tentatively' selected his photo, then said that she was 98% sure days later after viewing him in a lineup, and then testified that she 'had no doubt' Alexander was the assailant by the time of his trial.[8] After DNA testing excluded Alexander, which prompted a reinvestigation by the District Attorney's Office, a district court judge dismissed the indictment and ordered the release of Alexander in 2018, who at that point had served nearly 38 years in prison in large part because of this misidentification.[9]

Let's now turn to interrogations.[10] There has been far less work on how interrogation techniques elicit false eyewitness testimony than there has been on how they lead to false confessions,[11] yet investigators often interview both suspects and witnesses using the same Reid Technique[12] discussed in Chapter 2. As may be recalled, such a technique involves two general types of approaches. Maximization is a 'hard-sell' approach that includes the interrogator trying to scare or intimidate the witness, offering false claims about the evidence, and exaggerating the seriousness of not cooperating. Minimization is a 'soft-sell' approach in which the interrogator 'tries to lull' the witness into a 'false sense of security by offering sympathy, tolerance, face saving excuses, and even moral justification' (Kassin and McNall 1991, p. 235). Consider, for instance, the interrogation of Sasha Allison, whose eyewitness misidentification was the result of the use of the Reid Technique. Allison had been in a parking lot in the vicinity of the fatal shooting of Mervyn 'Mikey' Spence in the Toronto area in 2006.[13] After repeatedly denying that she had seen Eric 'Action' Morgan involved in the murder, the

[7] https://www.innocenceproject.org/cases/malcolm-alexander/.

[8] https://www.innocenceproject.org/cases/malcolm-alexander/.

[9] https://www.innocenceproject.org/cases/malcolm-alexander/.

[10] While my focus in this chapter is on eyewitness testimony, similar considerations can be made regarding alibi testimony that is extracted. See, for instance, Moore, Cutler, and Shulman (2014).

[11] As Loney and Cutler note, 'While much is now known about interrogations and false confessions, there has been comparatively little attention paid to the impact of coercive interview practices on eyewitness reports. There is reason to believe, however, that coercive interviewing might be even more influential with non-suspect witnesses than with suspects. Suspects are pressured to implicate themselves by confessing to the crimes under investigation. When the suspect succumbs to the coercive influence and confesses, the suspect puts him or herself at risk for detention, a plea agreement or trial, and prison. By contrast, the non-suspect witness who succumbs to coercive influences and falsely accuses or implicates a suspect does not face the negative potential outcomes that a suspect would face, but rather garners the support of the police and prosecutor. Thus, there are fewer deterrents for the non-suspect witness than for the suspect to succumb to coercion' (2016, p. 30).

[12] See Inbau et al. (2013).

[13] While my focus in this book is primarily on the criminal legal system in the United States, this case in Toronto makes clear that the issues being examined certainly have broader relevance.

detective interrogating her used maximization tactics to extract the desired testimony, including confronting Allison with accusations that she was withholding information or lying, rejecting her denial that she knew the perpetrator's identity, threatening her with charges of accessory after the fact if she was caught 'holding back,'[14] and telling her 'if we don't sort it out, you get yourself in trouble. I know it's scary' (Moore, Cutler, and Shulman 2014, p. 36). These 'aggressive and abusive' tactics were so effective at wearing Allison down that when the detective interrogating her stepped out of the room and she was alone—confused and afraid—a camera captured her talking to herself in an anxious whisper: 'Oh God, help me... I'm getting scared. Oh my God, I don't even know who he is talking about.'[15] The detective also used minimization tactics by offering Allison sympathy, justification, and excuses for why she was finding it difficult to disclose the perpetrator's identity. 'On multiple occasions and in various ways he told [Allison] that she was a good person and should do the right thing. He made reference to her being a mom to two girls, a parent with values who instills them in her daughters, and an example for others' (Moore, Cutler, and Shulman 2014, p. 36). Allison eventually told the interrogator what he wanted to hear: that the person with the sunglasses who was outside and involved in the shooting was Action.

In the cases of Beaver and Morgan, we see testimony being obtained in ways that bypass, exploit, or subvert the eyewitness's rational capacities. Let's now turn to a closer analysis of the kind of extracted testimony that we find here, and the way in which it leads to the widespread perpetration of agential testimonial injustice against testifiers in the United States criminal legal system.[16]

2. Manipulation, Deception, and Coercion

As may be recalled from Chapter 2, epistemic agency is commonly understood as being grounded in a subject's responsiveness to reasons or evidence. Epistemic agency is thus exercised with respect to a subject's testimony when that testimony is responsive to reasons or evidence. In contrast, epistemic agency is bypassed, exploited, or subverted when a subject's ability to be responsive to reasons is circumvented, abused, or undermined.

[14] https://www.thestar.com/news/crime/2014/11/21/how_aggressive_and_abusive_tactics_by_police_put_an_innocent_man_through_two_murder_trials.html.

[15] https://www.thestar.com/news/crime/2014/11/21/how_aggressive_and_abusive_tactics_by_police_put_an_innocent_man_through_two_murder_trials.html.

[16] I should note that I will be focusing on a distinctive kind of epistemic wrong suffered by eyewitnesses in what follows, but this is clearly not the only epistemic wrong at work in these cases. There are, for instance, also the downstream epistemic wrongs suffered by various other members of the criminal legal system—such as jurors—who are unaware of the extracted nature of the evidence in question and the impact this has on its reliability, and thus rely on it in their deliberations.

As I understand it, testimony is *extracted* when it has been obtained through an interpersonal interaction that bypasses, exploits, or subverts the testifier's epistemic agency, and manipulation, deception, and coercion are the three central ways in which interpersonal processes can extract testimony from a speaker. Earlier, manipulation was characterized as intentional, arational influence—the circumvention of another person's rational decision-making power for the manipulator's desired end. There is, however, another kind of manipulation, one that neither circumvents nor subverts a person's epistemic agency but weaponizes it.

Suppose, for instance, that my daughter intentionally leaves her laptop at her out-of-state friend's house so that I will allow her to return. She reasons as follows: I need my laptop to do my schoolwork; my mom places a high value on my education; thus, she will choose the option that enables me to keep up with my schoolwork, even if she wouldn't have otherwise selected this. In such a case, my daughter is carefully curating the options available to me—(i) allow her to return to her friend's house and keep up with schoolwork, or (ii) stay home and fall behind—knowing full well that the value I place on her education will tip the scales in favor of permitting her to return to her friend's house. A distinction has been drawn in the philosophical literature between, on the one hand, manipulation that targets the person and interferes directly with her psychological processes and, on the other hand, manipulation that targets the situation and interferes with the options available to the person.[17] This case of my daughter curating the options in my decision space is clearly an instance of the latter. What I want to emphasize here, however, is not a distinction of this sort, but, rather, how my daughter is *weaponizing* my epistemic agency, rather than bypassing or subverting it. She knows full well that I am rational and that her having access to her schoolwork is a powerful reason for me to consent to her returning to her friend's house. It is precisely because of my epistemic agency that her plan is so effective. In such a case, she is intentionally exerting rational influence over me to achieve her desired end, though not through the offering of compelling reasons; rather it is through the selective curation or orchestration of my decision space.

Cases such as this show that manipulation need not bypass or circumvent a target's epistemic agency, even if it often does. Because of this, we may find more promising accounts that do not require that the influence in question be arational. Robert Noggle, for instance, argues that '[t]here are certain norms or ideals that govern beliefs, desires, and emotions... manipulative action is the attempt to get someone's beliefs, desires, or emotions to violate these norms, to fall short of these ideals' (Noggle 1996, p. 44). Building on this view, Anne Barnhill maintains that 'manipulation is directly influencing someone's beliefs, desires, or emotions such

[17] Ware (1981), Faden and Beauchamp (1986), Mills (1995), and Baron (2003).

that she falls short of ideals for belief, desire, or emotion in ways typically not in her self-interest *or likely not in her self-interest in the present context*' (Barnhill 2014, p. 72, original emphasis). Here there is no mention of manipulation needing to be either covert[18] or arational, but only that the influence in question aim for the target person's beliefs, desires, and emotions to fall short of the norms and ideals governing them, which Barnhill explicitly understands in terms of not being in the target's self-interest. Given this, such views can countenance as manipulation the cases from Chapter 2 involving overt influence, as well as my daughter's exploiting my epistemic agency through the selective curation of my decision space.

There are, however, several problems with accounts of this sort. On the one hand, I can directly influence someone's beliefs, desires, or emotions such that she falls short of the ideals governing them and yet not be manipulative. My offering to read my friend's poems might directly influence her to be overcome with self-doubt and to abandon her creative writing, but if my gesture was sincere and not-ill-intentioned, she doesn't seem to have been manipulated into foregoing her poetry. On the other hand, I can be manipulative even if I directly influence someone's beliefs, desires, or emotions so that they *satisfy*, rather than fall short of, the ideals governing them. If I convince you to get vaccinated from COVID-19—which is a rational choice consistent with the scientific evidence you already possess—but I do so by hacking into your social media accounts and inundating you with images of people dying from COVID-19, I seem to have manipulated you despite the fact that I influenced you to achieve the ideals governing your beliefs. We can also ensure that Barnhill's account is satisfied in both cases by stipulating that it is not in my friend's self-interest to abandon her poetry and that it is in your self-interest to get vaccinated. Nevertheless, the presence of manipulation does not seem to track influencing people to fall short of the ideals governing their psychological and belief states.

Taking a step back, one feature that seems relevant, though surprisingly absent from many accounts of manipulation, is the actions of the one doing the manipulating. To put this point in a vivid, though very oversimplified, way: if I behave well in my influence, but in a way that makes you worse off, I haven't manipulated you, but if I behave badly in my influence, even in a way that makes you better off, I may still have manipulated you. In other words, the actions of the manipulator can be a determining factor regarding whether manipulation has occurred. In the cases above, for instance, the fact that I earnestly and with no ill-intent offered to read my friend's poetry seems to prevent her from being manipulated by me, even if my action directly influenced her psychological and belief states to fall short of the relevant ideals. And the fact that I am bypassing your agency to bring about

[18] I argued against the need for manipulation to involve covert influence in Chapter 2.

the desired end of you getting vaccinated seems to result in you being manipulated by me, even if my action directly influenced your beliefs to achieve your own relevant ideals.

For these reasons, the view developed by Yochai Benkler, Robert Faris, and Hal Roberts is promising, according to which manipulation is understood as '[d]irectly influencing someone's beliefs, attitudes, or preferences in ways that fall short of what an empathetic observer would deem normatively appropriate in context' (Benkler et al. 2018, p. 30). What this view has over rival ones is the addition of the actions of the one doing the manipulating. In particular, the influence of the manipulator would be deemed normatively inappropriate by an empathetic observer, where such an observer 'takes the first-person perspective of the target of the communication, and asks whether that person, knowing the entire situation, including the intentions and psychological techniques of the alleged manipulator, would welcome the allegedly manipulative communication' (Benkler et al. 2018, p. 31). While I regard the focus on the one doing the manipulating as a step in the right direction, I reject that this role should be played by the judgment of an empathetic observer, especially as understood here. Placing the assessment of appropriateness entirely in the hands of the one being manipulated, without any objective normativity guiding her judgment, throws the door wide open to an absurd expansion of what counts as manipulation. For instance, any person who is especially sensitive to feeling played, or prone to seeing influence, or primed to blame others might assess influence as normatively inappropriate even when it clearly is appropriate. Given this, it is best to focus on what a 'reasonable' observer would judge to be inappropriate rather than on one who is empathetic in this sense. The sense of reasonableness operative here is not a purely subjective notion but, instead, should be interpreted as it is frequently employed in the law to capture the objective measure of 'ways in which it is right for persons to think, feel or behave' (Westen 2008, p. 138). Manipulation can thus be understood as follows:

> Directly influencing someone's beliefs, attitudes, or preferences in ways that fall short of what a reasonable observer would deem normatively appropriate in the relevant context.

It is important to note that this account of manipulation subsumes cases involving arational influence. For instance, bypassing a person's rational capacities in order to bring about a desired end—such as a confession—is to directly influence her beliefs, attitudes, or preferences in a way that falls short of what a reasonable observer would deem normatively appropriate in the relevant context. More precisely, a reasonable observer would judge it to be epistemically and morally violating to treat a suspect as a puppet to be molded rather than as an agent with rational capacities deserving of dignity and respect. Given this, I will continue to describe certain manipulative actions as bypassing or circumventing a person's epistemic agency, as this is often a more vivid or substantive characterization insofar as it captures what is normatively inappropriate about the influence. But the more expansive account is how manipulation generally should be understood since it also subsumes cases like the one above where epistemic agency is weaponized, rather than bypassed, through the selective curation of options in a person's decision space.

It should also be noted that actions can be manipulative even if they don't succeed in bringing about the influence in question and thus are not straightforward instances of manipulation. *Being manipulative* can be understood as *aiming* at directly influencing someone's beliefs, attitudes, or preferences in ways that fall short of what a reasonable observer would deem normatively appropriate in the relevant context. This is important, as manipulative actions are subject to criticism even when, for various reasons, the target is able to withstand the tactics aimed at influencing him in a particular way.

But what, we might ask, is the wrong of manipulation when it includes actions ranging from the bypassing of epistemic agency to its being weaponized? When people are manipulated, it is common for them to describe feeling played, or to be deprived of authorship over their own actions, or to be comparable to a puppet with the strings in the hands of another. Noggle hints at this when he writes '[a]ll cases of manipulative action involve a certain kind of intention, namely, the intention to lead astray, to induce a violation of certain ideals' (Noggle 1996, p. 52). As we have seen, however, this is not quite right. I can manipulate you not by leading you astray, but by leading you *toward* your ideals and goals.[19] If you find out that I hacked into your social media accounts to inundate them with pictures of people dying from COVID-19, you would still rightly feel played or like a puppet even if your getting vaccinated as a result satisfies your psychological ideals. It is not, then, being *led astray* that is the problem, but being *led improperly*. This is why the actions of the one doing the manipulating are so crucial in understanding manipulation.

Susser et al. argue that the wrongness of manipulation is that it 'undermines our sense of authorship over our decisions' (2019, p. 18), which they claim can only be explained by 'the hiddenness' of the influence of the manipulator. More precisely, they claim that once we become aware of another person's plans to influence us, we incorporate them into our own decision-making, which then become 'a regular part of how [we] make up [our] mind[s]' (2019, p. 20). But this doesn't seem correct. Suppose my daughter asks me to pick her up from a friend's house this evening and I tell her that she will need to walk instead because I have

[19] I am assuming that getting vaccinated is one of your belief ideals since it is consistent with all of the scientific evidence you already possess. However, the details of this case can be modified in any number of ways to make the same point. For instance, I know that you want to lose weight to improve your health and so I hack into your social media accounts and inundate them with vivid pictures of people dying from health problems due to obesity to motivate you.

a prior commitment with a colleague. As she walks out the door in winter weather, she deliberately leaves her coat on the rack, turning to me with a smile knowing that this choice on her part will lead me to prioritize picking her up. When I cancel my commitment with my colleague and pick her up, am I the author of my own decision? In one sense, of course I am, as I chose to put my daughter's wellness ahead of my meeting with my colleague. But appealing to my sense of duty and guilt as a mother to get what she wants, even if she flaunts it, is to radically constrain the options for the story I am telling and, in this sense, it is to encroach on my authorship. If you have me under your thumb, making me aware that I'm under your thumb doesn't make me any less under your thumb. To put this in terms of manipulation, being overt about your influence over me doesn't necessarily make your influence any less powerful. As Sarah Buss notes, the manipulator interferes with the 'self-governed (and self-governing) activity we call "making up one's own mind about how to act"' (2005, p. 195). As we see in the case of my daughter, such interference does not need to be covert to be effective.

Now it is tempting to regard cases of this sort as inching toward coercion rather than being instances of manipulation.[20] But this is a mistake. Constraining your options doesn't, by itself, result in you being coerced. Recall from Chapter 2 that coercion is typically understood as the offering of 'irresistible incentives' (1978, p. 341) or eliminating all of the 'acceptable alternatives' (Wood 2014, pp. 21–23).[21] There is a reason why such accounts focus on the incentives being irresistible and the alternatives that are eliminated being acceptable and this is because not all incentives and alternatives result in coercion. It is only when there seems to be no way out—when all of the reasonable paths have been removed from a person's decision space and only one move forward remains—that a person is said to be coerced. In the case above, letting my daughter walk home in cold weather is an acceptable alternative. We can even stipulate that it is not so cold that she is at risk of harm, such as of getting frostbite, by doing so. I have not, then, been coerced into canceling my commitment with my colleague, but I have been manipulated into doing so. My sense of duty as a mother and my guilt for not helping my daughter when I can, combined with her deliberate choice to leave her winter coat at home, exert a powerful influence over my actions. Even if I end up being, in one sense, an author of this decision, this part of my story also has a co-author or ghostwriter, as the options in the narrative are radically constrained by another person's will. This conclusion is supported by the fact that my colleague would almost certainly hold me less responsible for canceling our meeting when I explained to him the reasons for doing so.

[20] See Sussler et al. (2019).

[21] I will offer a more detailed account of coercion in Chapter 4, but this standard view will suffice for present purposes.

In addition to manipulation and coercion understood in these ways, testimony is also extracted from eyewitnesses using deception. Recall from Chapter 2 that deception includes deceiving, which involves aiming to bring about a false belief in another person, as well as concealing information. Deception can involve everything from claims to have evidence against a suspect that the interrogators in fact do not have to threats of consequences of not cooperating that the investigators cannot, or will not, follow through on.

To make this vivid, let's look at the case of Troy Anthony Davis, which powerfully illustrates the impact that manipulation, deception, and coercion can have on lineups and interrogations, ultimately leading not only to misidentifications and wrongful convictions, but even to executions. Officer Mark MacPhail was working as a security guard at a Burger King in Savannah, Georgia when he was shot and killed in a nearby parking lot as he intervened to defend a homeless man, Larry Young, who was being assaulted.[22] Davis was found guilty on August 28, 1991 of one count of malice murder, one count of obstruction of a law enforcement officer, two counts of aggravated assault, and one count of possession of a firearm during the commission of a felony.[23] Despite this, there was no physical evidence linking Davis to these crimes, and his convictions were based solely on the testimony of witnesses. He was sentenced to death on August 30, 1991 and was executed on September 21, 2011.[24]

There were 10 eyewitnesses and two informants who testified against Troy Davis at trial. In subsequent affidavits, an astonishing nine of these twelve witnesses revealed that their testimony was false or inaccurate.[25] In an *amicus* brief, the Georgia Innocence Project identified three major problems with the trial that sent Troy Davis to death row, all of which focused on the witness testimony. The two that are most relevant for our purposes are: '(1) eyewitness testimony was influenced by suggestive photo arrays' and '(2) statements and testimony from eyewitnesses were the result of suggestive and coercive interrogation techniques designed to incriminate Troy Davis.'[26]

Dorothy Ferrell was one of the ten eyewitnesses in the Troy Davis case, having witnessed the scene immediately after the shooting. In a post-trial affidavit, Ferrell revealed that a detective came to her house after the shooting, showed her a single photo of Troy Davis, and reported to her that 'other witnesses had identified Troy Davis as being the shooter.' Ferrell was also pregnant and on parole, was threatened with arrest by the police, and reported that she was 'scared that if I didn't cooperate with the detective, then he might find a way to have me locked

22 Marlowe et al. (2013).
23 https://www.scotusblog.com/wp-content/uploads/2008/09/08-66_bio.pdf.
24 Marlowe et al. (2013, p. 8).
25 https://planckconstant.org/blog1/pdfs/Davis_Troy_Innocence_Network_Brief.pdf, p. 6.
26 https://planckconstant.org/blog1/pdfs/Davis_Troy_Innocence_Network_Brief.pdf, pp. 4–5.

up again.... I had four children at that time and I was taking care of them myself. I couldn't go back to jail.'[27]

Larry Young is the homeless man who was beaten by the same person who had killed Officer MacPhail and suffered a severe head wound and blood clot from the attack. After being handcuffed and locked in a police car for an hour, the detectives interrogated him at the police station for an additional three hours, withholding medical attention while he repeatedly denied being able to identify the assailant. In a post-trial affidavit, Young said that 'the cops... made it clear that we weren't leaving until I told them what they wanted to hear,' leading him to confirm the version of events presented by the police in which he remembered Troy Davis beating him that evening. '[T]hey suggested answers and I would give them what they wanted,' Young claimed.[28]

In both instances, there are clear problems with the way in which the eyewitness testimony is obtained. Ferrell was shown a single photo of just Davis rather than a lineup of six members with five fillers who resemble the description of the perpetrator. In this way, the process is clearly *manipulative* insofar as the showing of the photo is designed to selectively curate her decision space so that she identifies Davis. To the extent that detectives were counting on Ferrell reasoning to the conclusion that the single photo in the array must be the shooter, her epistemic agency was being weaponized. Ferrell was also manipulated when she was given an overt cue to pick him out when the officer told her that other witnesses had identified Davis as being the shooter. Such a cue was intended to bring about a desired result—the identification of Davis—while bypassing Ferrell's rational capacities.

More generally, we can identify several features of standard lineups that can be manipulative: the number of fillers, their similarity to the suspect, the ordering of the people, and the cues provided by administrators. Lineup administrators can steer witnesses toward the identification of a particular person, not by appealing to rational persuasion, but precisely by circumventing or weaponizing their epistemic agency. In the case of Antonio Beaver, for instance, the witness described her assailant as wearing a baseball cap and having a gap in his teeth. When Beaver was placed in a lineup with only three other men, and Beaver and only one other man were wearing baseball caps, the eyewitness was being influenced through the orchestration of the decision space itself. That is to say, the lineup administrators

[27] https://planckconstant.org/blog1/pdfs/Davis_Troy_Innocence_Network_Brief.pdf, pp. 17–18.

[28] These two accounts are representative of many of the tactics mentioned in the other seven post-trial affidavits. For instance, 16-year-old Benjamin Gordon testified against Troy Davis, but he later reported that he signed the statement after police interrogated him for several hours and 'told me that I was going to the electric chair.' Then, '[a]fter four or five hours, they told me to sign some papers. I just wanted to get the hell out of there.' Darrell Collins, who was also 16 years old at the time of the interrogation, said that police 'started yelling at me' during questioning, 'telling me that I was an accessory to murder and that I would pay like Troy... if I didn't tell them what they wanted to hear.' https://planckconstant.org/blog1/pdfs/Davis_Troy_Innocence_Network_Brief.pdf, pp. 22–23.

did not aim to secure the identification of Beaver through providing reasons and evidence but simply by narrowing down the very options that are available. When Beaver was the only person in the lineup who had a gap in his teeth, the eyewitness was clearly being steered by the administrator to choose him. Indeed, just as my daughter curated my options and thus expected me to pick her up from her friend's to avoid her walking home in the cold, so, too, is the witness expected to reason to the conclusion that her assailant is Beaver since he is the only person fitting the description. Similar considerations apply when Dorothy Ferrell was shown only one photo of Troy Davis and was told that other witnesses had identified him as being the shooter. Ferrell is being directed to identify Davis through the number of photos in the lineup—only one—and the cues of the officer.

Lineups can also involve deception, and there are three broad ways that this standardly arises: deception regarding previously existing evidence, deception regarding the lineup process, and deception regarding the consequences of not making an identification. If, for instance, an administrator falsely reports that other witnesses identified a suspect, then the eyewitness is being deceived about other evidence. If an administrator deliberately conceals the information that the suspect may not be in the lineup, then the eyewitness is being deceived about the lineup process. And if the eyewitness is lied to about the repercussions of not choosing a suspect, then she is being deceived about the consequences of not making an identification. For instance, Allison almost certainly would not have been charged with accessory after the fact if she was caught 'holding back' and failed to identify Action, but the investigators knew that this would be effective in producing the identification they wanted.

Finally, lineups involve coercion when all of the acceptable alternatives have been eliminated—such as not choosing a suspect at all, not choosing a particular suspect, and so on—and the eyewitness is left with only the option of identifying the person the administrator wants to be chosen. When Ferrell was threatened with arrest and the loss of her children if she didn't identify Troy Davis, for instance, she was left with no choice except to cooperate.

Turning to interrogation tactics, we see very similar patterns emerge. Maximization techniques, for instance, can function in all three ways. When the interrogator told Sasha Allison that he knows it is scary to cooperate and that she will get herself in trouble if she doesn't, it is plausible that manipulation, deception, and coercion were all operative in the extraction of her testimony. Assuming that Allison will not face any trouble if she fails to report seeing Action involved in the shooting, she is being influenced to offer testimony through the forming of a false belief. In this way, she is being manipulated to implicate Action through deception. In addition, if 'trouble' is interpreted as arrest, it is also plausible that Allison understood this as a threat in which her only option is to cooperate, thereby rendering her testimony coerced. In general, intimidation, offering false claims about the evidence, and exaggerating the seriousness of not cooperating are both manipulative and deceptive: the interrogator is steering the witness to a desired end—testimony with a particular content—through causing false beliefs. Scaring witnesses through threats of arrests, imprisonment, loss of children, and so on are coercive: eyewitnesses are left with no acceptable option but testifying. We also see such tactics in the interrogations of both Ferrell and Young. When Ferrell was threatened with arrest, either the officers lied to her, knowing that there were insufficient grounds for actually doing so, or they in fact planned to arrest her if she failed to give them the identification they wanted. In the latter case the threat of jail, along with the loss of her children, was coercive and in the former, it was both coercive and deceptive. The same is true of Young where the denial of medical attention, and the implication that it would be withheld until he told the interrogators what they wanted to hear, functioned coercively in the extraction of his identification.

Minimization techniques tend to rely on manipulation and deception more than coercion. Witnesses are lulled into a false sense of comfort and security, are offered disingenuous sympathy and face-saving excuses, and are provided with inaccurate moral justification. In these ways, they are manipulated into offering the testimony that the interrogators want through being caused to form false beliefs, especially about what is in their own self-interest. When the interrogators appealed to Allison's sense of being a 'good person' and a mom to two girls who is instilling values in them, for instance, they were very clearly providing her with a veneer of moral justification for identifying Action as the shooter.

At this point, I have argued that eyewitness testimony is often obtained through lineups and interrogation techniques that rely on manipulation, deception, and coercion. I now want to show how the resulting testimony plays a massively oversized role in the American criminal legal system, thereby inflicting distinctive epistemic wrongs on eyewitness testifiers.

3. Credibility Excess

When testimony is extracted, it bypasses, weaponizes, exploits, or subverts a testifier's epistemic agency. When an eyewitness is manipulated into identifying a suspect in a lineup through subtle cues and suggestions, she is being arationally influenced to conform to the administrator's aims. In other words, the administrator is not going through the eyewitness's rational faculties but around them, and in this way her capacity for being responsive to reasons and evidence is being *bypassed*. When an eyewitness is manipulated into choosing a person in a lineup through the inclusion of dissimilar fillers, her own epistemic agency is *weaponized* through the selective curation of her decision space. Specifically, the administrator is counting on her reasoning to the conclusion that the only suspect resembling her description must be the one she actually saw at the scene of the crime. When an eyewitness is deceived into identifying a suspect, perhaps through the presentation of false evidence that others have already pointed the finger at this person, her epistemic agency is being *exploited*. In particular, fabricating evidence that interrogators know will be compelling to a rational agent is exploiting the eyewitness's epistemic agency for the desired end of obtaining incriminating testimony. And coercion undermines epistemic agency by shifting the nature of the question and the relevant considerations from the theoretical to the strictly practical. For instance, the eyewitness is no longer asked to consider whether she remembers seeing the suspect with the gun, but whether she values her freedom and her children more than giving the interrogators what they want. This is not to go through agency, around it, or even to exploit it, but to *subvert* it. It is to say: at this moment, evidence and reasons about the original question are no longer on the table, and now you are simply a practical agent trying to keep your head above water. By bringing to bear swamping considerations that, in many respects, change the topic through the changing of options, epistemic agency is overthrown.

The extraction of testimony in these sorts of ways, by itself, constitutes an epistemic wrong perpetrated against the testifier. Obtaining testimony through manipulative, deceptive, and coercive practices is to treat testifiers as epistemic tools to be influenced by, and molded to, the aims and desires of others.[29] When reasons and evidence are ineffective or inconvenient, the extractor turns to trickery, lies, and brute force. The eyewitness is thus treated as not only deserving of neither epistemic respect nor of dignity but also as less than fully a person.

But there is a second, importantly different epistemic wrong operative here: the eyewitness testimony, once extracted, is often given an *unwarranted excess of credibility* in the criminal legal system. Otherwise put, eyewitness testimony is frequently regarded as far more honest and reliable than, epistemically, it ought to be. This can be seen in at least four different ways: eyewitness testimony is *weighed too heavily*; it is *resistant to counterevidence*; it *distorts other evidence*; and it *blocks the seeking, gathering, and proper interpretation of additional evidence*.

That eyewitness testimony is weighed far too heavily is made vivid by the fact that convictions in the criminal legal system are often secured entirely or largely on the basis of such testimony despite eyewitness identifications being both very susceptible to manipulation and highly unreliable. For instance, there is 'no published research showing that interview techniques involving maximization and minimization facilitate accurate and complete memories from eyewitnesses' (Loney and Cutler 2016, p. 30), yet the Reid Technique is one of 'the most widely used police interrogation procedure in North America' (Moore, Cutler, and Shulman 2014, p. 34). Moreover, as we saw earlier, lineups and interrogation

[29] It is quite common for the *moral* wrongness of manipulation, deception, and coercion to be discussed, but far less so for the distinctively epistemic wrong to be identified and explained.

techniques can be used to manipulate, deceive, and coerce witnesses into offering false testimony. In a recent study showing that coercive interrogations can produce false identifications, Danielle M. Loney and Brian L. Cutler write:

> Individuals well-acquainted with the research on the effects of maximization and minimization techniques on the risk of false confession should not be surprised by our findings. If coercive interrogation practices are effective at getting innocent suspects to falsely confess to their own detriment, it certainly follows that the same practices should be as effective, or perhaps more effective, at getting bystander witnesses to falsely implicate other suspects. Doing so produces few, if any, negative consequences to the witness who may be commended by the police for his or her cooperation. (2016, p. 34)

Research also shows that attitudes and beliefs are susceptible to influence and change through persuasion, especially when the source is regarded as high in credibility.[30] Given that interrogators are often in positions of power or authority, it is unsurprising that they can wield significant and substantive influence over witnesses.

Moreover, eyewitness identifications themselves are often 'dangerously unreliable,' evidenced by the fact that they are the 'leading case of false convictions in the United States' (Vallas 2011, p. 98). In her dissent in *Perry v. New Hampshire* (2012), for instance, Justice Sotomayor notes that '[t]his Court has long recognized that eyewitness identifications' unique confluence of features—their unreliability, susceptibility to suggestion, powerful impact on the jury, and resistance to the ordinary tests of the adversarial process—can undermine the fairness of a trial' (*Perry v. New Hampshire*, 565 U.S. 228, 249 (2012)). In addition, one of the factors most responsible for the unreliability of eyewitness identifications is 'cross-race bias' or 'own-race bias,'[31] whereby 'individuals have less difficulty identifying and remembering faces of their own race than those of a different, less familiar race' (Vallas 2011, p. 102). While eyewitness identifications are often unreliable, cross-racial identifications—which involve an eyewitness of one race identifying a criminal suspect of another race—are 'particularly untrustworthy' (Gonzales Rose 2016, p. 2291).[32] Indeed, 42% of wrongful convictions involving eyewitness misidentification also involved cross-racial misidentification.[33] Cross-racial identifications are especially unreliable when a white eyewitness identifies a

[30] See, for instance, Pornpitakpan (2004).

[31] See Vallas for a discussion of other factors, including 'stress and weapon focus; exposure duration and retention interval; the lack of correlation between eyewitness confidence and accurate identifications; and problematic post-event information, such as suggestive identification procedures' (2011, p. 102).

[32] See also Rutledge (2001).

[33] https://innocenceproject.org/dna-exonerations-in-the-united-states/.

Black suspect; more precisely, 'a Black innocent suspect has a 56% greater chance of being misidentified by a White eyewitness than by a Black eyewitness' (Wells and Olson, 2001 p. 231).

This is especially magnified in sexual assault cases, where the leading cause of wrongful convictions is the misidentification of defendants who are strangers to the victims.[34] In 79% of sexual assault exonerations, the identity of the person who committed the crime is the only issue at trial, with mistaken eyewitness identification involved in 88% of these cases.[35] Crucially, however, the rate of eyewitness errors is much higher for innocent Black defendants—79%—than for whites—51%.[36] While Gross et al. note that 'there are many possible explanations for this disturbing pattern,' they also maintain that 'the simplest is probably the most powerful: the perils of cross-racial identification' (2017, p. 12). The race of the victim also plays a significant role in wrongful convictions of this sort, as Black men were convicted of raping white women in half of all sexual assault exonerations involving eyewitness misidentifications.[37] Otherwise put, Black defendants convicted of raping white women are about eight times more likely to be innocent than white men convicted of raping women of their own race.[38]

Despite all of this, eyewitness testimony continues to play a powerful role in the criminal legal system, securing not only convictions but executions.[39] As Jasmine B. Gonzales Rose notes, '[w]itness identifications are considered so reliable that they are afforded hearsay exemption status'[40] and 'are among the most influential items of evidence that jurors rely upon in determining if a defendant is guilty of a crime,' with jurors apt to 'believe eyewitness testimony above all else, even in the face of significant doubt' (2016, p. 2290). Duff McKee summarizes the situation powerfully when he says, 'Eyewitness testimony may be the least reliable, and yet the most compelling' (1996).[41]

A second way in which eyewitness testimony is afforded an excess of credibility is through the distorted effect it has on other relevant evidence, especially recantations.[42] In particular, when a witness provides testimony that identifies a suspect as the perpetrator of a crime, it is often massively privileged over a later recantation, even when the original identification is the sole or primary evidence

34 Gross et al. (2017, p. 11).
35 Gross et al. (2017, p. 11).
36 Gross et al. (2017, p. 12).
37 Gross et al. (2017, p. 12).
38 Gross et al. (2017, p. 12). I will discuss this in greater detail in Chapter 5.
39 See, again, Marlowe, Davis-Correia, and Davis (2013).
40 A statement is regarded as non-hearsay if a 'declarant testifies and is subject to cross-examination about a prior statement, and the statement... identifies a person as someone the declarant perceived earlier' (Federal Rules of Evidence 801(d)(1)).
41 Elizabeth Loftus similarly writes, 'The problem can be stated rather simply: on the one hand, eyewitness testimony is very believable and can wield considerable influence over the decisions reached by a jury; on the other hand, eyewitness testimony is not always reliable' (Loftus 1979, p. 7).
42 A recantation 'denotes a formal, intentional renunciation by a witness of her former testimony' (Repka 1986, p. 1434).

on behalf of guilt and the recantation is supported by corroborating evidence.[43] Consider, for instance, the very well-known case of Cathleen Crowell Webb, who, at the age of 16, accused Gary Dotson in 1977 of abducting and raping her. Eight years later, while married, a born-again Christian, and riddled with guilt, she recanted her testimony, admitting that she fabricated the accusation out of fear of a possible pregnancy from a consensual sexual relationship at that time.[44] Despite her maturation and the very plausible explanation of the unreliability of her original testimony, the judge found that Webb's trial testimony was more credible than her recantation at an evidentiary hearing that Dotson requested.[45] Eventually, in 1989, Dotson became the first person in the United States to be exonerated on the basis of DNA evidence. One way to understand why the claims of a frightened juvenile were massively privileged over those of a secure, guilt-ridden, adult woman—especially when a man's freedom was on the line—is that the recantation was distorted by the unwarranted excess of credibility given to the original eyewitness testimony.

Importantly, however, the way the State treated Webb's testimony is not in any way unique or anomalous. In fact, legal scholars have noted the general and pervasive credibility deficit attached to recanting testimony, pointing to a general judicial skepticism that 'has become so universal that it appears to have given rise to an inference that recantation evidence is not trustworthy and should be treated as such absent the movant's ability to persuade otherwise' (Sinnott 1993, pp. 574–75).[46] This is supported by the fact that the recantation of testimony of key witnesses is widely disregarded by courts, with the view of the Court of Appeals of New York in 1916 often cited by way of support: 'There is no form of proof so unreliable as recanting testimony. In the popular mind it is often regarded as of great importance. Those experienced in the administration of the criminal law know well its untrustworthy character' (*People v. Shilitano*, 218 N.Y. 161, 170 (N.Y. 1916)). The deep suspicion of recantations also contributes to prosecutors wielding what Russell D. Covey calls the 'perjury sword,' which involves threatening eyewitnesses with prosecution and prison time for coming forward to recant

[43] See Repka (1986), Sinnott (1993), and Armbrust (2008).

[44] https://www.upi.com/Archives/1985/05/10/Cathleen-Crowell-Webb-today-said-she-was-a-liar/4234484545600/.

[45] See Armbrust (2008).

[46] See, for instance, Repka: 'Although courts are not required to presume the untrustworthiness of recantation testimony, the long-standing rule that such testimony is suspect and inherently unreliable ultimately produces the same effect' (1986, p. 1442); Armbrust: 'Courts usually approach recantations with a presumption that they are incredible, which means that any defendant pursuing a new trial based on a recantation is facing an uphill battle' (2008, p. 82); Covey: 'As evidence goes, recanted testimony is the ugliest stepchild' (2016, p. 863); *Carpitcher v. Commonwealth* where the Virginia Supreme Court writes, 'recantation evidence is generally questionable in character and is widely viewed by courts with suspicion because of the obvious opportunities and temptations for fraud' (641 S.E.2d 486, 492 (Va. 2007)); and *People v. Morgan* where the Illinois Supreme Court explains that '[r]ecantation of testimony is regarded as inherently unreliable' (817 N.E.2d 524 (Ill. 2004)).

their original testimony. As he says, 'the threat of perjury can be manipulated by the state in ways that undermine the reliability of criminal proceedings. This latter phenomenon can be seen in cases involving allegations of witness coercion by police officers or other state agents' (2016, p. 864).

Moreover, it is clear that the general rejection of recantations as unreliable in the courts is often grounded in nothing more than bias or prejudice, a point made vivid by Judge Seabury in *Shilitano*:

> Bearing in mind that the witnesses to crimes of violence are often of a low and degraded character and that after they have given their testimony they are sometimes influenced by bribery and other improper considerations, it is evident that the establishment of a rule which left the power to grant a new trial to a defendant to depend upon recantation by such witnesses would be subversive of the proper administration of justice.
>
> (*People v. Shilitano*, 218 N.Y. 161, 169 (N.Y. 1916))

There are at least two problems with what Judge Seabury says in this passage: first, the wholesale rejection of recantations seems to be entirely driven by bias and prejudice regarding witnesses to crimes of violence, whom he describes as having a 'low and degraded character.' Second, everything that is said here applies to both recantations and identifications, as the same witnesses offering the recantation also provided the original testimony, and witnesses can similarly be subject to bribery and improper considerations at both times.

Still further, the very reasons that show that the suspicion regarding recantations involves an unwarranted credibility deficit also point toward the illegitimate credibility excess that the original testimony receives. To see this, notice that most of the considerations on behalf of discounting recantations cut both ways and provide no reason for a general preference for the original testimony of eyewitnesses. For instance, (1) recantations are thought to reveal the untrustworthiness of the witness; (2) fears are expressed that the witness has recanted under duress or because of coercion; (3) close relationships between defendants and witnesses are cited as reason for skepticism; and (4) worries are expressed about the court being manipulated.[47] But each of these could equally be invoked to call into question the reliability of the eyewitness identification in the first place. If providing inconsistent testimony, for instance, undermines the witness's credibility, this does not in any way favor the earlier time over the later one. Moreover, at the original trial, witnesses can testify under duress or because of coercion,[48] can

[47] Armbrust (2008, p. 82). While Armbrust discusses three other reasons why recantations are discounted, none support the radical asymmetrical treatment of accusations and recantations by courts.

[48] As Armburst notes, however, 'courts tend to presume that witnesses recant because they are coerced, but they neglect to consider the possibility, and even dismiss the possibility, that police or prosecutors also use improper tactics to elicit witness statements' (2008, p. 96).

have a close relationship with the defendant, and can be manipulating the court. Indeed, we saw clear instances of (2) and (4) earlier where eyewitnesses in the cases of Davis and Morgan were coerced by interrogators into falsely identifying the defendants, thereby lying to the court in order to avoid prosecution and prison time themselves. To the extent that these considerations raise concerns about reliability, identifications and recantations should be in the same boat. Yet courts systematically treat them not only differently, but radically so.[49]

Indeed, if eyewitness testimony and recantations are treated with differing degrees of reliability, courts often have reason to favor recantations because of the threat of perjury witnesses face when they recant.[50] Knowing full well that recanting means acknowledging that a lie was told either at the original trial or now, a witness opens himself up to prosecution and prison time by coming forward. Given that the stakes are high, the possibility that a crisis of conscience is motivating the recantation should be taken very seriously. And yet the deep suspicion of recantations often closes off this possibility.

The third way in which the unwarranted excess of credibility afforded to eyewitness testimony is made vivid is through its significant resistance to counterevidence. Consider, again, the Troy Davis case, where there wasn't simply the evidence that the testimony of most of the witnesses on behalf of the prosecution had been extracted through manipulation and coercion—there was also a host of reasons to call into question the reliability of the eyewitness identifications themselves. Studies show, for instance, that the shorter the exposure to an event, the more difficult it is for humans to encode enough information for later recognition.[51] Moreover, forensic psychologists have documented that a witness's attention is drawn to any visible weapon during a crime and away from the facial and physical characteristics of the assailant. As Steblay (1992) notes, '[t]he presence of a weapon... make[s] a significant difference in eyewitness performance... particularly in crimes of short duration in which a threatening weapon is visible' (pp. 420–21). And research shows that heightened stress at the moment of perception decreases the accuracy of eyewitness identifications.[52] Given that Officer MacPhail was shot within seconds of the assault on Young in a dimly lit parking lot late at night, and that the shooter fled immediately, the conditions for reliable

[49] One might argue that identifications are more reliable than, and thus epistemically preferable to, recantations 'because the prior identification occurred closer to the event in question and is still fresh in the witness's mind' (Gonzales Rose 2016, p. 2291). While this may be true in some cases, it clearly does not apply when the original identification is the result of the sorts of manipulative, deceptive, and coercive tactics discussed earlier, or when the eyewitness is being dishonest in the first instance for other reasons, such as external threats.

[50] Again, for an extended discussion of the 'perjury sword,' see Covey (2016). As he notes, the 'knee-jerk rejection of recantation evidence is misguided not only because judges tend to misjudge the reliability of recantations, but also because the policy is a major contributor to the abuse by law enforcement officials of what I refer to here as "the perjury sword"' (p. 864).

[51] Memon et al. (2003).

[52] Deffenbacher et al. (2004).

eyewitness identifications were far from optimal. Moreover, several witnesses reported running for cover upon seeing or hearing the gun,[53] which would have also severely limited their views in a highly stressful situation. Indeed, Dorothy Farrell's identification of Davis, which she admits was in poor lighting from 160 feet away, was described as 'scientifically impossible.'[54]

In addition, there is a substantial body of evidence showing that witnesses who have previously seen a suspect may, through transference, mistake him for a perpetrator in a subsequent photo array or lineup.[55] Because of this, prior exposure to a suspect's image will make a later selection of this suspect more likely. In the Davis case, witnesses were repeatedly saturated with Davis's image in a multitude of ways, including through daily displays of Davis's image in print and televised news media, 'Wanted' posters prominently displayed around Savannah and at some of their places of employment, and a single photo display that one of the detectives used while canvassing the neighborhood after the shooting.[56] As the Innocence Project notes in their *amicus* brief, '[u]nder those circumstances, even well-intentioned witnesses free from police intimidation could unconsciously transfer the memory of Davis's image.'[57]

All of this raises very serious worries about the eyewitnesses in Davis's case. Even putting aside the tactics involved in extracting the testimony from the witnesses, the conditions themselves provide counterevidence for regarding them as reliable sources of identifications. Drawing on the framework developed in Chapter 2, there are undercutting defeaters for the testimony in question since there is a substantial amount of evidence that shows that eyewitnesses in these kinds of circumstances are unreliable. Yet not only was all of this counterevidence ignored by the State—with no additional evidence to show that the conditions in question were in fact appropriate for accurate identifications—Davis was convicted and executed on the basis of the eyewitness testimony alone.

Finally, eyewitness testimony blocks the seeking, gathering, and proper interpretation of additional evidence. Once the investigators had Davis on their radar, for instance, tunnel vision set in and they single-mindedly focused on building a case against him for the prosecution. Crucially, however, Davis was put on the radar of police through a tip from an alleged eyewitness, Sylvester 'Red' Coles,[58] who was identified as the actual murderer of McPhail by no fewer than nine other

[53] https://www.scotusblog.com/wp-content/uploads/2008/09/08-66_cert_amicus_innocence.pdf, p. 16.
[54] https://www.scotusblog.com/wp-content/uploads/2008/09/08-66_cert_amicus_innocence.pdf, p. 16.
[55] See, for instance, Dysart et al. (2001).
[56] https://www.scotusblog.com/wp-content/uploads/2008/09/08-66_cert_amicus_innocence.pdf, p. 20.
[57] https://www.scotusblog.com/wp-content/uploads/2008/09/08-66_cert_amicus_innocence.pdf, p. 21.
[58] There are also documents where his name is spelled Sylvester 'Redd' Coles.

witnesses in affidavits. Joseph Washington, for instance, testified 'I saw Sylvester Coles—I know him by the name Red—shoot the police officer. I am positive that it was Red who shot the police officer....'[59] April Hester Hutchinson reported that following the shooting, 'Red turned to me and asked me if I would walk with him up to the Burger King so "they won't think that I had nothing to do with it." That's exactly what he said...I told [the police] that I saw Red talking to my cousin Tonya and that Red was real nervous. I did not tell them about what Red had said to me because I was scared he would hurt me. I was thinking that if he did that to a police officer, what would he do to me? I didn't want to die like that officer, so I kept my mouth shut.'[60] And Anthony Hargrove testified, 'I know a guy named Red, from Savannah. His real name is Sylvester Coles. I've known Red for years and we used to hang out together. Red once told me that he shot a police officer and that a guy named Davis took the fall for it. He told me this about a year or so after the officer was killed....'[61] Coles's tip to the police should have been regarded as at least possibly the 'self-serving accusation against Davis' that it in fact seems to be,[62] but detectives instead used it to zero in on Davis, to intimidate witnesses and contaminate identifications in order to build their case against him, and to disregard a mounting pile of evidence that pointed to Coles as the shooter. This is the grip that eyewitness testimony has on the criminal legal process.

Moreover, the screening off of additional relevant evidence brought about by the credibility excess afforded to eyewitness testimony is fueled by a number of biases. As was previously noted, tunnel vision, which is a 'compendium of common heuristics and logical fallacies' (Martin 2002, p. 848) whereby 'investigators, prosecutors, judges, and defense lawyers alike...focus on a particular conclusion and then filter all evidence in a case through the lens provided by that conclusion' (Findley and Scott 2006, p. 292), often leads to the State's fixation on a suspect who is identified by an eyewitness at the expense of pursuing any other relevant leads. As Dianne L. Martin notes, '[t]his drive to confirm a preconceived belief in guilt adversely impacts on witness interviews, eyewitness procedures, interrogation of suspects, and the management of informers in ways that have been identified in virtually all known cases of wrongful conviction' (2002, p. 848).[63] Once a conviction is secured, often on the basis of only the eyewitness testimony, 'status quo bias' kicks in, where courts 'have difficulty deviating from a prior decision because that decision has become the reference point to which they compare and contrast newfound information' (Medwed 2005, pp. 701–02). This leads to judges

[59] https://www.amnestyusa.org/files/pdfs/affadavits.pdf.

[60] https://www.amnestyusa.org/files/pdfs/affadavits.pdf.

[61] https://www.amnestyusa.org/files/pdfs/affadavits.pdf.

[62] https://www.scotusblog.com/wp-content/uploads/2008/09/08-66_cert_amicus_innocence.pdf, p. 20.

[63] See, also, 'the tunnel vision problem has been widely noted in wrongful conviction cases. Officers and prosecutors either don't realize the significance or accuracy of exculpatory evidence or on occasion affirmatively conceal it because they are convinced of the suspect's guilt' (Raeder 2003, p. 1327).

who revisit a case in which they have already presided being likely to require a defendant to prove far more to support his claim of innocence than he would have if it were a new case.[64] This is clear in the Troy Davis case where the State followed through with executing him, even in the face of the recantation of nearly all of the eyewitness testimony grounding his conviction and nine affidavits implicating Coles. In addition, judges may have a bias to preserve a 'positive self-image' of themselves as fair and competent when evaluating the merits of post-conviction innocence claims relating to trials over which they previously presided.[65] This can lead them to being reluctant to believe that their decisions could have involved an injustice, thereby rendering them disposed to find evidence that would suggest otherwise lacking in credibility.[66]

Eyewitness testimony thus receives an excess of credibility in at least four different ways. First, it is weighed too heavily, as we saw in the case of Troy Davis. Not only does such testimony secure convictions by itself—with no physical evidence connecting the defendant to the crime—it is also taken to be sufficient for executions. Given how susceptible to manipulation and fallible eyewitnesses are, this is far too much weight to be given to their testimony, especially when the stakes are so high. Second, eyewitness testimony casts other evidence in a distorted light. Recantations, for instance, are regarded as obvious cases of perjury when, in fact, circumstances often make it far more likely that a witness is being honest at the later time, as we see with Cathleen Crowell Webb's testimony. Third, eyewitness testimony is resistant to counterevidence. When nine out of twelve witnesses recanted in the Davis case, and one of the three witnesses who did not recant is Sylvester 'Red' Coles, who is the suspected killer of McPhail, there is considerable counterevidence against the original verdict. But not only were the recantations dismissed, Georgia went through with executing Davis without even granting him a new trial. Finally, eyewitness testimony blocks the seeking, gathering, and proper interpretation of additional evidence. Once Davis was put on the radar of investigators, the presumption of his guilt thereafter guided the detectives as they single-mindedly focused on building a case against him, even when nine witnesses testified that Coles was the actual shooter of McPhail.

When an eyewitness's testimony is extracted and then afforded an unwarranted credibility excess, that person is the victim of agential testimonial injustice. I explained earlier that there is a specific kind of epistemic wrong that is suffered in the extraction itself, but there is a second kind of epistemic wrong in the testimony then being given an excess of credibility. For doing so is to regard the testifiers in question as givers of knowledge, or as worthy of being believed, only insofar as their epistemic agency is bypassed, exploited, or subverted. When

[64] Medwed (2005, pp. 701–02) and Armbrust (2008, p. 90).
[65] Medwed (2005, p. 701) and Armbrust (2008, p. 90).
[66] Medwed (2005, p. 701) and Armbrust (2008, p. 90).

eyewitnesses are speaking without being manipulated, deceived, or coerced—such as in their years-later recantations—their testimony is disregarded, doubted, or rejected. But when they are being used as puppets to fulfill the aims of others, and their testimony is obtained through trickery, lies, and brute force, they are regarded by the criminal courts as valuable contributors to the epistemic community. It is one kind of epistemic wrong to have your testimony induced by circumventing, exploiting, or subverting your epistemic agency, and another to then have you be regarded as trustworthy only when this is done. Agential testimonial injustice thus involves at least these two distinct epistemic wrongs.[67]

4. Other Forms of Extraction

While most cases of agential testimonial injustice involve the extraction of eyewitness testimony by administrators and detectives in lineups and interrogation rooms, it is important to note that these are not the only ways or stages of the criminal legal process where coercion, manipulation, and deception occur. To see this, consider the case of Albert Kirkman and Cedric Cal.

In 2016, I was teaching a course on mass incarceration at Stateville Correctional Center, a maximum-security men's prison in Crest Hill, Illinois, when I met Albert Kirkman. For the final paper in the course, Albert asked if I might bring him articles on eyewitness testimony and recantations to help him with his research and I soon discovered that this topic was not merely one of intellectual interest for him.

In 1994, Kirkman and his co-defendant, Cedric Cal, were convicted of two counts of first-degree murder and aggravated battery with a firearm for a shooting that occurred when they were both teenagers in 1992, resulting in the deaths of Cedric Herron and Sammy Walker and serious injuries being sustained by Willie Johnson.[68] Despite being shot nine times, Johnson survived and spoke with police at the hospital, identifying one of the shooters by his street name, 'Duke.' A few hours later, police pulled over a vehicle that was driven by Kirkman and had Cal riding as a passenger. While Kirkman initially denied going by the name 'Duke,' he eventually admitted that it was his street name when police saw 'Duke' tattooed on his left arm. After viewing a photo array at the hospital, Johnson identified both Kirkman and Cal as the shooters and they were subsequently arrested and charged.[69]

[67] While my focus in this book is on speakers who suffer agential testimonial injustice, this should not in any way be understood as minimizing the life-shattering wrongs suffered by those who are wrongfully convicted because of the extracted misidentifications.

[68] *People v. Kirkman*, No. 1-11-2362, 1 (Ill. App. Ct. 2013).

[69] *Cal v. Garnett*, 991 F.3d 843, 845 (7th Cir. 2021).

Despite being subpoenaed, Johnson failed to appear at the joint jury trial for Kirkman and Cal because, knowing that they were innocent, 'he did not want them to be convicted' and he expected that 'Cal and Kirkman would beat the case if he did not show up' (*Cal v. Garnett*, 991 F.3d 843, 847 (7th Cir. 2021)). Indeed, '[a] warrant had to be issued for his arrest before he finally appeared and testified' (*Cal v. Garnett*, 991 F.3d 843, 847 (7th Cir. 2021)). It is unsurprising that the prosecution took such an aggressive move, as Johnson's testimony was 'the only evidence linking Cal and Kirkman to the crime' (*Cal v. Garnett*, 991 F.3d 843, 845 (7th Cir. 2021)). Moreover, a defense witness testified that Johnson told him that Kirkman and Cal were not the shooters a month after the shooting, and a second witness for the defense, who was a neighbor, testified that she and her grandchildren spoke to Cal minutes after the shooting and 'that he stood with them observing the crime scene for 45 minutes—not the reaction expected from someone who participated in the shooting' (*Cal v. Garnett*, 991 F.3d 843, 846 (7th Cir. 2021)). Despite the shockingly thin case against Kirkman and Cal that 'rested solely' on Johnson's dubious eyewitness testimony, the jury found Kirkman and Cal both guilty and the court sentenced each of them to mandatory life without parole sentences.[70]

After 'retiring' from the Vice Lords,[71] moving out of Illinois, getting married, and becoming a stay-at-home father to two young children,[72] Johnson recanted his identification of Kirkman and Cal as the shooters in 2009, stating in an affidavit: 'I am coming forward now because Duke and Cal don't belong in prison for shooting me and killing my best friends. They didn't do it. They weren't there and [had] nothing to do with what went down that night.'[73] Under oath, Johnson swore that Keith Ford and an unknown second person—but not Kirkman or Cal—were the actual shooters. When Johnson was asked why he didn't initially name Ford as the shooter, he explained that he had lied at trial out of fear for his own life and his family's. 'According to Johnson, when he first identified Cal and Kirkman to the police, he "didn't know if [he] was going to die or not," and his mother and sister had already received threats, which he believed came from Ford. He testified that the threats from Ford started immediately after the shooting—while Johnson was still in the emergency room' (*Cal v. Garnett*, 991 F.3d 843, 847 (7th Cir. 2021)).

In 2009, Kirkman and Cal each filed a successive post-conviction petition based on actual innocence. At a joint evidentiary hearing in 2011, Johnson explained that he chose to come forward with the truth after so many years because he was no longer fearful now that he lived in Texas far away from Ford

70 *Cal v. Garnett*, 991 F.3d 843, 846 (7th Cir. 2021).
71 *People v. Kirkman*, No. 1-11-2362, 7 (Ill. App. Ct. 2013).
72 https://jenner.com/library/news/13885.
73 https://www.injusticewatch.org/commentary/2016/anatomy-of-an-audacious-alvarez-lie/.

and his associates.[74] In addition, Johnson testified that he received a call from an old friend, Ray Longstreet, who urged Johnson to 'tell the truth' and assured him that Ford would not retaliate. Johnson took this seriously because Longstreet was a 'well-known man in these streets' with 'a lot of power' (*Cal v. Garnett*, 991 F.3d 843, 847 (7th Cir. 2021)). Johnson's recantation was corroborated by sworn statements from both Johnson's sister and his girlfriend at the time of the crime, and it was consistent with the testimony of the defense witness who testified at the 1994 trial that Johnson told him about a month after the shooting that Kirkman and Cal weren't involved.

In 2011, the Illinois Circuit Court denied Kirkman's and Cal's petitions for post-conviction relief, finding Johnson's recantation not credible for three reasons. First, the court found Johnson's new testimony inconsistent and implausible. Johnson testified, for instance, that he received a threatening phone call while in the emergency room after the shooting, but his former girlfriend testified that she did not see Johnson receive any calls during her time with him at the hospital. Second, the court found Johnson's stated motive for lying at trial unconvincing because when he first implicated Cal and Kirkman at the hospital, he thought he was dying and thus had no reason to do anything other than tell the truth. And, third, the court found that Johnson recanted out of allegiance to the Vice Lords and not out of concerns related to justice.[75]

Rather than taking seriously the very real possibility that Kirkman and Cal had been wrongfully convicted, then Cook County State's Attorney, Anita Alvarez, 'pounced on Johnson with a vengeance, charging him with perjury—based solely on the fact that his 1994 testimony and his 2009 affidavit could not both be true.'[76] Twenty-three distinguished former judges and prosecutors were so outraged by Alvarez's aggressive move that they wrote her a letter, arguing that 'Mr. Johnson's conviction would chill future witness recantations, thereby depriving those who stand convicted of crimes they may not have committed of a fair opportunity to obtain post-conviction relief.'[77] Seemingly unconcerned by this fact, Alvarez moved forward with prosecuting Johnson. Facing up to a decade in prison and a $25,000 fine if convicted at trial, Johnson pleaded guilty to perjury in exchange for a 30-month prison sentence. As Rob Warden notes, 'In essence, what Alvarez did was subject Johnson to a modern form of torture.'[78]

This case is a paradigm of just about every problem with the way eyewitness testimony is treated in the criminal legal system in the United States. Willie Johnson's initial testimony against Kirkman and Cal was extracted in two

[74] *Cal v. Garnett*, 991 F.3d 843, 847 (7th Cir. 2021).
[75] *Cal v. Garnett*, 991 F.3d 843, 847–48 (7th Cir. 2021).
[76] https://www.injusticewatch.org/commentary/2016/anatomy-of-an-audacious-alvarez-lie/.
[77] https://www.injusticewatch.org/commentary/2016/anatomy-of-an-audacious-alvarez-lie/.
[78] https://www.injusticewatch.org/commentary/2016/anatomy-of-an-audacious-alvarez-lie/.

different ways. First, the threats from the real shooter, Keith Ford—who was worried that he would be identified—prevented Johnson from being able to offer testimony guided by evidential reasons. Instead, fearful for his own life, and concerned about the safety of his mother and sister, he capitulated and provided an identification grounded in the practical aims of preservation of life. Second, Johnson's testimony was extracted via the coercive tactics of the prosecutors, who, recognizing that they had no case without his testimony, literally issued a warrant for his arrest in order to force him to appear and to testify at trial. The threat of prosecution and incarceration, which was designed to leave him with only one real option, was clearly effective—Johnson not only testified at the trial, he said exactly what the prosecution wanted him to say.

Johnson's testimony then received a massive excess of credibility in the joint jury trial for Kirkman and Cal. First, his eyewitness identification was weighed too heavily: even though Johnson's testimony was the only evidence linking the co-defendants to the shootings, Kirkman and Cal were nonetheless both found guilty. When the paucity of inculpatory evidence is viewed against the background of the general unreliability of eyewitness identifications, it is clear that these verdicts are unwarranted. Moreover, the conditions for making the identification were far from ideal, as Johnson viewed the photo array while lying in a hospital bed after having been shot nine times and witnessing the murder of his two best friends. He also began to have his own doubts about testifying, which is why he failed to show up at the trail and needed to have a warrant issued for his arrest. Second, his eyewitness identification was resistant to counterevidence: even though one defense witness testified that Johnson told him that Kirkman and Cal were not the shooters a month after the shooting, and another defense witness testified that she and her grandchildren spoke with Cal minutes after the shooting, this was entirely disregarded. Again, drawing on the language introduced in Chapter 2, the court had undercutting defeaters that called into question the reliability of Johnson's eyewitness identifications, which is especially problematic given that the prosecution's case rested solely on his testimony.

The extraction of Johnson's initial testimony by the actual shooter and the prosecution, combined with the excess of credibility it is then afforded by virtue of the massively oversized epistemic role it plays in the convictions of Kirkman and Cal, results in a clear case of agential testimonial injustice.

This is compounded and magnified by the way that Johnson's recantation was treated. In particular, each of the three reasons cited by the Illinois Circuit Court for regarding Johnson as not credible in 2009 reveals a straightforward bias against Johnson's recanting testimony. For instance, one of the central examples to support the court's finding regarding Johnson's new testimony is that he testified that he received a threatening phone call while in the emergency room after the shooting, but his former girlfriend testified that she did not see Johnson receive any calls during her time with him at the hospital. But there are clearly a number of innocent explanations here, including that Johnson had just been shot nine times and had witnessed his two best friends murdered, so he may have been confused in this highly stressful situation about whether he received the threatening phone call in the emergency room or later after he was transferred to a hospital room. To conclude that he is a liar or unreliable, rather than simply mistaken, reveals the court's predisposition to discount Johnson's credibility when it doesn't suit the prosecution's purpose.

Even more concerning, however, are the court's second and third reasons for finding Johnson's recantation to be lacking in credibility, which seem simply to amount to an assault on his moral and epistemic character grounded in prejudice. The court, for instance, regarded Johnson's stated motive for giving false testimony at trial unconvincing because when he first implicated Kirkman and Cal at the hospital, he thought he was dying and so had no reason to lie. But Johnson was clear that he feared for the lives of his mother and sister at the 1994 trial, which for many people would be an even more powerful motivation to lie than one's own safety. That the court simply cannot see that the love Johnson has for his mother and sister can function as a compelling reason to lie, even when there is no further threat to his own safety, reveals a bias it seems to have against his moral character. For why else would the court assume that in the absence of concerns about his own self-preservation, Johnson had no reason to do anything other than tell the truth?

Moreover, the finding that Johnson's recantation had nothing at all to do with honesty, truth, and justice, but only his allegiance to the Vice Lords, is not only unwarranted, but also raises serious concerns about the court's own prejudices. Fifteen years have passed since Johnson's original testimony, and he now has the advantages of maturity, retirement from the Vice Lords, marriage, fatherhood, and a new life in Texas on his side, so there are independent reasons for being open to the possibility that it is the pangs of conscience, and not gang loyalty, motivating him to come forward. Indeed, his own explanation for recanting is the injustice of Kirkman and Cal being in prison for something they didn't do. Why would the court fail to recognize that the power of guilt for ruining the lives of innocent people, and a commitment to the truth and to trying to make amends, might be what is at work here? The only explanation is that the court illegitimately believed that such factors are far less likely to be operative in Johnson than gang loyalty is. Indeed, in discussing its basis for drawing the inference that Johnson was acting in the interests of the Vice Lords, the circuit court was said to be 'in the best position to observe the demeanor of the witnesses' (*People v. Kirkman*, No. 1-11-2362, 16 (Ill. App. Ct. 2013)). But, as noted in Chapter 2, demeanor evidence has been shown to be a highly questionable source, with numerous studies showing that 'experts' perform only slightly better than ordinary people at detecting deception and that ordinary people perform no better than chance at doing so.[79] Moreover, as Rand notes, 'there exists . . . a "Demeanor Gap" in situations of cross-racial demeanor evaluation that undermines accuracy in credibility determinations: specifically, jurors of one race, even those well-intended and free of racial animus, will be unable to dependably judge the demeanor of a witness of a different race because they are unable to accurately decipher the cues that the witness uses to communicate sincerity' (2000, p. 4). Given these very serious epistemic problems with judging a witness's credibility on the basis of demeanor, the court's grounds for regarding Johnson as not credible are further undermined.

Finally, we see the State's Attorney not only wielding the perjury sword against Johnson, but also following through on the threat and using it. The fact that Johnson's original testimony and his later affidavit conflict means that he lied either in 1994 or in 2009. Given the possibility that it is his earlier identification that was false, which was the only evidence linking Kirkman and Cal to the shootings, justice demands that Johnson's recantation be taken extremely seriously. But Alvarez instead 'pounced on Johnson with a vengeance' and charged him with perjury. Everything about this is at odds with truth and justice: the intimidation and threatening of Johnson, the disregard of the possible innocence of Kirkman and Cal, the wholesale dismissal of Johnson's claims that he is motivated by truth and justice, and the chilling effect this aggressive move will surely have on future witness recantations and thereby on other wrongful convictions.

As if all of this were not enough, there was one final act of extracted testimony: threatened by Alvarez with a decade in prison and a $25,000 fine, Johnson pled guilty to perjury in exchange for 30 months in prison. Recognizing the coerciveness of this tactic and the deterring impact it would have on other witnesses offering truthful recantations, Governor Pat Quinn commuted Johnson's sentence to time served on his final day in office. While Johnson had served slightly more than three months of his sentence, his conviction remained, as did the wrongful convictions and incarceration of two innocent people.[80]

At multiple stages of the criminal legal process, then, Johnson was treated as a giver of knowledge only when his testimony was extracted, first when he was coerced to testify through threats from the actual shooter and a warrant issued

[79] Vrij (2000), Memon et al. (2003), and Granhag and Strömwall (2004). It is also worth mentioning that this is another example of agential testimonial injustice being fueled by hearer-excess testimonial injustice, which, it may be recalled, involves a hearer giving himself an epistemic boost, especially relative to the amount of credibility afforded to a speaker. In particular, the circuit court seems confident in its ability to assess Johnson's credibility via his demeanor, despite all of the evidence indicating that experts perform only slightly better than chance at detecting deception. This leads the circuit court to confidently judge Johnson's recantation as lacking credibility, thereby contributing to him being a victim of agential testimonial injustice.

[80] https://www.injusticewatch.org/commentary/2016/anatomy-of-an-audacious-alvarez-lie/. While Kirkman and Cal have since been released from prison, they are still fighting to prove their innocence.

for his arrest and then when he pled guilty to perjury because of threats of incarceration and fines. When he freely exercised his epistemic agency and offered a recantation that was grounded in maturity, guilt, and a desire for truth and justice, he was regarded as a liar. This is classic agential testimonial injustice perpetrated against an eyewitness that directly caused life-shattering consequences for many of those involved, especially Kirkman and Cal. It is also, once again, hauntingly reminiscent of the way the testimony of enslaved persons in ancient Athens and Rome was regarded as so unreliable that it was admissible in judicial proceedings only if it was extracted via torture. In discussing the events that led to Johnson's incarceration, it is, then, unsurprising that Warden maintains that he was subjected to 'a modern form of torture.'

5. Moving Forward

Since much of the testimony of eyewitnesses in criminal cases in the United States is both extracted and given an excess of credibility, agential testimonial injustice is fairly widespread within the criminal legal system. This calls for reforms along dimensions of both of the epistemic wrongs that are inflicted on such testifiers. First, lineups and interrogation techniques should not be manipulative, deceptive, or coercive. Not only do such processes fail to be reliably connected to obtaining true testimony, but they also wrong testifiers by circumventing, exploiting, and subverting their epistemic agency. If testimony cannot be acquired through practices grounded in reasons and respect, resorting to trickery, lies, and brute force should not be 'plan B.' The agency, autonomy, and dignity of witnesses in the criminal legal system should never be compromised in the service of the practical aims of the State.

One way forward is to reliably follow the recommended lineup procedures discussed earlier, such as 'double-blind' administration, the inclusion of at least five fillers who match the eyewitness's description of the perpetrator, and a sequential presentation. In addition, states should move away from the use of a confrontational interrogation method on suspects and witnesses, such as the Reid Technique, and adopt an information-gathering one, such as the PEACE Method. The PEACE Method, whose acronym stands for Preparation and Planning, Engage and Explain, Account, Closure, and Evaluate, was developed in the United Kingdom and has been adopted in Australia, New Zealand, and Norway.[81] Whereas the goal of the Reid Technique is to elicit a confession, beginning with the presumption that the suspect is guilty and using minimization and

[81] https://medium.com/nonviolenceny/implementation-of-peace-methods-in-modern-justice-systems-fd17d9548f26.

maximization to achieve the desired end,[82] the PEACE Method's aim is 'to obtain accurate and reliable information from a victim, witness or suspect of an investigation in order to discover the truth.'[83] Investigators are instructed not to be 'oppressive' and to 'act fairly,' which involves not approaching an interview with prejudice and being 'prepared to believe the account that they are being given.'[84] Deception is also prohibited, so interrogators cannot lie about the evidence or the consequences of cooperation. These differences alone in interrogation techniques would very likely significantly reduce the number of false statements.[85] In addition, interrogations should be electronically recorded in their entirety, which improves transparency and creates an indisputable record of what happened during the interrogation process.[86] Recordings of interrogations promote the protection of the rights of suspects and witnesses, create a deterrent against the use of improper or coercive techniques, and alert investigators, prosecutors, judges, and juries to mental limitations or other vulnerabilities that might make the suspect or witness more susceptible to offering a false statement, all of which prevent false statements from leading to wrongful convictions.[87]

Second, the epistemic force of eyewitness identifications should be viewed within the broader context of their susceptibility to influence and unreliability. As we have seen, under the right circumstances, eyewitnesses will say whatever those in power want them to say. Given this, judges and jurors should be made aware through expert testimony that eyewitness testimony is highly fallible and that there are practices that are known to bring about misidentifications, especially when eyewitness testimony is the sole or primary evidence against a defendant. Research has found, for instance, that judges have limited knowledge of eyewitness testimony, with many unaware that eyewitness confidence is not related to eyewitness accuracy, that sequential lineups are more effective than simultaneous ones in reducing eyewitness misidentification, and that jurors cannot distinguish between accurate and inaccurate eyewitness testimony.[88] Similarly, studies have shown that jurors have limited knowledge of the factors that influence eyewitness accuracy, that they rely on factors that are poor indicators of eyewitness accuracy, such as eyewitness confidence, that they overestimate the ability of eyewitnesses to make accurate identifications, and that they cannot distinguish accurate from

[82] When the Reid Technique is used on witnesses, the aim is to elicit an identification of a suspect and it begins with the presumption that the witness has relevant information.

[83] https://www.fis-international.com/assets/Uploads/resources/PEACE-A-Different-Approach.pdf.

[84] https://www.fis-international.com/assets/Uploads/resources/PEACE-A-Different-Approach.pdf.

[85] Meissner et al., for instance, found that information-gathering interrogations 'preserved, and in some cases increased, the likelihood of true confessions, while simultaneously reducing the likelihood of false confessions. In contrast, the accusatorial approach increased both true and false confessions....' (2014, p. 459).

[86] https://innocenceproject.org/false-confessions-recording-interrogations/.

[87] https://innocenceproject.org/false-confessions-recording-interrogations/.

[88] Wise and Safer (2003).

inaccurate eyewitnesses in mock trials.[89] However, empirical studies show that the introduction of expert testimony about the reliability of eyewitness identification has a significant impact on verdicts and the epistemic status of jurors and their deliberation. For instance, eyewitness expert testimony reduces the number of guilty verdicts, and this is especially true in the case of violent, rather than nonviolent, crime.[90] In particular, expert testimony produced a greater reduction in the likelihood of convictions in cases of violent crime, which may be explained by the testimony encouraging jurors to pay more attention to the details of the eyewitness account rather than the more emotional aspects of the crime.[91] Eyewitness expert testimony also increases jurors' knowledge of eyewitness factors and explains how to use that knowledge in assessing eyewitness accuracy.[92] Despite this, the vast majority of courts are skeptical of eyewitness expert testimony, 'if not outright hostile to its admission' (Wise et al. 2007, p. 823).

In addition, the unwarranted bias against recantation testimony should be recognized as just this—a bias—and should be replaced with an assessment grounded in evidence of whether there are compelling reasons why a witness may have been dishonest in the original testimony but telling the truth in the recantation. This is crucial, as nearly all of the reforms in the criminal legal system in the past three decades focusing on avoiding and correcting wrongful convictions have arisen from cases involving DNA evidence.[93] However, '[t]he vast majority (probably 80%) of felony cases do not involve biological evidence that can be subjected to DNA testing' (Scheck 2002, p. 221).[94] Indeed, 'perpetrators of murders, drive-by shootings, convenience store robberies, muggings, and other common crimes almost never leave DNA trace evidence that could exonerate someone who has been . . . mistakenly identified by an eyewitness' (Wells et al. 2000, p. 589). Since the same problems that led to the wrongful convictions of innocent defendants who were later exonerated through DNA testing 'appear in the scores of convictions procured without biological evidence' (Medwed 2005, p. 675), those who are wrongfully convicted in non-DNA cases must have an alternative path for supporting their claims of innocence. Appreciating the susceptibility to influence and error of eyewitness identifications, and the potential force of recantations,

[89] Wise et al. (2007, pp. 824–25). [90] Loftus (1980, p. 13). [91] Loftus (1980, p. 13).

[92] Wise and Kehn (2020, p. 315). This study focused specifically on the 'I-I-Eye method' of eyewitness expert testimony, which has three central components: 'First, ascertain whether law enforcement conducted the eyewitness interviews in a manner that obtained the maximum amount of information from the eyewitness, did not contaminate the eyewitness's memory of the crime, or artificially increase the eyewitness's confidence. Next, determine whether the identification procedures in the case were fair and unbiased. Finally, evaluate what eyewitness factors during the crime are likely to have increased or decreased the accuracy of the eyewitness testimony' (Wise et al. 2009, p. 435).

[93] Armbrust (2008, p. 77).

[94] This can happen because there was no DNA evidence available at the initial crime scene, because evidence that was available has since been lost or destroyed, or because evidence that has been saved is too degraded for testing. See Armbrust (2008, p. 78).

would be a positive step in the direction of respecting the epistemic agency and dignity of witnesses and, thereby, of achieving truth and justice.

6. Conclusion

In this chapter, I provided an analysis of the tension we find between the privileged epistemic status that eyewitness testimony occupies in the United States criminal legal system and the fact that it is often unreliable as a source of evidence. I show that lineups and interrogations often extract testimony from eyewitnesses through practices that are manipulative, deceptive, or coercive, and that when such extracted testimony is given an unwarranted excess of credibility, the eyewitnesses in question are the victims of agential testimonial injustice. Testifiers who suffer from agential testimonial injustice are wronged both in having their epistemic agency bypassed, exploited, or subverted in the obtaining of their testimony, and in then being regarded as truthful only when they are not properly exercising their epistemic agency. Given that this is a fairly widespread practice, courts are systematically privileging forms of testimonial evidence that are derived from the straightforward application of State power. This calls for significant reforms along both dimensions—lineups and interrogations should go through the epistemic agency of eyewitness, rather than bypassing, exploiting, or undermining it, and the resulting testimony should be viewed as a highly fallible source of evidence that needs to be substantially corroborated. Such reforms have the result of not only treating witnesses as rational agents deserving of epistemic respect and dignity, but also of reducing the number of life-shattering wrongful convictions based on false eyewitness testimony.

4

Plea Deals, Coercion, and Systemic Testimonial Injustice

One of the most powerful and lasting images of the criminal legal system is the courtroom, where justice is meted out through a battle between the prosecution and defense under the watchful eyes of a jury and the public. The reality, however, is that convictions in the United States are rarely the result of such a process. Indeed, it is not an overstatement to say that trial by jury is on the verge of extinction,[1] with 97.4% of federal felony convictions in the United States obtained through guilty pleas[2] and state felony convictions not far behind.[3] These staggering numbers, combined with the fact that the American criminal legal system 'has become the most punitive in the world,'[4] raise urgent and important questions about the ethical and epistemological status of plea bargaining. Why, we should ask, are so many defendants forfeiting the exercise of their Sixth Amendment right, especially when facing extraordinarily harsh sentences?

The aim of this chapter is to address this question by taking a close look at the normative status of plea deals in the United States criminal legal system, with particular attention paid to the plea-bargaining process. I begin with the widely cited criticism that plea deals are coercive. Despite the frequency with which this worry is expressed, it is rare to see it situated within a deeper understanding of what makes a process coercive in the first place, and so I start with how to best understand coercion. After raising objections to existing accounts, I develop and defend a new view according to which coercion involves an unfair offer or threat that closes a person out of a reasonable decision-making space. I then apply this notion to the practices in the current criminal legal system in the United States, showing that plea bargaining involves the extraction of guilty pleas that are not only coercive but also manipulative and deceptive. Such practices subvert,

[1] See New York State Association of Criminal Defense Lawyers (2021).

[2] United States Sentencing Commission, 2019 Sourcebook of Federal Sentencing Statistics, https://www.ussc.gov/research/sourcebook-2019.

[3] As Rakoff (2014) says, 'While corresponding statistics for the fifty states combined are not available, it is a rare state where plea bargains do not similarly account for the resolution of at least 95 percent of the felony cases that are not dismissed . . . .' Similarly, according to the New York State Association of Criminal Defense Lawyers, 'Recent data shows that in New York State 99 percent of misdemeanor charges and 94 percent of felony charges are resolved by a guilty plea. New York is by no means an aberration. Across the country criminal trials are vanishing at an alarming rate' (2021, p. 3).

[4] Materni (2013, p. 264).

Criminal Testimonial Injustice. Jennifer Lackey, Oxford University Press.
DOI: 10.1093/oso/9780192864109.003.0005

circumvent, or exploit the epistemic agency of defendants, thereby resulting in their being victims of agential testimonial injustice. American plea bargaining thus involves a form of systemic testimonial injustice perpetrated against its citizens, often with life-altering consequences, that not only takes place on a massive scale, but is also State-sanctioned.

1. Coercion

Guilty pleas are said to function in the criminal legal system the way that other performative utterances do. Performative utterances are speech acts that perform the action a sentence uttered describes and, in this way, they change social reality.[5] A paradigmatic example is, 'I now pronounce you husband and wife.' In offering this utterance, I make it the case that you are now married and so my words have quite literally changed the world. According to Richard Nobles and Davis Schiff (2019), guilty pleas should be understood as speech acts that execute a performance. They write: 'The person who pleads guilty voluntarily and knowingly changes their normative position. By this act, they alter their status from a defendant to a convicted person' (Nobles and Schiff 2019, p. 109). Just as someone who utters 'I do' changes her status from single to married, a person who accepts a plea deal is said to change his status from defendant to convicted person. Crucially, however, Nobles and Schiff go on to say:

> Thereafter, and as a result of this voluntary act..., they will be treated as a person whose conviction has been established beyond a reasonable doubt...the defendant had been offered a choice. He chose...to exercise a power constructed via a power-conferring rule, and thereby altered his status, just as would occur if he had voluntarily made a will or entered into a marriage. Having executed a speech act that he has been informed will have this effect, he cannot now disclaim his new status, any more than the groom or bride who reluctantly undergoes or regrets a marriage can claim to be single.
>
> (Nobles and Schiff 2019, p. 109)

According to Nobles and Schiff, a guilty plea is a performative utterance because it is the result of a voluntary act—a choice to alter one's status through exercising a power. In this way, the voluntariness of a performative utterance is what grounds the change in status from defendant to convicted person. Consider, for instance, that the United States Citizenship and Immigration Services regard 'forced marriage' as a 'serious human rights abuse' and defines forced marriage as 'a marriage

[5] See Austin (1962).

that takes place without the consent of one or both people in the marriage. Consent means that you have given your full, free, and informed agreement to marry your intended spouse and to the timing of the marriage. Forced marriage may occur when family members or others use physical or emotional abuse, threats, or deception to force you to marry without your consent.'[6] Thus, just as marriage requires free and informed consent for its legitimacy, so, too, is voluntariness necessary for a defendant to execute a status-changing act through a guilty plea.

In spite of this, it is not uncommon for plea deals in our current criminal legal system to be regarded as coercive. A cursory internet search, for instance, results in titles such as 'Prisons are packed because prosecutors are coercing plea deals. And, yes, it's totally legal,'[7] or 'Coerced Out of Justice: How Prosecutors Abuse Their Power to Secure Guilty Pleas.'[8] In a recently released report by the New York State Association of Criminal Defense Lawyers, 'The New York State Trial Penalty: The Constitutional Right to Trial Under Attack,' the authors conclude that '[t]here is ample evidence that federal criminal defendants are being coerced to plead guilty because the penalty for exercising their constitutional rights is simply too high to risk' (2021, p. 6).[9] A similar theme is found in legal and philosophical scholarship. In the context of discussing judges using near-term expiration dates on plea deals that only get worse if refused, Richard Klein refers to these as 'coercive tactics of the judge(s) that were designed to achieve a plea' (2004, p. 1351). Cynthia Alkon writes that 'prosecutors regularly use hard bargaining tactics such as exploding offers, threats to add enhancements, take-it-or-leave-it offers, and threats to seek the death penalty. These hard bargaining tactics contribute to the often highly coercive atmosphere of plea bargaining that can lead innocent defendants to plead guilty' (2017, p. 401).[10] Casey M. Burns says that '[t]hreats of higher sentences or more charges negate the voluntariness, knowledge, and understanding required to find a plea agreement valid' (2018, p. 4). Kenneth Kipnis draws a comparison between the paradigmatic case of surrendering one's wallet to a gunman and plea deals:

[6] https://www.uscis.gov/humanitarian/forced-marriage.

[7] https://www.nbcnews.com/think/opinion/prisons-are-packed-because-prosecutors-are-coercing-plea-deals-yes-ncna1034201.

[8] https://www.aclu.org/news/criminal-law-reform/coerced-out-of-justice-how-prosecutors-abuse-their-power-to-secure-guilty-pleas/.

[9] Elsewhere in this same report, the authors reflect on the number of innocent people who plead guilty, writing that '[t]his disturbing figure casts doubt on the assumption that defendants who plead guilty do so voluntarily' (New York State Association of Criminal Defense Lawyers 2021, p. 6).

[10] Similarly, Schehr writes, 'we cannot forget the potential threat of coercion should a defendant reject the plea and elect to pursue trial. This threat is leveraged by the fact that the defendant will confront a "trial tax" if convicted and as a consequence, suffer a far graver punishment' (Schehr 2018, p. 57).

> [T]he same considerations that will drive reasonable people to give in to the gunman compel one to accept the prosecutor's offer... one can see that, like the gunman's acts, the acts of the prosecutor can 'operate coercively upon the will of the plaintiff, judged subjectively,' and both the gunman's victim and the defendant may 'have no adequate remedy to avoid the coercion except to give in.' In both cases reasonable persons might well conclude (after considering the gunman's lethal weapon or the gas chamber) 'I can't take the chance.' (1976, p. 99)[11]

Defendants also perceive prosecutorial and judicial tactics involved in the obtaining of plea deals as coercive. In *North Carolina v. Alford*, Justice Brennan wrote in dissent that 'the facts set out in the majority opinion demonstrate that Alford was "so gripped by fear of the death penalty" that his decision to plead guilty was not voluntary but was the product of duress as much so as choice reflecting physical constraint' (*North Carolina v. Alford*, 400 U.S. 25, 40 (1970)). Indeed, Alford himself said: 'I pleaded guilty on second-degree murder because they said there is too much evidence, but I ain't shot no man, but I take the fault of the other man. We never had an argument in our life and I just pleaded guilty because they said if I didn't they would gas me for it, and that is all... I'm not guilty, but I plead guilty' (*North Carolina v. Alford*, 400 U.S. 25, 29 n.2, (1970)). Even Conrad G. Brunk, who argues that the practice of plea bargaining is 'not intrinsically coercive,' maintains that he is 'not convinced that the conditions of voluntary, noncoerced choice are being met in present plea negotiation practice, nor even that they can be achieved by initiating reforms' (1979, p. 552).

Coercion is said to target voluntariness.[12] This is crucial, as the Supreme Court made the necessity of voluntariness in guilty pleas clear in the 1927 case of *Kercheval v. United States*: 'Out of just consideration for persons accused of crime, courts are careful that a plea of guilt shall not be accepted unless made voluntarily after proper advice and with full understanding of the consequences... the court will vacate a plea of guilty shown to have been unfairly obtained or given through ignorance, fear or inadvertence' (*Kercheval v. United States*, 274 U.S. 220, 223 (1927)). Similarly, in 1962 in *Machibroda v. United States*, the Court says, 'A guilty plea, if induced by promises or threats which deprive it of the character of a

[11] See also: 'We threaten [the defendant] with a materially increased sanction if he avails himself of his right and is thereafter convicted. This sentencing differential is what makes plea bargaining coercive. There is, of course, a difference between having your limbs crushed if you refuse to confess, or suffering some extra years of imprisonment if you refuse to confess, but the difference is of degree, not kind. Plea bargaining, like torture, is coercive' (Langbein 1978, pp. 12–13).

[12] Wendler and Wertheimer (2017, p. 115) discuss how coercion 'undermines' voluntariness, but some may regard this as too strong. For instance, even the paradigmatic case of turning over your wallet to a gunman who threatens your life may be said to involve some voluntary action on your part. After all, you could have chosen death over surrendering your wallet, or to run with your wallet, or to fight back, and so on. Given this, I will focus on coercion 'diminishing' rather than 'undermining' voluntariness. As should be clear, actions taken with radically diminished voluntariness raise serious questions about their voluntariness and validity.

voluntary act, is void' (*Machibroda v. United States*, 368 U.S. 487, 493 (1962)).[13] If guilty pleas must be voluntary in order to be valid, and coercion diminishes voluntariness, it is important to fully understand what is meant by the widespread claims that plea deals are clearly coercive. And yet, despite this, there is surprisingly little discussion in the context of plea deals of what exactly coercion is and how precisely such deals are coercive.

To get a better handle on this notion, it will be helpful to take a closer look at the philosophical and legal literature on the nature of coercion. To begin, coercion is said to target the options available to a person making a decision, or the decision space itself, rather than the way a person sees the decision space. According to Allen Wood, for instance, coercing someone means eliminating all of the 'acceptable alternatives' (2014, pp. 21–23).[14] When I say, 'give me your money or I'll shoot you,' there is really only one acceptable option here, and that is to comply with my demand for your money.

While this account captures something important about coercion, there is also reason to regard it as too inclusive. Suppose that you and I are returning from a grueling trek through the desert after being lost for 48 hours and we are both suffering from dehydration. There are only two bottles of water at our campsite, and I reach for the one on the right and begin drinking it. At this point, not drinking water is an unacceptable alternative, as that will leave you seriously ill, and so the only acceptable alternative is for you to drink the remaining bottle of water on the left, as I have eliminated the other acceptable option. Have I coerced you to drink the water? This seems a strange use of 'coercion.' It is not as though the remaining bottle of water is poisonous or dirty or in any way worse than the bottle I reached for, and you are drinking the water because you are thirsty, not because of any threats or pressure from me. Indeed, according to Harry Frankfurt, '[t]he victim of coercion is necessarily either moved in some way against his will or his will is in some way circumvented' (1998, p. 41). By leaving you with only the bottle of water on the left, I am not forcing you to do something that goes against or around your will, as you are indifferent to whether you drink the water

[13] For a detailed discussion of the history of the Supreme Court's rulings regarding voluntariness, coercion, and plea deals, see Becker (1988).

[14] Pallikkathayil (2011) distinguishes between what she calls 'physical coercion,' which operates by taking physical control of at least some part of another person's body, and 'volitional coercion,' which operates on another person's actions. Similarly, coercion is often regarded as importantly different than brute force. While coercion involves achieving a desired end with a threat or offer that goes through the will and rational faculties of the other person, brute force involves achieving a desired end with the direct use of force and without going through the will or rational facilities of the other person. In his influential book, *Arms and Influence*, Thomas C. Schelling distinguishes coercion and brute force as the 'power to hurt' versus the 'power to seize or hold forcibly' (1966, p. 6) and says that 'brute force succeeds when it is used, whereas the power to hurt is most successful when held in reserve. It is the threat of damage, or of more damage to come, that can make someone yield or comply' (1966, p. 3). He later writes: 'The difference between coercion and brute force is often in the intent as in the instrument' (1966, p. 5).

on the left or the right. So, even though I eliminated all acceptable alternatives, I didn't seem to coerce you.

We may avoid this problem by making explicit that coercion involves a threat or offer,[15] and so merely eliminating acceptable alternatives via an action such as reaching for a bottle of water isn't the right sort of example. Suppose, however, that a surgeon in the emergency room meets with the parents of a child and makes clear that he either operates on their child immediately or she will die. This offer really leaves the parents with only one acceptable alternative—allow the surgeon to operate on their child. But the surgeon doesn't seem to have coerced the parents.

Picking up on Frankfurt, it might be helpful to turn to understanding coercion in terms of its targeting of the will of the one being coerced. Joel Rudinow, for instance, argues that to coerce another person is to offer '*irresistible* incentives' (1978, p. 341, emphasis added). Similarly, Frankfurt himself focuses on coercion involving threats or offers that arouse in victims desires that are 'irresistible'; these desires are so powerful that those who are coerced are 'incapable of defying them,' and they will move victims to act on them regardless of whether they want to (1998, pp. 39–41). This is a highly subjective notion of coercion that depends on what individual people find irresistible and which desires a person's will is unable to defy. Frankfurt is quite clear about this. For instance, he discusses being able to coerce a person who is pathologically fearful of bees into performing an action by threatening her with a bee sting (1998, p. 39), or coercing someone driven by fame into complying with a proposal by offering to make him famous (1998, p. 42). What is key on his view is that the victim of coercion is 'motivated against his own will to do what he does' (Frankfurt 1998, p. 42). This psychological view of coercion seems, at least in the letter of the ruling, to be operative in the Supreme Court's landmark decision in *Brady v. United States*. While this case is widely known for the Court ruling that the risk of greater penalties, including threats involving the death penalty, is *not* sufficient for rendering the resulting guilty plea a product of coercion, the decision itself says that 'the State may not produce a plea by actual or threatened physical harm or by mental coercion overbearing the will of the defendant' (*Brady v. United States*, 397 U.S. 750 (1970)). Threats and offers that overbear the will of a defendant, and thereby result in mental coercion, are precisely what Frankfurt is interested in. And so there is a deep sense in which

[15] While there is some debate about whether both threats and offers, rather than only threats, can coerce, there are compelling reasons to include both. Consider, for instance, Robert Nozick's (1969, p. 447) example of a slave owner who beats his slave daily, but who one day proposes to forgo the daily beating if the slave will perform a task that is disagreeable, but not as disagreeable as a beating. While this is clearly an offer, it is also surely coercive. Moreover, massive imbalances of power or a history of systemic injustice can certainly make even simple offers to a person coercive. See also Lyons (1975), Zimmerman (1981), Feinberg (1986), Stevens (1988), O'Neill (1991), Frankfurt (1998), and Berman (2001).

Frankfurt and the Supreme Court—at least in this opinion—are in the same camp when it comes to understanding coercion.

Despite this, there are a number of serious worries with this psychological view of coercion, especially when used to assess practices within the criminal legal system.[16] First, this conception of coercion is excessively subjective and dependent on the individual. Before we can even begin to determine whether a person has been coerced, we need to know a fair bit about her particular psychology. We need to understand, for instance, what her desires are, how strong they are, how powerful her will is, and so on. This has the consequence that one can be coercive without having any idea whatsoever that one is having this effect and one can fail to be coercive despite every attempt to be taken this way.[17] If, for instance, a defendant happens to be offered a cup of coffee during plea bargaining that she finds irresistible due to a peculiarity of her psychology, we clearly would not want to hold anyone accountable for coercing her into a guilty plea. Indeed, a highly suggestible person who finds most offers irresistible would be virtually incapable of entering into a non-coercive deal about anything on this view. On the flip side, if a defendant is threatened with physical torture if he doesn't accept a plea deal, surely we want to regard this as a coercive tactic, regardless of whether the defendant's particular psychology is resistant to such threats. Even paradigmatically coercive scenarios cannot be regarded as coercive without understanding the victim's individual mental states. When someone says to me, 'give me your wallet or I'll shoot,' we cannot conclude that I was coerced into turning my wallet over without first establishing that my fear of being shot motivated me to act against my own will. Moreover, suppose a defendant has suffered significant trauma in her life that has left her prone to dissociation. This dissociation, in turn, enables her to disconnect from the fear of consequences, and so she is able to resist most threats far more easily than others. The psychological view has the result that this defendant's trauma renders her virtually incapable of being coerced by the State, a consequence we should reject not only because it could lead to the impact of trauma warranting overtly abusive actions, but also because it completely ignores State accountability.

Second, the psychological account has significant practical costs. Consider, for instance, how difficult it would be to establish that someone has been coerced,

[16] To be clear, I am not arguing that there is no sense of coercion captured by the psychological view, nor am I suggesting that there are no domains in which our assessments of whether someone was coerced might be best grounded in such a view. For instance, in determining whether an addiction has rendered someone less culpable for an action, the psychological view might be best. But it is surely not the only notion of coercion, nor is it the one that is best used in generally evaluating the actions and practices within the criminal legal system.

[17] It should be noted that one can coerce another person even if one does not succeed in bringing about the desired end in question. If I say, 'give me your wallet or I'll shoot,' I am engaging in coercive actions, and you are being coerced, even before we know what the outcome is, i.e., whether you turn over your wallet or not.

especially in the context of the criminal legal system. Most likely, a robust, comprehensive psychological profile would need to be completed by an expert and fairly detailed testimony would need to be offered about the specific coercive act in question. This would be a time-consuming and expensive process, and so those defendants with limited resources would be at a significant disadvantage in trying to prove that they were the victims of coercion. Moreover, given the subjectivity involved in people's desires and what they find irresistible, it would not be difficult to raise doubts about whether a person was coerced, thereby leading to very few instances where actual cases of coercion could be proven. For instance, a prosecutor might point to cases where a defendant was able to resist far more seemingly irresistible offers in the past to undermine the claim that he was coerced in the present case, even if the defendant was in fact coerced.

Third, this view of coercion lends itself to serious concerns about coercive practices hiding under the guise of being non-coercive because of prejudices, biases, and myths. For instance, there are longstanding racist myths that Black people are less sensitive to pain than are white people. Consider the views of Dr. Samuel Cartright, who was a physician writing extensively on the topics of race and slavery during the two decades before the Civil War. Of Cartright's many proslavery arguments were a number grounded in purported physiological differences between Black and white people, including a 'Negro disease' that made 'Negroes...insensible to pain when subjected to punishment' (Guillory 1968, p. 215).[18] Versions of these same myths persist in present-day beliefs and values, with studies showing that 'people assume a priori that Blacks feel less pain than do Whites' (Trawalter et al. 2012). Indeed, such racist beliefs are even prevalent within the medical community. A 2016 paper published in the *Proceedings of the National Academy of Science* showed that of the 222 white medical students and residents surveyed in a study, half of them endorsed at least one myth about physiological differences between Blacks and whites, including 'Black people's nerve-endings are less sensitive than White people's nerve-endings' and 'Black people's skin has more collagen (i.e., it's thicker) than White people's skin' (Hoffman et al. 2016). It is not difficult to imagine that such false beliefs, often grounded in a history of systemic racism, could be used to argue that overtly coercive practices are not in fact coercive in particular, racially motivated cases. If, for instance, a particular defendant is more insensitive to pain, then presumably that person would find threats of pain more resistible, and so it would be more difficult to coerce him. As should be clear, this opens the door to the possibility of deeply pernicious and abusive practices of coercion being justified through prejudices, biases, and myths.

[18] Consider, also, how the so-called 'father of gynecology,' J. Marion Sims, perfected his surgical techniques for repairing vesicovaginal fistula by using Black slave women as his research subjects without the use of anesthesia. See Ojanuga (1993).

Finally, this view of coercion shifts the focus almost entirely on to the individual being coerced and away from the tactics and processes of the coercer and the institutions that support them. Suppose, for instance, that two prosecutors use tactics during plea bargaining that might be regarded as morally egregious, including making overt threats involving the unjustified removal of the defendants' children from their respective homes. Suppose further that while both defendants plead guilty as a result of the tactics, one has a slightly more powerful will than the other and so could have resisted the threats. On the psychological view under discussion, only one defendant would have been coerced to plead guilty, and only one prosecutor would thereby be guilty of being a coercer. But this seems problematic, as the mere fact that a person has a slightly more powerful will should not prevent us from recognizing that she was coerced by threats, nor that the prosecutor is accountable for using coercive tactics. Indeed, it is crucial in assessing whether someone was coerced that we fully recognize the one doing the coercing, his actions, and the broader practices and systems that make possible the interpersonal coercive dynamic.

An importantly different notion of coercion is found in the Model Penal Code's section on duress,[19] according to which: 'It is an affirmative defense that the actor engaged in the conduct charged to constitute an offense because he was coerced to do so by the use of, or a threat to use, unlawful force against his person or the person of another, that a person of reasonable firmness in his situation would have been unable to resist' (2.09). As found in *Brady v. United States* and Frankfurt's work, this account centers on what the person being coerced is able to resist, but it deviates from the purely psychological account in two crucial respects. First, it explicitly brings into the account the coercer, the coercer's conduct, and a normative assessment of the conduct. In particular, the conduct needs to involve the use of, or threat to use, *force* that is *unlawful*. Second, it is not just any old notion of irresistibility that matters; it has to be force that a person of *reasonable firmness in his situation* would be unable to resist.

This view clearly avoids the problems found in the psychological account. For instance, it is not excessively subjective, as the force in question needs to be both unlawful and irresistible to a person of reasonable firmness in that situation. Thus, no matter how irresistible you find coffee, it is neither unlawful to offer you a cup nor is it irresistible to a person of reasonable firmness, and no matter how unusual you are in your insensitivity to physical harm, it is unlawful to threaten you with it and it is not irresistible to a person of reasonable firmness. This means that such a view also does not have the practical costs of needing a robust

[19] While the Model Penal Code's duress provision is not meant to provide a general definition of coercion (but is instead intended to provide an affirmative defense for a person who is coerced into committing a crime), it nonetheless points in the direction of an alternative conception of coercion that is instructive for our purposes.

comprehensive psychological profile to prove that someone has been coerced, as what is lawful and resistible to a person of reasonable firmness can be determined independently of this level of individual detail. Moreover, the worries about coercive practices hiding under the guise of being non-coercive because of prejudices, biases, and myths are not as pressing as they are with the psychological account since coercion is determined by more objectively assessable features. And the role that lawfulness plays in this account makes the tactics and processes of the coercer and the institutions that support them front and center.

Despite these advantages, however, there are also some significant concerns. First, the nature of the normativity underwriting coercion cannot be unlawfulness. There have, for instance, been plenty of lawful practices and institutions in the United States that have clearly been not only coercive but also morally heinous. Slavery was lawful, as was torture, yet surely this does not mean that they could not be used to coerce victims in the relevant sense. Consider, also, the NBC News headline mentioned above, 'Prisons are packed because prosecutors are coercing plea deals. And, yes, it's totally legal.' Were the account of coercion found in the Model Penal Code adopted, this headline wouldn't make sense since if plea deals are 'totally legal,' then, by definition, they are not coerced.[20] This is an unwelcome result, as we clearly want to leave conceptual space for practices and tactics that are both legal and coercive. Indeed, on this view, it would be difficult to make sense of a practice in the criminal legal system being more or less coercive than it used to be or having been coercive and no longer being so. For instance, in July of 2021, Illinois became the first state in the nation to make it illegal for law enforcement officers to lie to minors during interrogations.[21] It would be natural to describe this in terms of the state making progress in moving toward less deceptive and coercive practices during interrogations. But on the Model Legal Code's view of coercion, lying to minors was not coercive when it was legal, and then became coercive once it is illegal. In addition, threats of execution would be coercive in states with the death penalty and not coercive in states without it.

Nobles and Schiff advance the debate by arguing that 'one would only describe something as coerced if the harm that influences a person to make a particular choice is impermissible' (2019, p. 114).[22] However, while there are different ways to understand impermissibility, Nobles and Schiff themselves seem to conceive of it as inextricably linked with what is accepted within the criminal legal system.

[20] Of course, the other conditions of the account need to be satisfied as well, such as that a person of reasonable firmness situation would have been unable to resist the offer.

[21] https://www.cnn.com/2021/07/17/politics/illinois-bans-police-lying-interrogation/index.html.

[22] In a similar spirit, the D.C. Circuit Court of Appeals holds that '[t]o say that a practice is "coercive" or renders a plea "involuntary" means only that it creates improper pressure that would be likely to overbear the will of some innocent persons and cause them to plead guilty' (*United States v. Pollard*, 959 F.2d 1011, 1021 (D.C. Cir. 1992), *cert. denied*, 506 U.S. 915 (1992)).

They argue, for instance, that sentencing discounts are not coercive because the varying sentences fall within the accepted guidelines (2019, p. 121). In a similar spirit, the Supreme Court found in *Bordenkircher v. Hayes* that plea bargaining itself, including the threat by the prosecution to bring more serious charges, does not render the resulting guilty plea involuntary:

> [A]cceptance of the basic legitimacy of plea bargaining necessarily implies rejection of any notion that a guilty plea is involuntary in a constitutional sense simply because it is the end result of the bargaining process.... [B]y tolerating and encouraging the negotiation of pleas, this Court has necessarily accepted as constitutionally legitimate the simple reality that the prosecutor's interest at the bargaining table is to persuade the defendant to forgo his right to plead not guilty. (*Bordenkircher v. Hayes*, 434 U.S. 357, 365 (1978))

The reasoning here is that because plea bargaining has already been accepted by the Court, guilty pleas that result from this process are thereby voluntary and constitutionally legitimate.[23]

But, again, both views face problems analogous to those concerning unlawfulness. The mere fact that a sentencing discount is within a set of guidelines does not in any way mean that it is not coercive. If, for instance, a sentence that fell within the appropriate guidelines included torture, it would still be coercive, despite its legal permissibility. Similarly, the Court's reasoning in *Bordenkircher v. Hayes* does not in any way provide an independent reason to regard plea deals as voluntary or legitimate. Rather, the Court seems to be arguing that because plea bargaining has already been accepted, guilty pleas that straightforwardly follow from such a process are thereby acceptable. Again, however, the criminal legal system can make progress, and can evolve from more coercive practices to ones that are less so. Given this, the mere fact that a guilty plea is the direct result of an accepted plea-bargaining practice in no way shows that the practice itself is not coercive.

What we need, then, is an *independent notion of normativity*, one that recognizes that lawfulness or institutional acceptability cannot adequately ground coercion. This shouldn't be a surprise, as the law is a human institution that undergoes significant developments and changes over time. It should also be clear that the notion of normativity cannot simply be moral impermissibility, as there are plenty of actions—even threats and offers—that are morally impermissible but not coercive. For instance, while it may be morally impermissible to threaten

[23] Elsewhere in this same opinion, the Supreme Court holds that '[t]o punish a person because he has done what the law plainly allows him to do is a due process violation of the most basic sort.... But in the "give-and-take" of plea bargaining there is no such element of punishment or retaliation so long as the accused is free to accept or reject the prosecution's offer' (*Bordenkircher v. Hayes*, 434 U.S. 357, 363 (1978)).

you with something that is incredibly rude, or offer you something that I've stolen, these need not be coercive. So, let's turn to Alan Wertheimer's 'moralized' theory of coercion that is robustly normative but carves out a narrower space within this terrain than general moral permissibility. His account begins with questions such as, 'Does A have the right to make his proposal?' and 'Should B resist A's proposal?' (Wertheimer 1987, p. 7). These lead to Wertheimer's two-pronged account of coercion, the first prong capturing the wrongfulness of the proposal offered by the coercer and the second prong focusing on the absence of acceptable alternatives for the victim. More precisely, A coerces B when the following two conditions are satisfied:

> The Proposal Prong: A threatens B by wrongfully making B a proposal such that, unless B complies, B will be in a worse position than B was otherwise entitled to expect; and
>
> The Choice Prong: B is morally justified in complying and does comply with A's proposal.[24]

For our current purposes, let's focus on the Proposal Prong, as here is where Wertheimer introduces the crucial normativity needed for understanding coercion. In the paradigmatic case of coercion involving a gunman threatening to shoot unless you turn over your wallet, the proposal being offered is clearly wrongful—the gunman has no right to threaten you with death or to expect your wallet—and you will clearly end up worse off than you are entitled to expect unless you turn over your wallet—you have every right to expect to both keep your own personal property and to not be shot for doing so.

According to Wertheimer, then, understanding the wrongfulness of a proposal turns on the possession of rights. In a crucial passage where he is arguing that standard guilty pleas are not coerced, he notes an 'offhand comparison' in *Brady v. United States*, 'which deserves much more attention than it has received,' in which 'the Court goes on to say that... guilty pleas are 'no more improperly compelling than is the decision by a defendant at the close of the State's evidence at trial that he must take the stand or face certain conviction.' Compelled, yes; improperly and therefore illegally compelled, no.... For the defendant is not coerced when the prosecutor is exercising his right....' (1987, p. 137). Tony Honoré agrees that guilty plea deals are generally not coerced, noting in his discussion of Wertheimer's theory that 'a defendant on a criminal charge has no right to be exempt from trial by jury or, if convicted, from the sentence prescribed by law, which may even be the death penalty' (1990, p. 96).

[24] Wertheimer discusses these prongs throughout his (1987), but never formally presents his theory in this way. This version is found in Honoré (1990, p. 94).

Despite Wertheimer's explicit claim that his view is 'moralized,' however, we see a very similar pattern of arguing here as was noted earlier. Guilty pleas are not coercive, we are told, because prosecutors are simply exercising their rights as officers of the court in offering them. Similarly, given the current criminal legal system, a defendant has no right to be exempt from the sentences prescribed by law, including execution. So, wrongfulness understood within this sort of rights-based framework ends up being virtually indistinguishable from being unlawful. Indeed, arguing that a 'defendant is not coerced when the prosecutor is exercising his rights' or that rights of defendants are those that are 'prescribed by law' is to begin with the assumption that the system itself, and the practices within the system, are not themselves coercive. *But what we want an answer to is precisely whether this system, and these practices, are coercive.*

There are also important reasons to regard rights as both too crude and too rigid to do the work needed to ground the wrongfulness in coercion. There are plenty of cases of coercion that nonetheless seem to involve actions that are totally within the coercer's rights. A father, for instance, might threaten to withhold all financial support for his 18-year-old daughter if she continues to date her current boyfriend. It is entirely within the rights of a parent to make this threat, as he is under no obligation to financially support an adult child, but the daughter might still be rightly described as being coerced to break up with her boyfriend, as she is in no position to support herself at 18. Rights also tend to be an all-or-nothing matter—you either have the right, or you don't. Practices and tactics, however, are often described as more or less coercive. So, let's take a step back and reflect on what seems normatively improper about some paradigmatically coercive threats or offers.

One question that seems relevant in many cases of coercion is what burdens it is appropriate for a person to be expected to bear when making a decision. This is why proportionality seems to matter with respect to the threats or offers that are put on the table. Threatening someone with 20 years of incarceration for shoplifting seems coercive in a way that it doesn't seem to be for an act of domestic terrorism that leaves 70 people murdered. Offering someone who is incarcerated a payment of $350 for taking part in research on the attitudes of correctional officers seems coercive in a way that offering $25 does not.[25] What lies at the heart

[25] In their research on compensation for incarcerated research participants, Smoyer et al. note that 'the potential for coercion is magnified when participants are incarcerated' (2009, p. 1746) and found that compensation amounts when working with those who are incarcerated range from $5 to $50 (2009, p. 1750). The risk of coercive offers when working with participants who are incarcerated is so concerning that some researchers forgo compensation altogether. In their research with incarcerated women, for instance, O'Brien and Bates write, 'We had discussed the idea of an incentive to participate, but on the advice of former [incarcerated persons], we realized that any incentive within the prison would be seen as providing advantages that were not available to the general population and hence were potentially coercive for that reason. We did not realize that just the fact that [incarcerated persons] had someone to talk to (the interviewers) could be construed as a disparity owing to the lack

of these proportionality judgments is a question of *fairness*.[26] What burdens or demands can fairly be placed on a person? Is it fair to ask a person to consider her options for shoplifting with a threat of 20 years behind bars, and is it fair to ask an incarcerated person who is already in a highly vulnerable position to consider participating in a study about the attitudes of correctional officers with an offer of $350? The excessiveness of the penalty and the incentive here calls into question the fundamental fairness of the corresponding actions. This is crucial, as it is clear that there is a normative dimension to coercion that needs to focus on the actions of the coercer, which may also include the institutions or systems in which the coercer is acting.[27] Fairness meets this desideratum: the coercer's actions, as well as those of their institutions, can certainly be evaluated in terms of fairness. Moreover, we have seen that the normativity in question needs to be both independent of lawfulness and narrower than morality in general, which fairness also satisfies. Consider *Roper v. Simmons* in which the Supreme Court ruled in 2005 that the execution of people who were under the age of 16 at the time of their crime is unconstitutional. Presumably, it was unfair to have executed those convicted as juveniles before 2005, despite its then being lawful.

Now, it may be worried that fairness is too vague a notion to be helpful or explanatory in understanding coercion. But consider the accounts thus far noted. 'Impermissible' and 'improper' are left either intuitive or collapse into unlawfulness, and 'wrongful' is fleshed out primarily in terms of rights, which also threaten to depend on what is unlawful. Fairness is certainly clearer than 'impermissible' or 'improper.' For instance, John Rawls's famous 'justice as fairness' theory,[28] which is arguably one of the most influential political theories, takes fairness to be highly explanatory from a normative point of view insofar as it is what grounds justice. On the empirical side, fairness is taken to be a central foundation of morality in many psychological theories,[29] and humans generally show a significant desire for fairness and a strong aversion to inequity.[30] There is also a great deal of work in psychology demonstrating that children exhibit fairness concerns, with infants as young as 16 months old expecting resources to be allocated equally among recipients.[31] Indeed, even non-human animals, including domestic dogs[32] and non-human primates,[33] reveal an aversion to inequity that is disadvantageous to themselves. So, fairness is one of the most accessible pre-theoretical moral notions.

of the consistent availability of anyone to talk to, especially someone who might be trusted not to disclose information within the prison' (2003, p. 215).

[26] Proportionality may thus be viewed as essential to the fairness of the plea-bargaining system. See, for instance, Lee (2019).

[27] In contrast, Frowe uses 'happenstance' to describe 'cases in which there is a forced choice, but no wrongdoing' (2021, p. 3467).

[28] According to Rawls, 'the fundamental idea in the concept of justice is fairness' (1958, p. 164).

[29] See Piaget (1965) and Kohlberg (1969).

[30] Fehr and Schmidt (1999).

[31] Geraci and Surian (2011) and Li et al. (2016).

[32] Range et al. (2009).

[33] Jensen et al. (2006).

It should be emphasized, however, that fairness is not equivalent to equality. Of course, sometimes being fair requires equal distribution. If I have a limited number of goods to pass out, and there are no compelling normative reasons why some deserve or need more than others, then fairness might call for their equal distribution. But this does not mean that fairness just is, or always requires, equality. Egalitarianism, for instance, centers equality in morality and politics, holding that people ought to in some crucial respect be treated the same, or receive the same, or be treated as equals.[34] The 'Leveling-Down Objection,' however, is a well-known objection to egalitarianism according to which 'egalitarians must accept, implausibly, that it is an improvement, at least in some respect, if the better-off are reduced to the level of the worse-off without the worse-off becoming any better off' (Weber 2019, p. 1). If fairness were understood as equivalent to equality, the version of the Leveling-Down Objection that would be relevant here would be that the plea-bargaining process could be rendered fair by simply treating all suspects and defendants equally harshly rather than aiming for an independent notion of fairness. For instance, on an egalitarian model of fairness, threatening an eyewitness with incarceration could be rendered fair simply by threatening all eyewitnesses with incarceration. But this hardly seems fair if no eyewitness ought to be threatened with execution in the first place. Hence, fairness clearly is neither equivalent to equality, nor does it simply require the equal distribution of goods and penalties.

Moreover, it is just as clear that fairness is not taken to be equivalent to, or dependent on, lawfulness. It is rather commonplace for the criminal legal system to be described as unfair, especially in its radically disproportionate targeting of people of color, and plea deals specifically are often criticized for being unfair. Still further, fairness is not an all or nothing affair, as just as actions may be more or less coercive, so, too, they may be more or less fair. Offering one of my children six slices of pizza and the other none for no reason at all is more unfair than offering one of them three slices and the other one two.

Given all of this, I want to argue that fairness is a helpful starting place for understanding the normative dimension of coercion. More specifically, on my view, the wrongness or impropriety of coercion[35] involves the making of a threat or offer that is unfair. Now, Wertheimer also includes in his first prong that unless the victim complies with the proposal in question, she will be in a worse position than she was otherwise entitled to expect. Should we take this condition on board in understanding coercion? One problem with doing so is that there seem to be coercive threats and offers that undoubtedly leave the victim in a far better position than she was otherwise entitled to expect. Consider, again, the father who

[34] See Anderson (1999) and Scheffler (2003).

[35] As mentioned earlier, I leave open the possibility that there are other notions of coercion that are especially useful for other contexts, such as the coercive nature of addictions.

threatens to withhold all financial support for his 18-year-old daughter if she does not break up with her current boyfriend. Suppose that along every relevant dimension—happiness, meaning, financial stability, and so on—the daughter ends up far better off after breaking up with her boyfriend than she was otherwise entitled to expect. Perhaps he was emotionally unavailable, self-centered, prone to infidelity, and so on. Even if this turns out to be the case, we might still say that her father coerced her to break up with her boyfriend. Indeed, it is not difficult to imagine a broad range of actions that clearly leave one better than one was otherwise entitled to expect but are nonetheless coercive. If someone holds a gun to my head and says, 'Join the gym or I will shoot,' or 'Eat more greens or I will shoot,' I may end up far healthier after regularly working out and eating greens, but I was nonetheless clearly coerced into getting in shape. For these reasons, I think we should leave off the second half of Wertheimer's Proposal Prong.

The Choice Prong is intended to capture what many of the psychological conditions discussed above do. Wertheimer rejects the idea that, in standard cases of coercion, the victim's will was 'overborne' or that she 'had no choice or alternative,' writing:

> [D]espite the frequency with which the law refers to 'overborne wills' (or analogues to that phrase), a coercion claim rarely attempts to deny B's moral agency. Consider the restaurant cashier who hands over the money in his till in response to the threat of a gang of armed robbers. We do not blame him for what he does, of course, but not because he lacks moral agency. We do not blame him for what he does because, under the circumstances, he does nothing that is blameworthy. (1987, p. 270)

It is precisely because Wertheimer takes victims in standard cases of coercion to retain their moral agency that he rejects the purely psychologized views discussed earlier in favor of a moralized account of the Choice Prong. It is not, on his view, that victims of coercion have 'irresistible' desires aroused in them or have their wills overpowered, but, rather, that their response to the threats or offers in question is one that is morally justified. For instance, even if the restaurant cashier can resist the threat of armed robbers or is not motivated against his own will to do what he does, he was still coerced because he was morally justified in his response to hand over the money in his till. In this way, coercion is said to be compatible with the retention of a fairly robust sense of moral agency.

There is, however, another kind of agency that does seem to be clearly impacted by coercive threats and offers: epistemic agency.[36] Sure, coercion's success depends, in many respects, on the rationality of the person being coerced.

[36] Once we see how epistemic agency is bypassed, exploited, or subverted in coercion, I will circle back to moral agency and show how it, too, can be compromised.

Christian Coons and Michael Weber write that 'the instruments of coercion (threats, incarceration, and other penalties) are attempts to alter the context of choice, making it rational for you to comply. In this way, the coercer typically treats the coerced as rational. In fact, coercion depends on the target's being rational' (2014, p. 15). In other words, while coercion robs someone of choice, it is said to not affect that person's ability to engage in rational decision-making. Indeed, coercion is effective only insofar as the one being coerced is rational enough to appreciate that there is really only one acceptable alternative between turning over the money and being shot. As Susser et al. write, '[c]oercing someone forces them to act the way the coercer wants, not by undermining or circumventing their decision-making faculties, but by making the coercer's way the only acceptable one' (2019, pp. 15–16). But while coercion depends on the victim recognizing the rationality of giving into the threat or taking the offer in question, there are important ways in which their epistemic agency *is* compromised.

Recall from earlier chapters that epistemic agency is commonly understood as being grounded in a subject's responsiveness to reasons or evidence.[37] If you come to believe that there are anthropogenic causes of climate change on the basis of the force of the compelling data found in an academic journal, then you are exercising your epistemic agency in the formation of this belief. In contrast, epistemic agency is bypassed, exploited, or subverted when a subject's ability to be responsive to reasons is circumvented, abused, undermined, or otherwise compromised. Coercion interferes with the victim's ability to be properly responsive to all of the relevant reasons in their decision space.

Consider a case from Chapter 3 where an eyewitness is being asked to pick a suspect out of a lineup and is then threatened with jail time and the removal of her children from her home if she doesn't cooperate. In such a case, the eyewitness's decision space has radically changed, moving from one in which she is considering the evidential factors that bear on the question whether the suspect is in the lineup, such as height, weight, facial features, and so on, to one that includes an altogether different swamping consideration—her freedom and her children. Or consider the incarcerated person who is offered a payment of $350 to participate in a study on the attitudes of correctional officers. As was already noted, part of what is problematic about this offer is the excessiveness of the incentive, especially against the background of the standard amount of compensation offered for research participation. But this excessiveness, in turn, has the consequence of closing the incarcerated person out of a reasonable decision-making space. He is no longer weighing the factors that bear directly on the question of whether he should be a participant in the study, such as the risks to his safety, the contribution to the social sciences, the potential benefits to the broader incarcerated

[37] See, for instance, Hieronymi (2008), McHugh (2013), and Reed (2013).

population, and so on. Instead, a swamping consideration is put on the table—a sum of money that could radically improve the circumstances he finds himself in while incarcerated.

In both cases, the threat and offer not only change the options in the decision space, but they also change the decision space itself. The addition of the proposals in question has a swamping effect, thereby effectively screening off the other relevant normative considerations in the victim's deliberative process. But this doesn't happen in familiar epistemic and moral ways. Epistemic overpowering occurs when the epistemic force of a reason or piece of evidence is so powerful that it nullifies or substantially diminishes the epistemic force of other reasons or evidence. Suppose your friend believes that the COVID-19 vaccine is unsafe because his uncle, who is not a medical doctor, told him so, but then the Centers for Disease Control and Prevention (CDC) reports that it is safe on the basis of multiple trials and intense monitoring of millions who have received the vaccine. The CDC's testimony should undermine the force of the uncle's layperson concerns, as the CDC's basis is competent, reliable, and extensive while the uncle's is not.[38] Moral overpowering occurs when the moral force of a reason is so powerful that it nullifies or substantially diminishes the moral force of other considerations. Suppose that you made a promise to your friend to go holiday shopping this afternoon but then see a drowning child in the river on your way to the restaurant. The moral force of the duty to save the drowning child is so great that it overpowers the obligation to keep your promise to go shopping.

This sort of normative overpowering is not what happens in classic cases of coercion. Instead of appealing directly to epistemic or moral agency in these ways, threats or offers are made that introduce a *swamping* practical consideration that *screens off* all of the other normativity in the relevant decision space. Victims go from weighing the strength of the reasons for or against a particular question to factoring in a wholly different kind of consideration, one that is practical in nature and often involves a change in the stakes. The coerced eyewitness, for instance, may begin by considering the question, 'is this the person I saw fleeing from the scene of the crime' and engaging in epistemic deliberation about the evidence relevant to this matter, such as the height, weight, and facial features of the person she saw at the crime scene compared to those in the lineup. When the threat of jail time and the loss of her children are put on the table, a practical consideration is introduced to her decision space that screens off this epistemic normativity and fundamentally changes the question under deliberation. She is no longer aiming at a true identification and engaged in evidential weighing to arrive at that end but is now desperately trying to figure out how to keep her family intact. The options in her decision space have changed, but so, too, has the

[38] Otherwise put, your friend has a *normative defeater* for the testimony of his uncle. See Chapter 2 for a discussion of normative defeaters.

decision space itself transformed. The swamping consideration that has been added to her deliberation screens off the epistemic normativity of the other reasons in this space, leaving her with only one viable path forward.[39] In so doing, the victim is closed out of a reasonable decision-making space whereby all of the relevant reasons can be taken into account.

More precisely, closing a victim out of a reasonable decision-making space involves the introduction of a swamping consideration that is practical in nature and that thereby screens off all of the other relevant normativity in the space. The case of the eyewitness above powerfully illustrates how the swamping consideration of a threat of jail time and loss of one's children can screen off the epistemic normativity governing a true or correct lineup identification. But similar considerations apply with respect to moral normativity. Suppose an innocent defendant is offered a deal to plead guilty and accept 30 years behind bars or face execution at trial. The risk of execution might function so powerfully that it serves as a swamping consideration in the defendant's decision space. He may no longer be considering epistemic and moral questions about truth and justice such as, 'should I plead guilty to a murder I didn't commit,' 'is it just to be incarcerated for decades for something I didn't do,' 'is it morally permissible to knowingly allow someone who actually committed murder to be free,' and so on. Instead, he is singularly focused on the practical matter of how to avoid execution. In this way, the epistemic and moral normativity involved in the acceptance of the plea deal are screened off by the swamping effect of the possibility of the death penalty.

The introduction of a swamping consideration often brings along a change in the practical stakes in the relevant decision space. Crucially, 'change' here does not always mean 'increase,' at least not when the stakes are understood in their totality. For instance, the stakes might be higher for the eyewitness when the threat of jail time and loss of her children are put on the table, but the stakes were high for the innocent suspect even before the addition of this swamping consideration. Similarly, the threat of execution might raise the personal stakes for the innocent defendant being offered the plea deal, but, again, the stakes have always been high for the murder victim's family, the person who actually committed the murder, and so on. In this way, while the stakes are often raised by a swamping consideration for the deliberator herself, the overall stakes can be high even before a victim is closed out of a reasonable decision-making space.

I want to propose a new view, then, where coercion is understood as *the making of an unfair threat or offer that closes victims out of a reasonable decision-making space*. As should be clear, this is a normative view of coercion, as it explicitly requires that the threats or offers in question be ones that are unfair. But it also captures what psychological views or conditions are after in requiring that

[39] As the New York State Association of Criminal Defense Lawyers write, 'the mere decision to charge triggers a domino effect making a guilty plea the only rational choice in most cases' (2021, p. 9).

the threat or offer close victims out of a reasonable decision-making space. Indeed, this may just be one way of understanding what it means for an option to be 'irresistible' or the only 'acceptable' one. A proposal may not literally be psychologically irresistible, but all of the other relevant considerations may be swamped by it, thereby leaving only the force of the proposal on the table. Similarly, when all of the other reasons in question are screened off by the radical increase in stakes for the deliberator by a threat or offer, then it may be apt to describe there being only one acceptable option remaining. At the same time, 'reasonable' here is not a purely subjective notion but can instead be understood as it is often employed in the law, whereby it is 'not an empirical or statistical measure of how average members of the public think, feel, or behave. Average is not the same as right or appropriate. Regrettably, average persons have been known to think, feel, and behave very differently from the way that the polity to which they are duty-bound believes they should, and when they do, they are answerable to the polity for their failings. Rather, reasonableness is a normative measure of ways in which it is right for persons to think, feel or behave' (Westen 2008, p. 138). The notion of 'reasonable' in my account, then, is a normative notion that can be captured by how a person ought to rationality regard the options in the decision space.

At this point, one might wonder why closing a person out of a reasonable decision-making space isn't sufficient to be coercive. In particular, why does the offer or threat *also* need to be unfair? Consider a drug addict who is engaging in behavior so harmful that she will almost certainly die within the next month. Her parents issue the following threat: either get clean or we will call the police and report the drugs in the house. The threat of being arrested might function here as a swamping consideration, screening off all of the other reasons in her decision space, such as her enjoyment of her drug of choice, the withdrawal symptoms she will face, and so on. In this way, the drug addict is closed out of a reasonable decision-making space. But given that getting clean will save their daughter's life, the threat made by the parents is not unfair, and so it also doesn't seem to be coercive. In contrast, suppose that a drug addict's surgeon offers to the parents of a child that he either perform surgery on their daughter immediately or not at all. While the condition that the surgery will be treating is not life-threatening, the surgeon is one of the few specialists in the world who can perform it. His reason for proposing this exploding offer to the parents, however, is that he wants the data from the surgery for some research he plans to publish before an upcoming performance review. Such an offer seems coercive, but also unfair.

Suppose, however, that a villain credibly threatens to kill 50 innocent hostages she has taken unless you kill the villain's enemy.[40] This certainly seems to be

[40] See Bazargan (2014).

coercive, but the sense in which it is an unfair threat concerns the innocent hostages and the villain's enemy far more than it does you. This is an instance of what has come to be known as *moral coercion*. According to Saba Bazargan, '[i]n cases of non-moral coercion, C1 forces C2 to choose between perceived costs to her own interests, whereas in cases of moral coercion, C2 has to choose between perceived costs to the interests of third-party innocents' (2014, p. 6). In a case of this sort, the threat or offer being put on the table involves the potential of significant harm to hostages and enemies of the villain, and so there are third-party innocents whose interests are a central part of the options in your decision space. Similar considerations apply in a number of morally coercive tactics commonly used in warfare, such as certain forms of terrorism and the use of human shields.[41] Helen Frowe maintains that '[a]n agent A morally coerces another agent, B, when A manipulates non-epistemological facts in order that B's moral commitments enjoin B to do what A wants B to do, and B is motivated by these commitments' (2021, p. 3465). Such a conception of coercion importantly differs from the non-moral notion discussed here, as epistemological asymmetries between prosecution and defense certainly contribute to threats and offers being coercive, and practical commitments are often the driving force behind their acceptance. The point that should be emphasized here, however, is that moral coercion is distinct from non-moral coercion and it is not typically what is at issue in cases of plea deals.[42]

Relatedly, recall the case of the 18-year-old whose father issues the threat that she either breaks up with her boyfriend or he will withhold all financial support. One might agree that this is coercive but push back against it involving a threat that is unfair. After all, if the boyfriend will ultimately make the 18-year-old less happy than she would be without him, then ending the relationship seems to be in her best interest. Doesn't the father's threat thus seem fair because of these consequences, despite being coercive? By way of response, notice that there are countless instances of threats or offers that would leave those targeted significantly better off. People with gambling problems might be better off if the State intervened to manage their finances, young adults who obsessively play video games and cannot retain employment as a result might be better off if their parents stepped in and controlled their daily lives, those who are depressed might be better off if their friends forced them to take medication, and so on. Each of these 'better off' outcomes could be presented as an offer or a threat, such as the parents telling the gamer that he needs to relinquish control of his daily life to them or they will evict him. But even if the gamer would end up significantly better off because of the parents' threat, there is still an important sense in which it is unfair.

[41] See Bazargan (2014, p. 2).

[42] I say 'typically' since some plea deals do involve the costs to the interests of third-party innocents, such as one's family, co-defendants, community, and so on.

In particular, it violates the gamer's *autonomy*. Recall from Chapter 2 that autonomy involves self-governance or the ability to be directed by desires and conditions that are part of one's authentic self rather than simply imposed externally. Even among moral theories that are deeply opposed, autonomy often occupies a prominent role and is understood to be a central normative value.[43] Of course, there may be times when violating someone's autonomy may be necessary, such as when a person's actions put their life or the lives of others in imminent danger. The fact that this is necessary, however, does not eliminate the sense in which the threat or offer still violates a person's autonomy and is, to this extent, unfair.[44] Otherwise put, because of autonomy's fundamental or central status in morality, a threat or offer that forces a person to choose self-preservation at the expense of self-governance is unfair and, therefore, a candidate for being coercive.[45]

2. Plea Deals

As we saw in the earlier quotations, it is not uncommon for plea bargaining to be regarded as coercive in the current criminal legal system. In what follows, I will examine some of the central dimensions of plea bargaining through the lens of the account of coercion defended in the previous section with the aim of determining the extent to which guilty pleas are being coerced.

The 'trial penalty' refers to the substantial difference between the sentence received when a defendant opts for a trial versus that offered through a plea deal.[46] This penalty is now said to be 'so severe and pervasive that it has virtually eliminated the constitutional right to a trial' (New York State Association of Criminal Defense Lawyers 2021, p. 17). To illustrate the trial penalty, consider the

[43] See, for instance, Kant (1785/1983) and Mill (1859/Mill 1975).

[44] In the context of discussing coercion in relation to treating people with addictions, Janssens et al. highlight the centrality of autonomy: 'Over the last two decades, many countries have adopted new laws that regulate the use of coercive measures in psychiatric care. These laws have been guided by the principle of autonomy. Patients are considered autonomous unless there is sufficient proof to the contrary. This also implies that patients who refuse admission or treatment cannot be coerced. In the USA, like in many European countries, the right to non-intervention is considered absolute unless harm has been caused, as a result of the disorder, or there is a high enough risk or harm. The new autonomy based laws reflect the philosophy of J S Mill. Individuals have sovereignty over themselves unless others are harmed' (Janssens et al. 2004, p. 453).

[45] Here is another type of case: Suppose that my daughter has been kidnapped. Isn't it both fair and yet coercive for me to threaten the kidnapper with physical violence if he doesn't disclose my daughter's location? Again, this is a case in which violating the kidnapper's autonomy may be justified, even if it is unfair to force him to compromise his status as a moral agent.

[46] For instance, according to the United States Sentencing Commission's data on federal sentencing, the average post-trial sentence was more than triple the average post-plea sentence in most primary offense categories in 2015 (New York State Association of Criminal Defense Lawyers 2021, p. 15). Nevertheless, '[b]ecause plea negotiations are off the record and because most cases plead out, data regarding plea offers is largely unavailable, so there is no way to accurately calculate the full extent of the trial penalty' (New York State Association of Criminal Defense Lawyers 2021, p. 16).

case of Eric Weakley and Michael Hash. On July 14, 1996, Thelma Scroggins, who was a 74-year-old retired mail carrier and church organist, was murdered in her Lignun, Virginia home. Her purse and truck were missing, and she had been shot four times in the head.[47] Weakley and Hash, childhood friends who were 16 and 15 at the time of the murder, were arrested four years later in 2000.[48]

Their ordeal began when investigators visited a local prison to interview Alesia Shelton, who had been convicted of shooting a man in the head six times, a crime that the police thought was similar enough to the Scroggins murder to warrant questioning her. Shelton initially denied knowing anything about the murder of Scroggins, but one of the detectives suggested that she might get a reduced sentence if she provided information about her cousin, Hash. After the tape was shut off for a supposed cigarette break, the interview resumed and Shelton now claimed that she had overheard her cousin, Hash, discussing his involvement in Scroggins's murder along with his friend, Weakley.[49]

Instead of interviewing Hash, however, the police decided to begin interrogating Weakley, who 'was 19 years old with a reputation as a follower, someone who could be easily intimidated.'[50] They 'hounded' and 'stalked' Weakley until his employer fired him. In an effort to put an end to the harassment, he relented to a polygraph exam, which he subsequently failed, leading him to finally break and confess to the robbery and murder of Scroggins. Once this confession was extracted from Weakly, the prosecution offered him a plea deal: testify against Hash and another defendant and plead guilty to second-degree murder, a charge that carried at most 20 years behind bars, or face life in prison. On June 13, 2001, Weakley pleaded guilty to second-degree murder and ended up serving six years and eight months because of his cooperation with authorities.[51]

In contrast, Hash opted for a trial, twice rejecting a plea deal from the Commonwealth to amend the capital murder charge to second-degree murder, which would have resulted in him spending roughly 6–12 years in prison. Hash said, 'I would never admit to something I did not do, period. There was never a question in my mind of whether or not I was going to go to trial.'[52] On February 9, 2001, the jury found Hash guilty of capital murder and he was sentenced to life in prison without parole.

[47] https://www.law.umich.edu/special/exoneration/Pages/casedetail.aspx?caseid=3977.

[48] https://www.happyscribe.com/public/wrongful-conviction-podcasts/wrongful-conviction-false-confessions-eric-weakley-and-michael-hash.

[49] https://www.happyscribe.com/public/wrongful-conviction-podcasts/wrongful-conviction-false-confessions-eric-weakley-and-michael-hash.

[50] https://www.happyscribe.com/public/wrongful-conviction-podcasts/wrongful-conviction-false-confessions-eric-weakley-and-michael-hash.

[51] https://www.law.umich.edu/special/exoneration/Pages/casedetail.aspx?caseid=3977.

[52] https://www.wtkr.com/2018/12/22/one-innocent-man-gets-six-years-for-murder-the-other-life/.

Weakley was released from prison in 2006 and in 2011 he signed a formal statement recanting his confession and testimony against Hash, saying, 'All of the information I gave at trial about the crime scene was given to me during interviews with police and prosecutors.'[53] With assistance from the University of Virginia Innocence Project, Hash's attorneys filed a writ of *habeas corpus* for his release. On August 20, 2012, Senior U.S. District Judge James C. Turk voided Hash's conviction citing 'outrageous' police and prosecutorial misconduct.

What we see here is a paradigmatic case of the trial penalty at work. Both defendants were innocent of the crimes for which they were convicted, and both were offered a deal to plead guilty to second-degree murder, which would lead to serving 6–12 years in prison. One accepted the plea, received 20 years, and was out in six; the other turned down the deal, opted to exercise his constitutional right to a trial, and was penalized for doing so by receiving a life sentence.[54]

The severity and prevalence of the trial penalty is one of the driving forces behind the virtual extinction of jury trials. Faced with the possibility of a radically harsher sentence if convicted at trial—sometimes even including death—defendants will often go with the lighter and far safer option.[55] Indeed, as we see in the case of Weakley and Hash, the pressures involved in plea bargaining, and the likelihood of significantly lengthier sentences at trial, lead even innocent defendants to plead guilty.[56] Of the 375 DNA exonerations in the United States to date, 44 pled guilty to crimes they did not commit.[57] Moreover, the Innocence Project highlighted the stories of 31 people who pled guilty despite being innocent, serving a combined total of more than 150 years in prison before being exonerated, and the vast majority reported that they were seeking to avoid a lengthy sentence or the death penalty.[58]

[53] https://www.insidenova.com/news/crime_police/one-innocent-man-gets-six-years-for-murder-the-other-life/article_e1296e4e-0548-11e9-983c-6fe37cf5d0bd.html.

[54] See also Klein, where he discusses such a tactic being used even in juvenile courts: 'A Juvenile Court judge in Georgia [said]: "I tell the minor, I will up the sentence if you take it to trial, because you could have pleaded and saved us all this trouble"' (2004, p. 1350).

[55] In Chapter 2, I drew a comparison between how the extracted confessions of suspects and defendants are treated in the criminal legal system with the way the testimony of enslaved persons was regarded in judicial proceedings in Ancient Greece and Rome. Douglas A. Blackmon discusses the similarities between modern-day guilty pleas and 'confess judgments,' whereby 'the accused confesses his responsibility before being tried. The local judge then accepted payment and forfeiture of a bond from the white surety, rather than render a verdict on the alleged "crime." In return, the African American farmer would sign a contract to work without compensation for the white landlord for however long it took to pay back the amount of the bond.... The records of thousands of prosecutions [in the 1880s] show it was... likely that an arrested black man—knowing he had no possibility of true due process, or acquittal—agreed to confess judgment specifically to avoid the far more dire alternatives that he knew lay in wait. It was the nineteenth-century equivalent of modern plea bargains, in which a defendant agrees to a lesser sentence ahead of trial in order to be spared any possibility of the most severe punishment' (2009, p. 67).

[56] See Covey (2009) for a discussion of plea bargaining's 'innocence problem.'

[57] https://innocenceproject.org/dna-exonerations-in-the-united-states/.

[58] https://innocenceproject.org/when-the-innocent-plead-guilty/.

In addition to the trial penalty, prosecutors will often engage in 'charge stacking' or 'charge piling' to secure guilty pleas.[59] This will typically involve bringing a large number of often redundant charges against a defendant, thereby increasing the quantity of charges and, therewith, the length or severity of the possible sentence.[60] Given that 'prosecutors are the most powerful officials' in the criminal legal system, and that they 'exercise almost boundless discretion' when it comes to the nature and number of charges brought against defendants (Davis 2013, p. 832), prosecutors can vastly change the stakes of opting for a trial through charge stacking.[61] For instance, in addition to armed robbery, a prosecutor might stack on aggravated assault, theft, possession of a weapon, use of a firearm during the commission of a crime, and so on, which drastically increase the number of years the defendant is facing if convicted.[62] Prosecutors might also overreach beyond what the law and evidence support, inflating the substance of the charges themselves. For instance, in the above scenario, the far more serious and questionably applicable charge of kidnapping might be added to the others, once again tipping the scales against the defendant, especially if found guilty at trial.[63]

In determining whether the trial penalty and charge stacking or overreaching contribute to plea bargaining being coercive, we should ask two questions: first, are the threats or offers being made in plea bargaining unfair and, second, are such threats or offers closing defendants out of a reasonable decision-making space?

One feature of focusing on fairness that helps us better understand coercion is that it is often connected with power and resources. A threat or offer made by someone with a great deal of power over you is more likely to be unfair than one made by a peer. For instance, we might regard it as unfair for a professor to ask a student in his class for a personal favor while thinking nothing of a peer doing the same thing. Similarly, what it is fair to expect may depend on a person's available resources. Elon Musk paying his Tesla employees minimum wage, for instance, may be regarded as unfair in a way that it would not be for an owner of a small, struggling business to do with her employees. In assessing whether plea deals are coercive, then, it is helpful to note the radical asymmetry in power and resources found between the State and most defendants coming to the bargaining table. While prosecutors enjoy 'almost boundless discretion' regarding whether charges

[59] This phenomenon is also called 'redundant charging,' which is the 'prosecutors' nearly unrestricted ability to manufacture closely related charges based on the same course of conduct' (Seigel and Slobogin 2005, pp. 1108–09) or 'horizontal overcharging,' which is 'multiplying "unreasonably" the number of accusations against a single defendant' (Alschuler 1968, p. 85). I should note that there may be some cases where charge stacking is appropriate. See, for instance, Lee (2018).

[60] See Crespo (2018).

[61] Similarly, the New York State Association of Criminal Defense Lawyers argue that the 'virtually unfettered prosecutorial charging discretion' is a significant factor in 'the corrosive effect of the trial penalty' on the criminal legal system (2021, p. 7).

[62] See Crespo (2018).

[63] See Crespo (2018).

are brought, what they are, and whether a plea offer is even an option, defendants are largely at the mercy of the State.[64] Moreover, unlike prosecutors, who often have robust epistemic, legal, and financial resources available to them, many defendants are low-income, less educated, and unemployed,[65] and so their ability to mount an adequate investigation and defense is severely compromised. When facing charges that have the potential to be dramatically life-altering, it is reasonable to ask whether it is fair for defendants to be starting at such a major disadvantage in terms of power and resources.

In addition, consider the plausible moral principle, due to Aristotle, that likes ought to be treated alike.[66] If, for instance, two students produce work identical in quality, fairness seems to require that I assess them comparably, just as I should sanction them similarly if these same two students are then found to have cheated under the same conditions. To fail to do so would be to violate this principle by not treating like cases alike—a violation at the heart of much discrimination that is deeply problematic. The mere fact, then, that two prosecutors have the discretion to bring dramatically different charges against relevantly similar defendants for the same crime, often simply to incentivize the acceptance of a plea deal, raises pressing questions of fairness.

These questions are exacerbated by some of the consequences that come with charge stacking and overreaching. First, there is the unfair prejudice that a defendant might face at trial, as 'the more counts in the indictment, the quicker the jury may be to assume that the accused must be guilty of *something*' (Leipold and Abbasi 2006, p. 355, original emphasis). Second, multiple counts require multiple blocks of evidence, and this not only necessitates greater resources from the defense, it also might lead to jury confusion, as jurors are more likely to confuse which pieces of counterevidence relate to which charge.[67] This is especially concerning when the charges are of a similar character. For instance, in *Drew v. United States*, appellant Drew brought an appeal from a District Court conviction on one count of robbery and one count of attempted robbery on the grounds that the counts were improperly joined. The court ruled in Drew's favor in part because of jury confusion:

> It is not mere conjecture to say that the jury may have been confused in this case. A perusal of the record shows that witnesses' responses at times indicated confusion as to which crime counsel were referring to in their questions; the two crimes were repeatedly referred to as of the same order; and the prosecutor in his summation not unnaturally lumped the two together on occasion in his

[64] Crespo notes that 'As plea bargaining scholars consistently recognize, prosecutorial charging discretion... "translates into power in the plea bargaining context"' (2018, p. 1315).
[65] https://www.prisonpolicy.org/reports/repeatarrests.html.
[66] For a helpful discussion of this principle, see Winston (1974).
[67] See Leipold and Abbasi (2006, pp. 355–56).

> discussion of the evidence.... If separate crimes are to be tried together... both court and counsel must recognize that they are assuming a difficult task the performance of which calls for a vigilant precision in speech and action far beyond that required in the ordinary trial.
>
> (*Drew v. United States*, 331 F. 2d 83, 93–94 (D.C. Cir. 1964))

Relatedly, '[a] defendant who is guilty of one charge but innocent of another may find it difficult to present separate defenses to separate charges, particularly if he wants to take the stand on the second count but not the first' (Leipold 2005, p. 1143). For instance, if he takes the stand on one count for a crime he did not commit, he opens himself up to cross-examination on another one that he did.[68]

Finally, there are powerful psychological and epistemic consequences that result from the 'anchoring' effect of charge stacking or overreaching. Defendants evaluate deals by focusing on a reference point, or anchor, that determines the reasonableness of subsequent offers.[69] A prosecutor may begin with an inflated offer of 25 years for robbery because of charge stacking or overreaching, knowing that the defendant is likely to reject it as unreasonable. When the prosecutor returns with an offer of 20 years, this will sound more reasonable. When the prosecutor finally scales back to 15 years, the defendant may be very eager to accept this deal because the initial anchor was 10 years longer. If, however, the prosecutor had started with a fairer offer of 18 years[70]—one that wasn't inflated through charge stacking or overreaching—what would seem reasonable would have been radically different, and so 15 years may very well have been rejected as a bad deal. As Andrew Crespo notes, 'it is the difference between the threat and the subsequent offer that constitutes the prosecutor's power: The larger the differential, the more likely the defendant is to plead guilty—whether he is in fact guilty or not' (2018, p. 1314). Moreover, 'multiple charges intimidate defendants,' thereby making them more likely to accept the scaled back offer (Seigel and Slobogin 2005, p. 1126).

Thus far, the discussion has focused primarily on assessing plea bargaining in relation to the fairness dimension of coercion, but there is the second question of whether defendants are closed out of a reasonable decision-making space during the process. And here it is instructive to note that when charge stacking and overreaching are coupled with the trial penalty, the offers proposed by prosecutors often dramatically alter both the options on the table for defendants as well as the stakes in their deliberative space. In particular, when the number and nature of charges in question are threatening not only years of a defendant's liberty, but also

[68] See Leipold and Abbasi (2006, p. 356).

[69] See Bibas (2004, pp. 2517–18).

[70] Moreover, as Crespo notes, 'most criminal codes authorize sentences much higher than what a typical prosecutor—or a typical person, for that matter—would actually want to see imposed in a given case' (2018, p. 1312).

just about everything else he holds dear in this world, and taking the case to trial is likely to only make his situation worse—possibly leading even to execution—he can plausibly feel backed into a corner with only one real path forward. As the New York State Association of Criminal Defense Lawyers write, '[w]hen a prosecutor offers to reduce a multi-decade prison sentence to a number of years—from 30 years to 5 years, for example—any choice the defendant had in the matter is all but eliminated' (2021, p. 6). This is evidenced by the overwhelming number of defendants who accept plea deals with lengthy prison sentences instead of taking their cases to trial, including those who are innocent. When the options and stakes of plea offers are resulting in innocent defendants forfeiting the exercise of an important constitutional right, these facts alone should give us pause about whether plea bargaining is resulting in deliberation within a reasonable decision space.

3. Epistemic Deficits

There are a number of serious epistemic deficits that suspects and defendants suffer when considering and ultimately accepting plea deals that also raise urgent questions about coercion. First, as we saw in the context of false confessions, the Supreme Court sanctioned the presentation of false evidence of guilt to suspects during interrogations, a tactic often referred to as 'the false evidence ploy.'[71] Indeed, the Reid Technique, which is 'currently the most widely used police interrogation procedure in North America' (Moore et al. 2014, p. 34), encourages the ploy as it is 'clearly the most persuasive' interrogation tactic within 'the area of deception' (Inbau et al. 2013, p. 255). However, what makes this particularly pernicious in the context of plea deals is that defendants do not have a right to exculpatory evidence or impeachment information prior to the acceptance of plea agreements.[72] This means that an interrogator can falsely tell a suspect that the State has DNA evidence linking him to the crime, a confession from a co-defendant, fingerprints, shoe prints, his semen in the victim, a failed polygraph, an eyewitnesses identification, and so on,[73] all while incurring no obligation to disclose that these are lies before the plea deal is accepted. The false evidence ploy combined with the legally sanctioned withholding of impeachment information and exculpatory evidence results in suspects and defendants deliberating about

[71] See Leo and Ofshe (2008) and Wynbrandt (2016).

[72] See the Supreme Court ruling in *United States v. Ruiz*, 536 U.S. 622, 629–33 (2002), which holds that the disclosure of impeachment information before a guilty plea is not constitutionally required. Moreover, as Bibas notes, '[w]hile the facts of *Ruiz* involved only impeachment information and evidence supporting affirmative defenses, the Court's reasoning would apply with almost as much force to classic *Brady* exculpatory material' (2004, p. 2494, note 125).

[73] See Wynbrandt (2016, pp. 551–52).

plea deals not only with the evidential decks seemingly stacked against them, but also while in the dark about the epistemic situation that they are actually in. This is in contrast to convictions obtained through trial, where the Supreme Court has ruled that the government must disclose both exculpatory[74] and impeachment[75] evidence to the defendant.[76] Moreover, it has been shown that a defendant's perception of the likelihood of a conviction at trial plays a particularly important role in decision-making regarding plea deals.[77] This can lead to the presentation of false evidence—especially evidence that will likely be viewed as compelling by a jury—having a powerful psychological impact on a defendant's reasoning during plea bargaining.

In addition to lying about the presence of incriminating evidence of guilt, interrogators engage in deception with respect to the consequences of a suspect not cooperating. For instance, on September 1, 1989, Ada JoAnn Taylor agreed with prosecutors to plead guilty to the rape and murder of a 68-year-old woman, Helen Wilson, in Beatrice, Nebraska and to testify against her co-defendant, Joseph White, at trial in exchange for a sentence of 10–40 years in prison.[78] In discussing her guilty plea, Taylor says, 'When they first started interrogating me, they kept telling me they'd make me the first female on death row. I did not know that Nebraska didn't have a female death row. They just kept pushing it on a very regular, almost daily, basis that I might as well come clean that they were going to put me on death row and I might as well face it.'[79] After spending 19 years in prison for a crime she didn't commit, Taylor was exonerated in 2009. What we see here is Taylor being lied to about the consequences of not cooperating with law enforcement. In deliberating about whether to plead guilty to the rape and murder of Wilson, Taylor was in the epistemic dark about the actual stakes of her situation. What's even worse, the consequence of not taking the plea was falsely presented to her as being about as ominous as possible—execution by the State. Thus, Taylor suffered a massive epistemic deficit regarding the stakes involved when weighing the cost of clinging to the truth versus pleading guilty despite her innocence. It is also widely known that the threat of the death penalty wields enormous power, with William Stuntz noting that '[c]apital punishment's largest consequence is not the few dozen executions that happen each year in the United States but the many life sentences imposed after plea bargains designed to avoid death sentences' (2011, p. 260).

Moreover, 'nondisclosure disproportionately harms the innocent since, almost by definition, guilty defendants know more about the facts surrounding a crime

[74] See *Brady v. Maryland*, 373 U.S. 83, 87 (1963).
[75] See *Giglio v. United States*, 405 U.S. 150, 154–55 (1972).
[76] See also Cassidy (2019).
[77] See, for instance, Kramer et al. (2007).
[78] https://www.law.umich.edu/special/exoneration/Pages/casedetail.aspx?caseid=3676.
[79] https://www.guiltypleaproblem.org/?id=ada_joann.

than do those who are factually innocent' (Douglass 2007, p. 582).[80] While defense attorneys can invest costly resources to engage in their own fact-finding missions to challenge or undermine the false evidence presented, prosecutors are permitted to put time limits on offers.[81] This leads to defendants being offered plea deals that expire before their counsel can conduct or complete thorough investigations. Still further, despite the name 'plea deal' or 'plea bargaining,' there is often very little negotiation that takes place, with prosecutors presenting a 'take it or leave it' offer with a near-term expiration date that only gets worse if refused. As Alkon writes, 'prosecutors will regularly say, "If your client doesn't take this deal today, I will add that prior and he will be looking at double the time"' (2014, p. 597). These 'exploding offers' dramatically increase the pressure that defendants experience, especially when the alternatives, such as far lengthier sentences or even the death penalty, are in the decision spaces. Indeed, the higher the stakes, the greater the pressure, with prosecutors reporting that there is 'no negotiation over a plea in death-eligible cases; a plea bargain, if offered [is] presented as "take it or leave it"' (Ehrhard 2008, p. 320). In addition, pressures are directed not only at the defendants, as prosecutors will also threaten family members and other loved ones with prosecution if they do not cooperate.[82]

There are also countless cases of judges using similar tactics. In a particularly tragic case in New York in 1998, Derrick Smith, 19, was offered three to six years in prison by Judge Budd G. Goodman for a drug charge that was good for only that day. While Smith rejected the offer as too long, he faced four to nine years if he was convicted at trial. As he was being led out of the courtroom, Smith turned to his mother and said, 'Mom, I can't do it,' broke free from two court officers escorting him, and leapt out of a sixteenth-floor window of the Manhattan Criminal Court building to his death.[83] Similarly, in *People v. Lewis*, the defendant, Derrick Lewis, moved to vacate the judgment against him on the grounds that, among other things, the 'court coerced him into pleading guilty.' In particular, the judge is reported to have told Lewis's counsel: 'Tell the defendant that if he doesn't take the 15 years to Life, I promise if he is found guilty after trial, I will give him 25 to Life for the murder and 12-1/2 to 25 for the attempted murder, running consecutive' (*People v. Lewis*, 630 N.Y.S.2d 605, 607 (N.Y. Sup. Ct. 1995)).

Still further, defense attorneys typically meet with their clients shortly after they have been arrested and so at the outset they are at a 'considerable informational disadvantage to the prosecutor' (Rakoff 2014). If a client is detained, the

[80] See also Bibas: 'Guilty defendants generally know that they are guilty, and are aware of the likely evidence against them, so they can predict the probable trial outcomes. But defendants who are innocent, mentally ill, or were intoxicated during the crime may have little private information about the state's evidence' (2004, p. 2494).

[81] See Alkon (2014, p. 597).

[82] See Alkon (2014, p. 597, note 230).

[83] https://www.nytimes.com/1998/10/31/nyregion/prisoner-leapt-to-death-despite-plea-for-suicide-watch.html.

defense attorney has very limited opportunities—subject to the visiting hours and other restrictions imposed by jails—to interview the client and get access to evidence that would be crucial in assessing the rationality of accepting a plea deal. In contrast, the prosecutor will often have 'a full police report, complete with witness interviews and other evidence, shortly followed by grand jury testimony, forensic test reports, and follow-up investigations' (Rakoff 2014). This leads to not only a radical epistemic asymmetry between prosecutors and defense attorneys, but also to prosecutors heading into plea negotiations with an overabundance of confidence about the strength of the case.

In addition to the possibility that defendants are deceived about both the evidence against them and the stakes of their situation—with no right to access this information before accepting a plea—the standard of proof is significantly lower for convictions via plea deals than through trials.[84] Whereas proof beyond a reasonable doubt is required for a criminal conviction via trial, felony criminal convictions as a result of plea deals require only a probable cause determination, usually from a preliminary hearing or a grand jury proceeding.[85] Probable cause is 'more than a bare suspicion but less than evidence that would justify a conviction.'[86] Given that there are powerful reasons for criminal convictions to require proof beyond a reasonable doubt, and criminal convictions obtained via plea deals require a standard of proof dramatically lower, it is shocking from an epistemic point of view that plea deals have become the norm in the criminal legal system.[87] Indeed, this means not only that defendants and their attorneys might be groping in the dark because of the withholding of exculpatory evidence and impeachment information, but all of the relevant parties—including prosecutors—may be epistemically handicapped by a lackluster or otherwise inadequate investigation. For if the considerable resources needed to prepare for a costly and lengthy trial can be spared, and a conviction can be secured on the basis of simply having more than a bare suspicion, then the investigative and discovery process can be quite minimal. This leads to the loss of valuable information and knowledge, not only for the parties involved, but for the criminal legal system as a whole.

Relatedly, the epistemic safeguards of a trial are virtually non-existent in plea negotiations. Instead of the prosecution and defense counsel engaged in a robust discovery process, where a jury of peers adjudicates guilt on the basis of an adversarial presentation of evidence that is presided over by a neutral judge, plea deals involve a defendant 'adjudicat[ing] his own case by declaring himself guilty. He

[84] As Albert W. Alschuler writes: 'The plea bargaining system effectively substitutes a concept of partial guilt for the requirement of proof of guilt beyond a reasonable doubt. It is marvelously designed to secure conviction of the innocent' (2003, pp. 1413–14).

[85] See Schehr (2018, pp. 64–65).

[86] *Black's Law Dictionary* (1999).

[87] Constitutional questions can also be raised here: '[W]hen juxtaposed with the Supreme Court's compelling case for proof beyond a reasonable doubt as the constitutionally mandated standard for conviction at a criminal trial, the standard of proof required to convict between 95 and 97 percent of criminal defendants via plea bargaining is unconstitutional' (Schehr 2018, pp. 64–65).

also agrees to his own sentence, or at least to its principal terms' (McConkie 2017, pp. 3–4). In addition, a trial is a public process, with complete records maintained to allow for external review and correction of error on appeal.[88] But prosecutors and defense attorneys agree on the terms of plea deals in private without a judge, jury, or members of the public to assess the relevant evidence, and typically no written records of the details of the plea bargaining are kept except the terms of the final agreement.[89] As the New York State Association of Criminal Defense Lawyers write, 'A system that insulates a prosecution from the searing light of a public trial invites the misuse and abuse of the criminal law' (2021, p. 8).

Combining the account of coercion defended earlier with these overwhelming epistemic deficits suffered by defendants, the full extent to which plea deals are coercive should be clear. The deals themselves are massively unfair, as they are being offered under conditions of radical epistemic asymmetries. When defendants are lied to about the evidence against them or the consequences they are facing, there is simply no explanation that can be given that justifies why defendants are forced to deliberate about life and death decisions while being the victims of deception. But even when deceptive practices aren't used, the significant informational disadvantage that defendants are often at in the bargaining process, the 'take it or leave it' nature of the offers, and the near-term expiration dates all conspire to place defendants in situations that are unfair, especially against the backdrop of the incredibly high stakes at issue. Moreover, this unfairness is directly targeting the decision-making space of the defendant. The options on the table are manipulated through the inflation of charges, and the decision space itself is fundamentally altered through the inclusion of a consideration that swamps all other ones, such as the possibility of the death penalty or a natural life or *de facto* life sentence. This is brute State power being wielded against defendants, perhaps even most effectively against those who are innocent, to achieve desired ends that are neither morally nor epistemically justificatory, such as saving time and money.[90]

4. Agential Testimonial Injustice

In previous chapters, I introduced and developed the concept of agential testimonial injustice. A speaker is the victim of agential testimonial injustice when testimony is extracted in a way that bypasses, exploits, or subverts the speaker's

[88] See Taylor (2020, p. 507). [89] Taylor (2020, p. 508).

[90] See, for instance, Crespo: 'The defendant enjoys a constitutional right to competent representation at government expense, a constitutional right to present and cross-examine witnesses, and, perhaps most notably, a constitutional right not to be convicted unless the prosecutor convinces a jury that he is guilty beyond a reasonable doubt.... All of those protections, however, disappear if the prosecutor successfully induces the defendant to waive his trial and plead guilty. Indeed, *avoiding those costly procedural checks is often the prosecutor's primary objective*' (2018, p. 1339, emphasis added).

epistemic agency and is then given an unwarranted *excess* of credibility. Manipulation, deception, and coercion are the three central mechanisms by which interpersonal processes extract testimony from a speaker in this way.

While most of the earlier discussion of plea bargaining focused on its coercive nature, we have also seen that the criminal legal system is structured so that plea deals are often the result of practices that involve manipulation and deception. Options, stakes, and decision spaces are manipulated through charge stacking and overreaching as well as by the powerful psychological and epistemic consequences that result from their 'anchoring' effect. If a prosecutor begins with an inflated offer of 40 years through charge stacking and then scales down to 20 years, knowing full well that this will dramatically increase the likelihood of arriving at an agreement that will save time and costs, intentional, arational influence is being exerted on the defendant for the desired end of the prosecutor—the acceptance of the plea offer. This is paradigmatically manipulative behavior. The prosecutor is circumventing the defendant's rational decision-making power through the anchoring effect of charge stacking and is, in this sense, bypassing his epistemic agency. Moreover, this is exacerbated by the presentation of exploding offers, where the near-term expiration dates raise the pressure and the stress involved in a life-altering decision space simply to increase the probability of reaching a deal.

But plea bargaining also involves manipulation that goes directly through the defendant's rational capacities. It is obviously rational to prefer 20 years over 40 years of incarceration, or to prefer the certainty of a limited number of years in prison to the very real possibility of natural life or execution. When charge stacking or overreaching is used to curate the options on the table, and the trial penalty is looming in the background, the prosecutor is manipulating the defendant's decision space for his desired end. In such a case, the prosecutor knows that rational agents, especially risk-averse ones, will often opt for a shorter sentence over a longer one and for certainty over gambling, especially when the disparity of outcomes is so stark. In this way, the defendant's epistemic agency is being exploited rather than bypassed. Otherwise put, it is precisely because of the defendant's rationality that the prosecutor's influence is so effective.[91] This is especially concerning in light of the fact that 'innocent defendants . . . are on average more risk averse than guilty defendants' (Bibas 2004, p. 2495).

In addition, plea bargaining involves an attack on epistemic agency through tactics that are overtly deceptive. As discussed earlier, defendants can be lied to about both the evidence possessed against them and the consequences they face,

[91] As William Peeples, a student in the Northwestern Prison Education Program, notes about his own plea deal in a case where he was innocent but was told by his public defender that the probability was high of his being sentenced to 30 years in prison at trial: '[W]hat sane person would not cave in, especially an 18-year-old Black kid? I could not risk all that time trying to prove my innocence, and the State knew it!'

with no requirement that the truth be disclosed before the acceptance of a plea deal. Again, this involves the targeting of epistemic agency. Rather than going through the rational faculties of a defendant via the presentation of evidence that is in fact compelling, the State resorts to weaponizing the rationality of the defendant for the aim of eliciting a guilty plea. In this way, the false evidence ploy exploits the defendant's epistemic agency by relying on the fact that a rational person will recognize that compelling evidence of guilt will likely lead to a worse outcome at trial than the current one on the bargaining table.

Finally, the earlier discussion makes clear how the coercive nature of plea bargaining subverts epistemic agency. Defendants are presented with unfair offers or threats that have a swamping effect that screens off the other relevant normative considerations in the victim's deliberative process. This changes both the options in the defendant's decision space as well as the decision space itself. In particular, the addition of the proposals in question prevents defendants from being able to properly engage with the normative force of the full range of the reasons on the table and often brings along a dramatic increase in the first-personal stakes of the situation. In particular, these coercive practices often result in the questions under deliberation shifting from being evidential or moral to strictly practical in nature: defendants are no longer free to weigh the rational or moral power of the considerations but are instead forced to make decisions that are aimed at simply trying to minimize the life-altering harm they face.

Let's now turn to the second component of agential testimonial injustice: the excess of credibility afforded to plea deals. Despite all of the forces at work in extracting testimony from defendants through plea bargaining, the criminal legal system treats guilty pleas as representing the defendants' actual states; in other words, the system regards a defendant who pleads guilty as in fact guilty. This is importantly different from a confession, even a true one, which is evidence of guilt, but is not itself a plea of guilt. As the Supreme Court notes in *Kercheval v. United States*, 'A plea of guilty differs in purpose and effect from a mere admission or an extra-judicial confession; it is itself a conviction. More is not required, the court has nothing to do but give judgment and sentence' (*Kercheval v. United States*, 274 U.S. 220 (1927)).

This is further evidenced by the general finality with which plea deals are viewed within the criminal legal system.[92] After a guilty plea is entered, 'barriers to appeal are nearly insurmountable' (Wynbrandt 2016, p. 547). Indeed, plea deals often explicitly include a requirement that defendants waive a number of rights.[93] For instance, in the first empirical analysis of appeal waivers—which are clauses in plea deals whereby defendants waive their rights to appellate and post-conviction review of sentencing errors—King and O'Neill (2005) analyzed data

[92] See, for instance, Erickson (1973).
[93] See New York State Association of Criminal Defense Lawyers (2021, pp. 5–6).

from 971 randomly selected federal cases and found that defendants waived their rights to appellate review in nearly two-thirds of the cases settled by plea agreement. Even defendants in capital cases may entirely waive post-conviction review as part of a plea agreement.[94] In *Whitmore v. Arkansas*, for example, the court found 'no reason to disturb the judgment of the Supreme Court of Arkansas' that the defendant made a 'knowing, intelligent, and voluntary' waiver of his right to appeal, when he 'was questioned by counsel and the trial court concerning his choice to accept the death sentence, and his answers demonstrate that he appreciated the consequences of that decision,' and 'indicated that he understood several possible grounds for appeal, which had been explained to him by counsel, but informed the court that he was "not seeking any technicalities"' (*Whitmore v. Arkansas*, 495 U.S. 149, 165–66 (1990)).

Even for those defendants who don't explicitly waive their rights, there are often significant barriers to post-conviction review. While there is tremendous variation at the state level, '[s]ome states explicitly exclude those who plead guilty from their post-conviction statutes, denying them the opportunity to have DNA testing performed on evidence from their cases, denying them access to the courts, or denying them the opportunity to file habeas corpus petitions' (Stephens 2013, p. 340). This is powerfully exemplified in the case of the so-called 'Dixmoor Five,' briefly discussed in Chapter 2. On December 8, 1991, the body of 14-year-old Cateresa Matthews was found in a field near her home in Dixmoor, Illinois; she had been raped and shot in the mouth.[95] About a year later, Jonathan Barr, James Harden, Shainnie Sharp, Robert Taylor, and Robert Lee Veal, all between the ages of 14 and 16, were arrested in connection with the case. After lengthy interrogations, Veal and Sharp agreed to plead guilty and to testify against the other defendants in exchange for shorter sentences, while Barr, Harden, and Taylor were convicted at trial.[96] What is of particular interest for our purposes is that in 2011, the defendants who were convicted at trial successfully petitioned the courts to have DNA evidence from the crime retested, which not only excluded all five defendants, but also matched a man with a prior rape conviction. Barr, Harden, and Taylor quickly filed motions to vacate their convictions, but the state of Illinois 'argued that the defendants who pleaded guilty were barred from participating in those postconviction proceedings' (Stephens 2013, p. 311). In particular, prosecutors argued that the post-conviction statute providing relief from judgments should be understood as barring those who plead guilty from filing motions for post-conviction relief precisely because the DNA testing statues had been interpreted as excluding those who plead guilty from petitioning the

[94] See King (2014).

[95] https://www.law.northwestern.edu/legalclinic/wrongfulconvictions/exonerations/il/the-dixmoor-five.html.

[96] Stephens (2013, p. 309).

court for forensic testing.[97] So, even when defendants aren't pressured into waiving their post-conviction rights as a condition of their plea deals, state statutes are often interpreted as doing just this. Thus, despite the fact that the DNA evidence in the Dixmoor Five case equally supported the innocence of all five defendants, the guilty pleas entered by Veal and Sharp functioned as barriers to the reversal of a massive miscarriage of justice.

The general finality of plea deals and the uphill battle to reverse the often life-altering consequences of a guilty plea point to a potentially deeper form of credibility excess: like false confessions, guilty pleas are weighed far too heavily in the criminal legal system. In particular, guilty pleas often overpower other evidence, are resistant to counterevidence, and are isolated or blocked from other relevant evidence.

Consider, for instance, the case of Brian Dement, which differs from that of the Dixmoor Five in some important respects. In 2002, 21-year-old Deanna Crawford was found naked from the waist down and strangled to death in a shed next to an abandoned barn in rural West Virginia.[98] The case remained unsolved for five years until Brian Dement, a 26-year-old man who had been diagnosed with learning disabilities, antisocial personality disorder, attention deficit disorder, bipolar disorder, and depression and anxiety, told state troopers that he and three other men had been involved in Crawford's murder.[99] After confessing, Dement agreed to plead guilty to murder, but two days after entering his guilty plea in 2007, he recanted his confession and said that he made up the entire story to please authorities. Nevertheless, despite the complete absence of physical evidence linking Crawford's death to any of the four defendants, and based largely on Dement's testimony—which was riddled with inconsistencies—each of the defendants was sentenced to 30 years or more in prison.[100]

In February of 2018, testing found that DNA from semen on Crawford's pants and from a cigarette butt near the isolated crime scene belonged to Timothy Smith, who was incarcerated at an Ohio prison at the time and was convicted of raping a child.[101] These DNA results led Cabell County Judge Alfred Ferguson to overturn the convictions of Dement's three associates, but he refused to grant a new trial to Dement, citing the fact that he confessed and pled guilty: 'I wouldn't have had any problem at all if he would have pled not guilty and gone to trial and been convicted and then you find this DNA. He would have had a new trial. Just like the other defendants. But his case to me . . . is different from the other three because they have always maintained their innocence' (*Dement v. Pszczolkowski*, No. 19-0785 W. Va. 20, 2021).

97 Stephens (2013, pp. 311–12).

98 (*Dement v. Pszczolkowski*, No. 19–0785 W. Va. 5, 2021).

99 https://www.injusticewatch.org/interactives/trading-away-justice/west-virginia.html.

100 https://www.injusticewatch.org/interactives/trading-away-justice/west-virginia.html.

101 https://www.injusticewatch.org/interactives/trading-away-justice/west-virginia.html.

Unlike the case of the Dixmoor Five, where the prosecution tried to block access to relevant DNA evidence, Dement's case is one where the DNA evidence had been tested and excluded him, but Judge Ferguson *denied its evidential value*. In this way, Judge Ferguson's ruling powerfully illustrates the credibility excess afforded to guilty pleas. In particular, there is an absence of evidence in support of Dement's guilt: there is not a single piece of physical evidence linking him or his associates to the crime. There is evidence that Dement's confession is false: in addition to the learning disabilities and mental health issues that Dement faced, which are connected with an increase in the likelihood of falsely confessing to a crime,[102] his confession was riddled with inconsistencies. And there is compelling evidence of his innocence: the DNA from semen on Crawford's pants and from a cigarette butt near the isolated crime scene belonged to Smith, who was previously convicted of raping a child, and was compelling enough for Judge Ferguson to overturn the convictions of Dement's three associates. In spite of all of this, Dement's guilty plea is regarded as so epistemically weighty that it grounds his murder conviction, overpowers evidence that his confession is false, is resistant to evidence that directly points to the guilt of another person, and is isolated by the court from exculpatory DNA evidence. That this represents a massive unwarranted excess of credibility being afforded to Dement's guilty plea is even clearer against the background of the way plea bargaining functions in the criminal legal system. If plea bargaining often results in unfair offers that close defendants out of a reasonable decision-making space, relying on manipulative, deceptive, and coercive practices to get there, then defendants are pleading guilty to crimes under conditions of radically compromised epistemic agency. This provides even further reason to regard a response such as Judge Ferguson's as involving an excess of credibility.

Notice, moreover, that if guilty pleas are speech acts whereby persons who plead guilty voluntarily and knowingly changes their status from a defendant to a convicted person, then plea deals that are involuntary, or insufficiently voluntary, because they have been extracted are not in fact changing the normative status of those who plead guilty. In this way, defendants are being treated as though they have been convicted when in fact they are not.

One intuitive objection here is to resist the conclusion that defendants receive an unwarranted excess of credibility in cases of false confession or guilty pleas and receive credibility deficits when they recant. For, it may be argued, it clearly flies in the face of self-interest to confess to a murder that one did not commit or to plead guilty to a violent crime of which one is innocent. In both cases, one is facing a multitude of serious consequences, including incarceration, separation from one's family and friends, and even death, and so it can be inferred that, except in highly unusual cases, one would confess or plead guilty to a crime only

[102] See Chapter 2.

if one had in fact committed it. Moreover, recantations of confessions or guilty pleas also make a great deal of sense from a self-interested point of view, as they aim to avoid, or reverse, the negative consequences of criminal convictions. Given this, confessions and guilty pleas should, from an epistemic point of view, be given a great deal of credibility, as they are quite likely to be true, and recantations should be met with suspicion, as they are rather likely to be false. It is, therefore, not clear that confessions and guilty pleas are being given a massive unwarranted excess of credibility in the criminal legal system, and so we have reason to question whether suspects and defendants are indeed the victims of agential testimonial injustice.

While this response may seem intuitive at first, it should be clear from the earlier details about plea deals, as well as the discussion in Chapter 2 about confessions, that defendants often come to believe that it *is* in their self-interest to confess or to plead guilty to a crime. For instance, they are told that through cooperation with authorities, they will avoid the death penalty, a natural life sentence, a *de facto* life sentence, the loss of their children, and so on. Given the realities of the trial penalty, defendants are often clearly rational in believing that pleading guilty is in their self-interest, even when they are innocent.

Defendants who plead guilty to crimes in the current criminal legal system are thus often victims of agential testimonial injustice. Their pleas are extracted through processes that are manipulative, deceptive, and coercive, and are then given a massive excess of credibility. As we saw in previous chapters, there are at least two epistemic wrongs that victims of agential testimonial injustice suffer. First, the extraction itself constitutes an epistemic wrong, as obtaining guilty pleas through manipulative, deceptive, and coercive practices is to treat testifiers as epistemic tools to be influenced by, molded to, and cornered into meeting, the aims of others. In many such cases of extraction, the rational capacities of defendants are weaponized against them not only for the desired ends of the State, but also for their own demise. The second kind of epistemic wrong involves the excess of credibility given to the extracted testimony. Here, defendants are epistemically wronged by virtue of being regarded as givers of truth or knowledge only under conditions of radically compromised epistemic agency. Otherwise put, when defendants are taken to be worthy of being believed only when they offer testimony because the brute power of the State has been wielded against them, they are treated as lying outside of the epistemic community where the giving and taking of reasons is central. Moreover, the epistemic wrong of the credibility excess here provides yet another case in which the traditional deficit model of testimonial injustice is shown to be deeply inadequate.[103]

[103] See Fricker (2007) for the deficit model of testimonial injustice and Chapter 5 for a discussion of the alternative multi-directional model.

It is also crucial that the systemic nature[104] of the agential testimonial injustice at work in plea bargaining is fully appreciated here. Sure, a single prosecutor may engage in charge stacking or put an exploding offer on the bargaining table, but these individual acts take place within a criminal legal system that has created, sanctioned, and perpetuated these acts of agential testimonial injustice inflicted on defendants every day. That charge stacking and exploding offers are allowed in the first place, for instance, is part of the system in which prosecutors operate. Moreover, that the trial penalty is a reality in American courtrooms is not due to a few isolated actors but, rather, to the criminal legal system as a whole. Still further, that it is legal to outright lie to defendants about the evidence against them and the legal consequences they face is built into the laws governing plea-bargaining practices. All of this gives rise to a system whereby guilty pleas are extracted and given a massive excess of credibility, resulting in the State itself committing acts of agential testimonial injustice on its citizens.[105]

5. Conclusion

The plea-bargaining process in the United States criminal legal system involves a magnitude and depth of injustice that cries out for urgent and radical change. Guilty pleas are not the result of anything that can rightly be called a 'deal,' but are instead the product of the wielding of state power that leaves defendants cornered, desperate, and in the dark, leading even innocent people to accept a plea deal rather than face the alternatives. That this is the system in which over 95% of federal and state felony convictions in the United States are obtained means that vast numbers of Americans across the nation are victims of a state-sanctioned form of agential testimonial injustice, often with life-shattering consequences. This calls for a dramatic shift in the way in which defendants are viewed in the criminal legal system, one where epistemic agency is centered rather than circumvented, subverted, and weaponized. It is only through the recognition and respect of one another's personhood and rational capacities that we can truly take the steps needed to achieve justice.

[104] See Anderson (2012) for a discussion of the systemic dimension of epistemic injustice and Fricker (forthcoming) for an analysis of false confessions as a form of institutionalized testimonial injustice.

[105] See List and Pettit (2011) and Lackey (2021) for more on how groups can function as agents.

5

Race, Gender, and the Multi-Directional Model of Credibility Assessments

On the standard view, the way that bias or prejudice and social identity intersect to impact credibility determinations has two central components: first, a hearer has a bias or prejudice that targets the social identity of a speaker and, second, this results in a deficit of credibility afforded to the testimony in question.[1] Indeed, the wrongness of testimonial injustice on this model derives from these two features. It is wrong to be racist or sexist, for instance, and it is wrong for this racism or sexism to lead to a speaker getting less than she deserves.

In contrast, agential testimonial injustice includes neither of these features and thus does not explain the epistemic wrongs inflicted on speakers through either bias and prejudice or through being deprived of one's epistemic due. Instead, the epistemic wrongs of agential testimonial injustice result from a speaker having her testimony extracted in a way that circumvents, exploits, or undermines her epistemic agency and then being regarded as knowledgeable only under such conditions of compromised epistemic agency. This attack on a speaker's agency results in an undermining of her autonomy and dignity and, ultimately, her status as a person.

Nevertheless, biases and prejudices that target a speaker's social identity can and frequently do interact with agential testimonial injustice, but often in complicated and non-linear ways. In this chapter, I will take a close look at the way that biases, prejudices, and myths about race and gender cause, fuel, and exacerbate agential testimonial injustice, leading to a multi-directional attack on the credibility of some of the most vulnerable defendants, witnesses, and victims in the United States criminal legal system.

1. The Multi-Directional Model

According to the standard view of testimonial injustice, when a bias or prejudice toward members of oppressed groups targets their testimony and is unjust, it is always manifested in one direction—as a deficit. Let's call this the *one-directional*

[1] See Fricker (2007).

Criminal Testimonial Injustice. Jennifer Lackey, Oxford University Press. © Jennifer Lackey 2023.
DOI: 10.1093/oso/9780192864109.003.0006

model. Fricker's view is the *normative* version of this sort of one-directionality,[2] as it focuses on justice and how we *ought* to treat one another's testimony. But there is also a *descriptive* version, according to which bias or prejudice toward members of oppressed groups that targets their testimony *in fact* manifests itself—either always or largely—in the direction of a deficit. While such a descriptive view is widely discussed across a variety of contexts, here I will focus on it in relation to the criminal legal system.

Legal scholar Amanda Carlin uses a critical race theory lens to argue that the formal exclusion of people of color historically found in the courtroom now manifests as a functional exclusion where the rules and expectations are white social and behavioral norms. In particular, nonwhite performance in courtrooms—including, for instance, demeanor and speech patterns—is regarded as inappropriate, and credibility determinations are thereby used as tools of exclusion where the testimony of people of color is discredited. To illustrate this, Carlin focuses on the treatment of Rachel Jeantel, who was the last person to speak to Trayvon Martin before he was killed and was widely regarded as the prosecution's star witness in the George Zimmerman trial. However, 'Jeantel did not resemble your typical star witness. She was not well educated, or white, or a man. By contrast, she was a large, dark skinned teenage girl, whose language was peppered with slang' (2016, p. 452). Given this, Jeantel was immediately regarded by the court as an 'outsider,' her testimony was discredited, and her performance on the stand was used to justify Zimmerman's acquittal. Carlin concludes that 'the systematic undercutting of black testimony undermines black credibility. . . . . What makes black testimony non-credible or unintelligible is its distinction from whiteness . . . .' (2016, pp. 476–77).[3]

Similarly, Jasmine Gonzales Rose argues that 'a witness of color is automatically considered less credible' (2016, p. 2259). Using examples of flight from racially targeted police profiling and violence and cross-racial witness identification, Gonzales Rose shows how certain kinds of evidence receive racially disparate treatment in the criminal legal system, resulting in the systematic exclusion or discrediting of the testimony of people of color. For instance, a defendant running from the police is often presented in court as evidence of guilt, but it is not at all uncommon for innocent people of color to flee law enforcement due to fear of racially targeted harassment and violence, especially in overpoliced communities.[4] The omission of this 'racialized reality evidence' from the record makes clear how

[2] For a discussion of Fricker's view, see Chapters 1 and 2.

[3] Despite this, Carlin maintains that '[n]ot surprisingly, the question of credibility is understudied, particularly as it intersects with race' (2016, p. 468). Over a decade earlier, Chet K.W. Pager made a similar point: 'While the problems of jury lie-detection and jury bias have been extensively discussed independently, little attention has been drawn to the *intersection* between race and credibility' (Pager 2005, p. 374).

[4] See *Commonwealth v. Warren*, 58 N.E.3d 333, 342 (2016).

the testimony of people of color's lived experiences of systemic racism is regularly excluded at trial. Moreover, in the context of cross-racial identifications, jurors generally find white witnesses more credible than non-white witnesses, even when the testimony in question is far-fetched or suggests unreliability.[5] Despite this, 'there is no established mechanism [in the criminal legal system] for challenging racially biased credibility determinations' (Johnson 1996, p. 266).

Deborah Tuerkheimer also focuses on credibility deficits arising from bias or prejudice that targets the social identity of speakers, but she adds a further element—testimony with a particular *content*. She argues that women's testimony regarding sexual violence is systematically subject to credibility discounting at every stage of the criminal legal process, where 'credibility discounting' is understood as an 'unwarranted failure to credit an assertion... [that] stems from prejudice' (Tuerkheimer 2017, p. 3). Moreover, Tuerkheimer shows how the incredulity operative in the legal response to rape has migrated from formal legal rules to informal practices, with much the same result—'an enduring system of disbelief' (2017, p. 1). Law enforcement officers, for instance, tend to doubt women's reports of sexual assault, which curtails investigations and leads to infrequent arrests and prosecutions. Thus, insofar as rape victims are effectively denied the protective resources of the State when their complaints are dismissed because of prejudice, Tuerkheimer concludes that credibility discounting perpetuates inequality and should be regarded as a distinct, actionable form of discrimination.

In addition, intersectionality[6] clearly impacts credibility assessments, with Carlin noting that '[i]ntersectional experiences of women of color place them at the bottom of the credibility hierarchy' (2016, p. 476). Indeed, the credibility deficit that women of color face, especially Black women, is often grounded in deeply entrenched and pernicious stereotypes that impact their testimony at every level of the criminal legal system. As Marilyn Yarbrough and Crystal Bennett say, '[w]hether she is plaintiff, defendant, or witness, the African American woman in the courtroom faces numerous obstacles to being considered a believable, reasonable person' (2000, p. 647). Even more directly, Jennifer Nash writes that 'there is a lengthy cultural history of disbelieving black women' grounded in the stereotype that 'black women... are liars' (2009, p. 7). This is an extension of the one-directional model: bias or prejudice can target multiple social identities at once, thereby leading to an *even greater deficit* in the credibility that speakers who lie at their intersection are afforded.

Testimony with a particular content can also combine with intersectionality and prejudice to result in still further credibility deficits. A common stereotype of Black women, for instance, is based on Jezebel, the biblical wife of King Ahab, who 'was a purely lascivious creature: not only was she governed by her erotic

[5] See Gonzales Rose (2016, p. 2255). [6] See Crenshaw (1989).

desires, but her sexual prowess led men to wanton passion' (Roberts 1997, pp. 10–11). This stereotype of Black women directly impacts the assessment of their testimony regarding sexual assault. '[J]udges and jurors will wonder whether a Black woman is promiscuous and of low moral character, such that she, herself is responsible for being raped or sexually assaulted, or in the extreme, whether she is even capable of being raped or assaulted' (Jacobs 2017, p. 46). So, while sexist prejudices lead to the discrediting of women's reports of sexual assault in general, racist stereotypes work to further undermine the testimony of Black women's testimony about sexual violence in particular.

Put simply, we see four different permutations of the one-directional model here:

(1) testimony + social identity + bias or prejudice = credibility deficit;

(2) testimony *with a particular content* + social identity + bias or prejudice = greater credibility deficit;

(3) testimony + *multiple relevant social identities* + bias or prejudice = even greater credibility deficit;

(4) testimony *with a particular content* + *multiple relevant social identities* + bias or prejudice = still greater credibility deficit.

On this picture, there are different ways that testimony combines with social identities and biases or prejudices to yield credibility deficits. Sometimes, the social identity of a speaker is especially salient, as we see with the way the testimony of people of color is treated across many dimensions of the criminal legal system. At other times, the social identity of a speaker interacts with the content of the testimony in question in important ways, as we see with the systematic discounting of women's reports of sexual violence. And at still other times, multiple social identities, either in isolation or in conjunction with testimony with a particular content, interact so as to result in major credibility discounting, such as with reports by Black women in general and, even more so, with their reports about sexual violence. Despite these important differences, however, all roads here ultimately lead in one direction: toward credibility deficits.[7]

And yet, the reality is in fact much more complicated, giving rise to what we might call the *multi-dimensional model*. On this model, the wrongs inflicted upon speakers do not involve a linear regression of deficits leading to an ever-increasing discounting of credibility, but a multi-directional attack that twists and turns, resulting in excesses and deficits that perpetrate injustice alike.

[7] Johnson is explicit about this when she talks about the 'overwhelmingly unidirectional nature of race and credibility inferences' (1996, p. 346).

The first nuance to add to this picture is that intersectionality is important, not only within the individual testifier in question, but also across relations within the criminal legal system. For the sake of clarity, let us call the former *intrapersonal* intersectionality and the latter *interpersonal* intersectionality.

A central way in which interpersonal intersectionality is relevant for credibility assessments is with respect to the intersection of the social identities of the *parties involved in the crime* in question—the one reporting the crime, or the victim, and the suspect or defendant. For instance, there is a long history of the testimony of white women who report being sexually assaulted by a Black man being given an *excess* of credibility,[8] with the judge in the infamous Scottsboro rape trial unabashedly expressing this:

> Where the woman charged to have been raped, as in this case is a white woman, there is a very strong presumption under the law that she would not and did not yield voluntarily to intercourse with the defendant, a Negro; and this is true, whatever the station in life the prosecutrix may occupy, whether she be the most despised, ignorant and abandoned woman of the community, or the spotless virgin and daughter of a prominent home of luxury and learning.
>
> (Carter 1969, p. 36)

Racist beliefs that a white woman would not voluntarily have intercourse with a Black man result in a massive excess of credibility being afforded to white women who report being raped by a Black man.[9] In other words, even if there should be a general presumption that women are telling the truth when they report being the victim of a sexual assault, white women should not be given *more* credibility than they deserve simply because of the races of the parties involved in the crime in question. Such an inflation of the credibility of the testimony of white women is often fueled further by racist myths and stereotypes of Black sexuality as 'wild, uncontrollable, bestial, and even criminal' (Patton and Snyder-Yuly 2007, p. 862) and the resulting belief that white women are vulnerable and must thereby be protected from Black men.[10] These forces conspire so that 'by preconceived notion, a man of color accused of rape, by a white woman, is presumed *guilty* beyond a reasonable doubt' (Hale and Matt 2019).[11]

[8] See, for instance, Carter (1969), Wriggins (1983), and Radelet et al. (1994).

[9] This is an instance of distributive testimonial injustice, which was developed in Chapter 1 and involves a speaker being afforded an excess of credibility relative to another.

[10] See Davis (1985) and Patton and Snyder-Yuly (2007).

[11] The accuracy of cross-racial credibility assessments is also relevant here. As Rand argues, 'there exists... a "Demeanor Gap" in situations of cross-racial demeanor evaluation that undermines accuracy in credibility determinations: specifically, jurors of one race, even those well-intended and free of racial animus, will be unable to dependably judge the demeanor of a witness of a different race because they are unable to accurately decipher the cues that the witness uses to communicate sincerity' Rand 2000, p. 4). When this is coupled with the fact that demeanor is often 'the determinative factor in

Despite this, the power of the one-directional model persists. For instance, despite her extended discussion of the case of Tom Robinson in *To Kill A Mockingbird*—where Robinson is a Black man accused in 1935 Alabama of raping Mayella Ewell, who is white—Fricker (2007) focuses entirely on the credibility deficit that Robinson receives in explicating the notion of testimonial injustice and not at all on the credibility excess that Ewell receives.[12] Arguably, however, the inflated credibility that Ewell receives largely explains the course of events that unfolds, leading ultimately to Robinson's death. It is, after all, Ewell's testimony that she was raped that sets in motion Robinson being arrested and tried, and it is the central evidence used to ground his conviction. Moreover, Ewell's credibility assessment in virtue of being a white woman is clearly causally linked to Robinson's denials being rejected. If Ewell had been Black, for instance, then we can imagine a very different outcome having obtained. It is thus 'the relatively high credibility accorded white women's accusations of rape against Black men' (Wriggens 1983, p. 122, note 116), and not merely the credibility discount suffered by Robinson, that explains the jury returning a guilty verdict in *To Kill A Mockingbird*.

In a similar spirit, immediately after Tuerkheimer articulates a version of the one-directional model—'The legal response to rape has long been shaped by entrenched disbelief of women who level accusations of sexual assault'—she notes 'one important exception... for cases of white women alleging rape by black men' (Tuerkheimer 2017, pp. 20–21).[13] But this one important exception crucially complicates the one-directional model. While it is true that the criminal legal system often treats 'rape complainants with incredulity,' (Tuerkheimer 2017, p. 21), other biases and prejudices can be so powerful that this phenomenon is completely turned on its head. According to Sheri Lynn Johnson, for instance, 'African Americans... are... stereotyped as less honest and more criminal than the majority' (Johnson 1996, p. 316).[14] Sexist stereotypes about the incredulity of rape

appraising trustworthiness' (Timony 2000, p. 919), and has long been regarded as a central 'method of ascertaining the truth and accuracy' (*Arnstein v. Porter*, 154 F.2d 464, 470 (2d Cir. 1946)) of witness testimony, inaccurate cross-racial demeanor evaluations can be a powerful force at work in wrongful convictions. For a discussion of the role that demeanor evidence generally plays in assessing witness credibility, see (Blumenthal 1993). See also *Mattox v. United States* where the Supreme Court holds that in-person confrontation gives the accused an opportunity to 'compel... [the witness] to stand face to face with the jury in order that they may look at him, and judge by his demeanor... whether he is worthy of belief' (*Mattox v. United States*, 156 U.S. 237, 242–43 (1895)).

[12] To be fair, the reason Fricker focuses on the credibility deficit Robinson receives, rather than the excess Ewell is afforded, is because only Robinson is the victim of testimonial injustice in such a case. However, for the purpose of developing an alternative to the one-directional model, it is important to expand the discussion to include the role that interpersonal intersectionality can have on credibility determinations. For detailed analyses of Ewell's credibility excess, see Johnson (1996) and Medina (2011).

[13] See also Radelet et al. (1994) and Johnson (1996).

[14] Rand similarly discusses three negative stereotypes about Black witnesses that directly affect credibility assessments: '(1) the stereotype that African-Americans are less intelligent than whites, which would be invoked if the Black witnesses were called upon to recall and describe events accurately; (2) the stereotype that African-Americans are not trustworthy and honest, which would have

victims can thus intersect with racist myths and stereotypes of dishonesty and criminality about Black men[15] to result in a testifier who would otherwise be regarded as a liar—such as a white woman reporting sexual violence—instead receiving a massive inflation of credibility. Again, think of *To Kill A Mockingbird* here: despite the fact that Mayella Ewell sustained injuries on her face inflicted by a left-handed person, and Tom Robinson's left arm is disabled, she was believed when she insisted that it was Tom Robinson who attacked her.[16] In this way, social identity combined with bias or prejudice does not neatly and straightforwardly lead to distrust; instead, it can lead to a credibility excess, even a massive one.[17]

This is an example of how interpersonal intersectionality can give rise to an instance of the multi-dimensional model, thereby directly challenging (1) above. In particular, while the one-directional model notes that testimony + social identity + bias or prejudice leads to a credibility deficit, we see that the testimony of a white woman, combined with biases or prejudices about both her as vulnerable and in need of protection, and about Black men as 'uncontrollable, bestial,' and 'criminal,' can lead to her being afforded a massive excess of credibility that is unwarranted in reports involving sexual violence.[18]

Similar results are found when we turn to (2). As we saw in Chapter 2, for instance, confessions are regarded as the 'gold standard' of evidence or the 'queen of proofs' in the United States criminal legal system. Even when there is

obvious implications for any sort of trial testimony; and (3) the stereotype that African-Americans are violent, such that any allegation regarding violence would be bolstered by its consistency with the stereotype' (2000, p. 42).

[15] As George Yancy powerfully writes: 'Let a Black commit a crime and it is said to have been predictable. Let a white commit a crime and it becomes anomalous, an exception, something that was off the map of expectation' (2008, p. 866).

[16] It may be objected that surely at least some of the court officials and jurors did *not* believe Mayella Ewell, but nonetheless wanted to see Tom Robinson convicted because of their broader racist attitudes about Black men and white women. While this may be true, this does not undermine the claim that Mayella Ewell's testimony was afforded a massive excess of credibility. As discussed in Chapter 2, even if some individual members of the court room did not *believe* her, Robinson's conviction revealed that her testimony nonetheless played an inflated role within the trial and was thus afforded an action-driven excess of credibility. In other words, outright belief is not necessary for testimony to be given an excess of credibility by virtue of playing an unwarranted and oversized epistemic role within the criminal legal system more broadly.

[17] Again, see the earlier quote from the judge in the infamous Scottsboro rape trial.

[18] It should be emphasized that only some excesses of credibility wrong the speaker or result in agential testimonial injustice. As presented, for instance, the weight that Mayella Ewell's testimony against Tom Robinson is afforded may not involve an epistemic wrong being inflicted upon *her*. (Of course, it is possible that the backstory is that her testimony is extracted by her father or community because of the racist stigma of a white woman having a sexual relationship with a Black man.) But in understanding the multi-directional model that I am developing in this chapter, it is important to see the intersectional dimensions of credibility assessments more generally, as sometimes they can lead to epistemic wrongs or exacerbate agential testimonial injustice. For instance, as I will discuss in the next section, an extracted confession might receive an excess of credibility, which is even greater if the confessor is Black, and is greater still if the victim is white. In this way, the intrapersonal intersectionality of the speaker—a Black man confessing to a violent crime—can combine with interpersonal intersectionality—a Black man being accused of raping a white woman—to result in an even greater epistemic wrong being inflicted upon the speaker.

overwhelming evidence that a defendant who confessed to a crime is innocent—including, as we saw in the case of Juan Rivera, massive inconsistencies between the proffered testimony and the facts of the case and DNA evidence that does not match the defendant—guilty verdicts are not uncommon. This shows that testimony with a particular content, such as confession evidence, is often afforded an unwarranted credibility excess.[19] But what I want to do now is show how this testimony can combine with biases or prejudices that target testifiers' social identity to further bolster the multi-directional model.

2. Race

A particularly powerful case that makes clear how the excess of credibility afforded to extracted confessions can be exacerbated by racist myths and biases involves Barry Lee Fairchild. Since this case provides an instructive illustration of the scale and scope of credibility excesses as understood on the multi-directional model, it is worth examining in some detail.

On February 26, 1983, an Arkansas State Trooper pursued two Black males who were traveling at high speed in a vehicle belonging to a 22-year-old white woman, Marjorie Mason, but the occupants were able to flee on foot. The following day, Mason's body was found behind an abandoned farmhouse in Lonoke County; she had been kidnapped, robbed, raped, and shot twice in the head. Fairchild, a young Black man with an IQ between 60 and 80,[20] was apprehended on March 4, 1983 in Pope County, Arkansas, where he was first taken to a local hospital for treatment of a head laceration, then to the Pope County sheriff's department, and ultimately transported to the Pulaski County jail.

The following day, on March 5, 1983, Fairchild provided a videotaped confession admitting involvement in the crimes and implicating an acquaintance, Harold Green, whom he accused of shooting Mason unexpectedly. Green was never charged, as he was imprisoned in another state at the time of the murder.[21] Fairchild then went with police and sheriff's authorities on a tour of the abduction site, after which he gave a second videotaped statement at the Pulaski County jail.

Upon meeting with his appointed counsel in 1983, Fairchild immediately asserted his innocence and reported that his confession of involvement in Mason's

[19] Broadly speaking, the excess of credibility afforded to confessions can also be seen as an instance of content-based testimonial injustice, which was developed in Chapter 1.

[20] See *Fairchild v. Lockhart*, 744 F. Supp. 1429, 1434–5 (E.D. Ark. 1989), *aff'd*, 900 F.2d 1292 (8th Cir. 1990).

[21] https://www.washingtonpost.com/archive/politics/1994/01/09/in-arkansas-a-death-row-struggle-and-doubt/772108c9-1db5-4f2e-8ffe-0c512c842a1b/.

abduction, rape, and murder was coerced.[22] Fairchild filed a motion to suppress his confession, alleging that Sheriff Tommy Robinson and his chief assistant, Major Larry Dill, repeatedly kicked him in the stomach, hit him in the chest and on the arm with a shotgun, and threatened to kill him.[23] The motion to suppress the confession was denied, Fairchild's confession was introduced into evidence, he was convicted of being involved in the kidnapping, rape, and murder of Mason, and was sentenced to death. Despite a number of appeals, Fairchild was executed by the State of Arkansas by lethal injection on August 31, 1995.[24]

Unfortunately, these events would not be particularly remarkable in the United States criminal legal system if this were the end of the story, as there is a long history of this sort of police brutality involved in the extraction of confessions, especially when the victim is white and the suspect is Black. But what does make this case especially noteworthy, particularly for our purposes here, is the sheer quantity of additional testimony that was offered in support of Fairchild's accusations of police violence, and the way in which a single extracted confession was used to undermine and discredit all of it.

Following a number of unsuccessful appeals of his conviction, Fairchild's attorneys quite fortuitously learned of an FBI probe of police brutality in the Pulaski County Sheriff's Department. After it was revealed that other Black men had been subjected to treatment similar to Fairchild's by the sheriff and his deputies, including Fairchild's own brother, Robert, the Eighth Circuit stayed Fairchild's execution and remanded the case for an evidentiary hearing. At this hearing, Fairchild's attorneys presented details of egregious police brutality, with 13 other suspects testifying to being subject to coercion by the Pulaski County Sheriff's Department in connection with the investigation of Mason's kidnapping, rape, and murder. These men reported being verbally threatened, slapped, choked, punched, kicked, stomped upon, beaten with clubs, fists, telephone books, night-sticks, and threatened with a gun. Two suspects from contemporaneous cases also testified to police brutality by the Pulaski County Sheriff's office. Racial slurs were used throughout these interrogations, such as 'N-----, you're going to talk.'[25] In addition, there was substantial evidence buttressing the truthfulness of all of this testimony, including eyewitness accounts of the abuse that corroborated the victims' accounts and reports of physical signs of abuse by others, such as documented records by medical personnel.

When the totality of the evidence was taken into account, 30 Black witnesses testified that officers of the Pulaski County Sheriff's Department verbally and physically brutalized Black suspects during investigations, while 14 white officers

[22] See *Fairchild v. Lockhart*, 857 F.2d 1204, 1207 (8th Cir. 1988).
[23] See *Fairchild v. Lockhart*, 857 F.2d 1204, 1207 (8th Cir. 1988).
[24] https://www.nytimes.com/1995/09/01/us/arkansas-executes-man-who-argued-he-was-retarded.html.
[25] Johnson (1996, p. 282).

either failed to remember details of their contact with the suspects in question or denied engaging in, witnessing, or hearing any abuse.[26] Judge Garnett Thomas Eisele presided at the district court hearing and concluded that there was a lack of evidence that Fairchild's confession was coerced. There are a number of very serious concerns with Judge Eisele's opinion, including that he applied 'a far more rigorous standard in assessing the credibility of Fairchild's Black witnesses than in assessing the state's white witnesses' and 'even applied different and conflicting standards in discrediting the testimony of the various Black witnesses' (Johnson 1996, p. 288). What is especially striking here, however, is the role that the single confession played not only in determining whether Fairchild was guilty of the crimes in question, *but also in assessing all of the other testimony supporting his claim that his confession was coerced.* In particular, rather than using the additional evidence of police brutality, both in the Mason investigation and in contemporaneous cases, as support that Fairchild's testimony about his confession being coerced was credible, Judge Eisele '*first* determined that the confession was not coerced and *then* avoided reconsideration of this conclusion by discrediting all thirty of the Black witnesses' (Johnson 1996, p. 287–88, original emphases).[27]

Once again, we see the unshakeable and extraordinary power of confession evidence. Despite an overwhelming amount of testimony that is not only consistent with and corroborative of Fairchild's account, the judge *began* with the veracity of the confession and then relied on this as an epistemic lens through which all of the other evidence was filtered. For instance, instead of regarding consistency of reports among the Black witnesses as indicative of truth, Judge Eisele used this as evidence of a conspiracy. In describing one witness, John Walker, he writes: '[He is] somewhat of a salesman. He has a pleasant demeanor and manner of talking. But he will go beyond the truth. He and his "supporting" witnesses had a clear objective of aiding petitioner in this high-profile case.' Fairchild's confession is thus the starting point, and the excess of credibility it is afforded is wielded to undermine, discredit, and disregard all of the other supporting testimony. Indeed, Judge Eisele ultimately found that 'all witnesses questioned during the Mason murder investigation who alleged that they had been beaten in the same manner and by the same officers as Fairchild were simply lying' (Johnson 1996, p. 288).

Fairchild's confession was thus extracted via coercion—indeed, through brute physical force—and was then given a massive excess of credibility, so much so that it was used as a basis for both discounting 30 other supporting witnesses and for his ultimate execution. This is a paradigmatic example of what we earlier identified as agential testimonial injustice. But what we also see is the powerful role

[26] Johnson (1996, p. 284).

[27] 'The truth of this assertion is abundantly clear from the record, because the judge relegated his assessment of the *new* evidence and testimony to a document separate from and subsequent to the document in which he presented his findings regarding Fairchild's allegations that his confession was coerced' (Johnson 1996, pp. 287–88).

that race can play in exacerbating agential testimonial injustice and giving rise to countless other forms of harmful credibility misassessments. Among the many ways in which it is clear that racism was overtly at work here are the racial slurs that were peppered throughout the interrogations, the testimony from Black witnesses and white witnesses receiving radically different treatment, and Black witnesses being described in 'condescending and biased' language, such as being 'a large man who appears to be hot headed,' as having a 'poor and distorted memory,' or as being 'high strung, impressionable and possessed of a faulty memory' (Johnson 1996, pp. 289–90). Racism thus shaped and colored the way the proffered testimony was extracted, heard, and assessed throughout the entire process, beginning with Fairchild's arrest and ending with his execution.

Moreover, this case provides a striking illustration of the multi-directional model. Whereas (2), (3), and (4) of the one-directional model focus on how testimony with a particular content can interact with multiple social identities and bias or prejudice to give rise to a credibility deficit, we see how the dominant misassessment of credibility here is an excess afforded to Fairchild's confession, which, in turn, is used to at least partially justify the credibility deficits of the Black witnesses who corroborated his account. This is precisely why the model I am defending is *multi-directional*. It does not deny that biases and prejudices that target a speaker's social identity can, and often do, result in a deficit of credibility. What it adds to this picture is that sometimes these very same biases and prejudices target the same social identity and end up with a speaker being given a credibility excess, even an extraordinary one. Racist stereotypes of criminality about Black men,[28] for instance, can lead to the unjustified acceptance of a confession to a violent crime, while racist myths of dishonesty about Black men can give rise to the illegitimate discrediting of the testimony of supporting witnesses. What we have, then, is testimony with a particular content—a confession—being offered by a speaker with multiple relevant social identities in the context in question—a Black man—being give an unwarranted excess of credibility because of racism. This can then be exacerbated by other dimensions of the multi-directional model. For instance, Black defendants convicted of murder are 50% more likely to be innocent than other convicted murderers,[29] and an important factor that explains this disparity is the race of the victim. 'African Americans imprisoned for murder are more likely to be innocent if they were convicted of killing white victims. Only about 15% of murders by African Americans have white victims, but 31% of innocent African-American murder exonerees were convicted of killing white people' (Gross et al. 2017, p. 2). Thus, a Black man confessing to a crime with a white victim may be given an excess of credibility three times over—one that targets his social identity as a Black man viewed through the stereotype of

[28] See, for instance, Oliver (2003) and Smiley and Fakunle (2016).

[29] Gross et al. (2017).

criminality, one that inflates the evidential status of a confession, especially when given by someone who is already believed to be disposed to be violent, and one that focuses on the race of the victim. These credibility excesses are then used as tools to further promote the State's power, providing the foundation for a broad range of downstream credibility deficits.

3. Gender

An importantly different, though no less powerful, illustration of the multi-directional model can be seen in a widely discussed case featured in 'An Unbelievable Story of Rape'[30]—an article that won both the 2015 George Polk Award for Justice Reporting and the 2016 Pulitzer Prize for Explanatory Reporting[31] and was also turned into a Netflix series, *Unbelievable*.

The case begins with 18-year-old Marie[32] reporting to police that a man broke into her apartment in Lynnwood, Washington, bound, blindfolded, and gagged her, and then raped her.[33] One of the two detectives responding to the call, Sgt. Jeffrey Mason, advised Marie to go to the hospital for a sexual assault examination, and the medical report documented abrasions to her wrists and vagina. In the days that followed, however, family members and friends noticed that Marie wasn't behaving as they would have expected from a rape victim. At times she was crying in ways that 'didn't sound real' or 'sounded like a lot of drama' and at other times she exhibited 'no emotion,' was 'detached,' and avoided eye contact. Marie's previous foster mother, Shannon McQuery, and current foster mother, Peggy Cunningham, conferred and while they 'had not known Marie to be a liar,' they also realized that they 'weren't alone in wondering if Marie had made up' the rape complaint. Peggy decided to call Mason to question 'whether the "rape" had occurred' and to report that Marie 'had a past history of trying to get attention.' Based on this phone call, combined with an inconsistency in Marie's story—she had previously told detectives that she had called her ex-boyfriend after cutting the laces that were binding her, but described in her written statement calling him while being still tied up—Mason called Marie in for further questioning.

Marie was brought to a conference room and was almost immediately confronted by Detective Jerry Rittgarn, who told her that there were inconsistencies in her statements and reports from other witnesses. He told her that he believed she had fabricated the rape allegation, later writing in his report, 'Based on her answers and body language it was apparent that [Marie] was lying about the

30 https://www.themarshallproject.org/2015/12/16/an-unbelievable-story-of-rape.

31 https://www.themarshallproject.org/2016/04/18/the-marshall-project-wins-a-pulitzer-prize.

32 'Marie' is the victim's middle name.

33 Unless otherwise noted, all facts and quotes about the case of Marie in this section are from: https://www.themarshallproject.org/2015/12/16/an-unbelievable-story-of-rape.

rape.'[34] Indeed, '[t]he focus of the investigation became her credibility. And instead of interviewing Marie as a victim, they began interrogating her as a suspect.' Marie was threatened with jail time and withdrawal of housing assistance if she failed a polygraph. After asking whether there was *really* a rapist on the streets, Marie quietly responded 'no,' and, without reading Marie her *Miranda* rights, Mason and Rittgarn requested that she write out the truth about what happened, admitting that she had previously lied. In her new statement, she said that 'she dreamed that someone broke in and raped me.' When Rittgarn asked why she didn't admit that she made up the story, Marie 'crying, said she believed the rape really happened. She pounded the table and said she was "pretty positive."' When Rittgarn asked if she was pretty positive or actually positive, Marie responded that it's possible that she was in fact raped and she blacked it out. After further interrogation, Marie finally gave the detectives the statement they were seeking: 'I have had a lot of stressful things going on and I wanted to hang out with someone and no one was able to so I made up this story and didn't expect it to go as far as it did. . . .' The detectives were finally satisfied, writing that they 'were confident that [Marie] was now telling us the truth that she had not been raped.'

Marie's ordeal, however, did not end with the false recantation of her rape report. Not long after the interrogation, Marie received notice that she was being charged with false reporting, which was punishable by up to a year in jail. Being 'certain Marie had lied,' Sgt. Mason signed the criminal citation. Ultimately, Marie accepted a deal offered by the prosecution: if she received mental health counseling for her lying, agreed to supervised probation, stayed out of trouble, and paid $500 in court costs, the charges would be dropped.

Two and a half years later, Marie was notified by the same police department who had charged her with lying that her rapist, Marc O'Leary, had been caught in Colorado. During a search of O'Leary's house, police found photos of Marie, bound and gagged on a bed, with her learner's permit on her chest. O'Leary ultimately pleaded guilty to 28 counts of rape and associated felonies. In December of 2011, he was sentenced to 37.5 years in prison in Colorado and, in June of 2021, he was sentenced to 40 years for a rape in Kirkland, Washington and to 28.5 years for the rape of Marie.

The first point to notice is that, in addition to all of the obvious wrongs suffered, Marie was clearly the victim of agential testimonial injustice. Her recantation of her sexual assault was extracted through coercive interrogation techniques and was then afforded a massive excess of credibility. To see this, notice that at the outset of the second interview, Marie was aggressively interrogated by detectives who already believed her to be a liar. This is made clear by both internal and external reviews that were requested after O'Leary's arrest by Lynnwood Police

[34] https://www.themarshallproject.org/2015/12/16/an-unbelievable-story-of-rape.

Chief Steven Jensen regarding his department's handling of the investigation of Marie's assault. The internal review found that Sgt. Mason had been unduly influenced by Peggy questioning whether the rape had actually occurred, leading to the second interview of Marie being 'designed to elicit a confession of false reporting.' According to the external review, what happened to Marie was 'nothing short of the victim being coerced into admitting that she lied about the rape.' The threats of jail and the withdrawal of housing assistance were said to be 'coercive, cruel, and unbelievably unprofessional,' and the fact that Marie recanted wasn't surprising given the 'bullying' and 'hounding' she experienced. Moreover, the detectives 'elevated "minor inconsistencies,"' which are quite common among victims, 'into discrepancies, while ignoring strong evidence the crime had occurred.'

These reviews are unequivocal: Marie's recantation was extracted. She was 18 years old, had been violently assaulted while home alone in her apartment, and was being interrogated without counsel or support. All of these factors contributed to the unfair threats of jail time and possible homelessness closing her out of a reasonable decision-making space. In particular, the power of the threats swamped all of the other considerations in her deliberations, including the fact that she was actually raped, leaving her with only one path forward. Rather than focusing on the epistemic dimensions of her experience—such as features of her rapist that she remembers or details about the morning of her attack—a practical question is thrust on the table that overpowers everything else: are you willing to risk your freedom and your housing? Feeling cornered and desperate, and knowing that she is already branded a liar, Marie is coerced into giving the detectives what they so clearly wanted—a recantation.

The belief that Marie is a liar fuels the bullying and hounding of the detectives, giving rise to tunnel vision and an excess of credibility being afforded to the recantation. Recall from Chapter 2 that tunnel vision is a 'compendium of common heuristics and logical fallacies' (Martin 2002, p. 848) whereby 'investigators, prosecutors, judges, and defense lawyers alike...focus on a particular conclusion and then filter all evidence in a case through the lens provided by that conclusion. Through that filter, all information supporting the adopted conclusion is elevated in significance, viewed as consistent with the other evidence, and deemed relevant and probative. Evidence inconsistent with the chosen theory is easily overlooked or dismissed as irrelevant, incredible, or unreliable' (Findley and Scott 2006, p. 292). This is clearly at work in the case of Marie. There was compelling evidence that supported Marie's report that was ignored or dismissed—the rear sliding glass door to her apartment was found ajar, the wooden railing on her back porch was covered in dirt, except for a three-foot wide area that looked like it had been brushed off while someone climbed over it, the abrasions on Marie's wrists and vagina found during her medical exam, and so on. In contrast, a vague suspicion by Marie's former foster mom, and a minor inconsistency that could easily be the result of actual trauma, were massively elevated in evidential significance, providing a lens through which everything else was filtered for Detectives Mason and Rittgarn. Hesitation, lack of eye contact, and fidgeting were interpreted as evidence of dishonesty rather than as a natural response to being alone, cornered, bullied, and threatened. This gives rise to not only overlooking evidence that Marie was actually raped, but also to magnifying and elevating the status of evidence that may suggest otherwise. At best, the evidence justifies the detectives in suspending belief about the status of Marie's recantation until further investigation can be conducted. That the detectives were 'confident' in the truth of Marie's second report, and that Mason was 'certain' that Marie lied about being raped, makes clear that her recantation was given a massive unwarranted excess of credibility.

This conclusion is further supported by the fact that Marie was charged with making a false report of rape, an aggressive move that sends an unequivocal message, one that was picked up by local media outlets. One local newscast announced, 'A Western Washington woman has confessed that she cried wolf when it came to her rape she reported earlier this week' while another wrote 'Police: Lynnwood rape report was a hoax.' The same woman offers two different reports—one corroborated by physical evidence, the other supported by vague suspicions rooted in sexist tropes about the way rape victims ought to act, and the recantation receives uptake while the report of a violent sexual assault is dismissed. There is simply no epistemic story that can be told to justify this radical asymmetry.

What is particularly noteworthy for our purposes here is the contrast between the way Marie's recantation was regarded by her interrogators and how recantations in other areas of the criminal legal system are treated. Recall from Chapter 3 that recantations are widely regarded as unreliable and untrustworthy by courts, with the view of the New York Court of Appeals often cited by way of support: 'There is no form of proof so unreliable as recanting testimony. In the popular mind it is often regarded as of great importance. Those experienced in the administration of the criminal law know well its untrustworthy character' (*People v. Shilitano*, 112 N.E. 733, 736 (N.Y. 1916)). If the recantations of those who confessed to a crime or provided an eyewitness identification are almost universally dismissed as unreliable, then why, we might ask, was Marie's recantation given such an elevated epistemic status? Otherwise put, why are some recantations given a credibility deficit, while others are afforded an excess of credibility?

At least one answer to this question is that the direction of the credibility assessment often tracks biases and prejudices. For instance, when suspects or defendants are Black, and 'African Americans . . . are . . . stereotyped as less honest and more criminal than the majority' (Johnson 1996, p. 316), then credibility deficits and excesses often reflect these stereotypes. When a Black man confesses to a violent crime, or points the finger at a neighborhood associate, being apt to believe that Black men would be involved in criminal activity is likely to give rise to a massive elevation of the credibility of such statements. At the same time, these very same stereotypes are often a driving force behind the illegitimate rejection of recantations of confessions and eyewitness identifications: if Black men are taken to be more likely to be both dishonest and criminally engaged than others, then of course they are likely to be dishonest about their involvement in criminal activity.

When it comes to the sexist myths and stereotypes operative in the assessment of women's testimony about sexual assault, however, we see a reversal of the direction of these credibility assessments. Women are thought to commonly lie about being the victims of sexual violence,[35] and so their reports of assault are met with incredulity. This leads to credibility deficits regarding women reporting sexual assault. The flipside of this, then, is that these same myths and stereotypes lead to the recantations of these reports, such as Marie's, being given a shockingly elevated epistemic status. Contrary to *People v. Shilitano*, then, recantations *in general* are not regarded as unreliable in the criminal legal system but, rather, only those that accord with already existing racist and sexist stereotypes are.

Racist and sexist myths and stereotypes can then interact with other biases, heuristics, and aims that impact the way evidence is viewed and weighed. Confirmation bias, for instance, involves the 'seeking or interpreting of evidence in ways that are partial to existing beliefs, expectations, or a hypothesis in hand' (Nickerson 1998, p. 175). When a Black man flees from police, for instance, this is viewed through the lens of an already existing belief in his criminality, and thus this is interpreted as powerful evidence of his guilt rather than as a rational response for an innocent person of color to have in the face of racially targeted harassment and violence. Similarly, when women are already thought to be liars when it comes to reporting sexual violence, lack of eye contact, inconsistencies in memory, and unusual behavior is seen as evidence of deception rather than as an expected response to what is often life-altering trauma.[36]

While Marie's case is widely discussed because of the award-winning article and Netflix series about it, she is certainly not alone in being a rape victim who then also becomes a victim of agential testimonial injustice. On her 16th birthday in 1997, a man followed Fancy Figueroa home from school, broke into her Queens home, and violently raped her.[37] A medical exam confirmed that she was two weeks pregnant by her then boyfriend, which led police detectives to believe that Figueroa was lying about the rape to explain the pregnancy.[38] Eventually, Figueroa was pressured to write a note saying she made up the account of the

[35] See, for instance, Page (2008) and Tuerkheimer (2017). Jordan (2004) discusses how police are disposed to view the behavior of rape victims through a narrow lens that emphasizes suspicion and disbelief.

[36] Tunnel vision, discussed earlier and in Chapter 2, can also be operative here.

[37] https://www.law.umich.edu/special/exoneration/Pages/casedetail.aspx?caseid=4474.

[38] https://www.law.umich.edu/special/exoneration/Pages/casedetail.aspx?caseid=4474.

rape. She was then prosecuted for filing a false report and sentenced to pick up trash for three days.[39] In 2004, evidence taken from Figueroa during her medical exam matched Vincent Elias, who not only pled guilty, but was already serving 15 years for raping two other teens.[40]

Figueroa's recantation was extracted through deceptive and manipulative tactics. Despite the fact that she insisted that she was raped, detectives doubted her from the outset: 'They told me if I wrote down on a piece of paper that I was lying, they would help me look for this guy.'[41] Instead, her written statement was used to charge her with filing a false report, which she was pressured to plead guilty to in exchange for the case being dismissed and three days of community service. While Figueroa 'forgives the two detectives who pressured her to recant,' she also says, 'There was a point where I was just so upset with them . . . I felt they hurt me more than the rapist hurt me. He just came and left, but for six years nobody believed me.'[42]

Crucially, however, Figueroa *was* believed, but only when she recanted. Sexist stereotypes combined with confirmation bias appear to be at work here, as the detectives had no intention of investigating her rape or looking for the man who attacked her because they didn't believe she was the victim of a violent assault in the first place. Saying that they would help her 'look for this guy' was clearly a deceptive tactic, which was used in tandem with Figueroa's vulnerable position to manipulate her into saying what they believed all along—that she was a liar. Moreover, rather than recognizing that two conflicting statements by the same person requires some rational reason to prefer one over the other, the detectives simply wholeheartedly embraced the truth of the recantation, charging Figueroa with filing a false report and then further eliciting a guilty plea from her. Her recantation was thus not only extracted from her through lies and manipulation, it was then given a massively elevated epistemic status. In this way, it is a paradigmatic instance of agential testimonial injustice.

4. Other Forms of Extraction: Recantations by Victims in Domestic Violence Cases

It is important to note that recantations are not only extracted by investigators, prosecutors, or other officers of the court. Consider, for instance, recantations by victims in domestic violence cases, which are so prevalent that they are

[39] https://www.law.umich.edu/special/exoneration/Pages/casedetail.aspx?caseid=4474.

[40] For other cases of this sort, see https://www.nytimes.com/2017/11/24/opinion/sunday/sexual-assault-victims-lying.html and https://archive.org/details/JohnL.QuinlanCryRape_OneWoman_sHarrowingQuestforJustice_byBillLueders.

[41] https://www.law.umich.edu/special/exoneration/Pages/casedetail.aspx?caseid=4474.

[42] https://www.law.umich.edu/special/exoneration/Pages/casedetail.aspx?caseid=4474.

'considered an epidemic' (Rutledge 2009, p. 149). Indeed, '[v]ictims of domestic violence are more prone than other crime victims to recant or refuse to cooperate after initially providing information to the police.... [E]vidence suggests that 80 to 85 percent of battered women will recant at some point' (Lininger 2005, p. 768).[43] There are a number of factors at work here, including financial dependence on the perpetrator,[44] concern that the state will remove children from a household that has experienced domestic violence,[45] and the victim's expectation of an inadequate response by the criminal legal system.[46] Crucially, however, victims of domestic violence often recant because of coercive, manipulative, and deceptive tactics employed by the very perpetrators of their abuse.[47]

Threats of retaliation from perpetrators,[48] for instance, are a significant factor in recantations of domestic violence, with the Supreme Court noting that '[t]his particular type of crime is notoriously susceptible to intimidation or coercion of the victim to ensure she does not testify at trial' (*Davis v. Washington*, 126 S.Ct. 2266, 165 L Ed.2d 224, 2006). In a random sample of criminal behavior reported by women in 100 restraining order files, one of the four central motivations behind men's violence and abuse is 'retaliation or coercion against women's pursuit of court or police remedies' (Ptacek 1999, p. 79). Women repeatedly report that their abusers were physically violent with them for calling the police and threatened to kill them if they cooperate with officers of the court, thereby 'seeking *vengeance against women for being held accountable to the law*' (Ptacek 1999, p. 85, original emphasis). When such physical harm and threats of murder by perpetrators lead to victims recanting their reports of domestic violence, their testimony has been extracted in a way that is clearly coercive. Drawing on our notion of coercion from Chapter 4, it is surely unfair to threaten someone with violence for pursuing justice from a prior incident of violence, and a threat of this

[43] See also De Sanctis: '[V]ictims of domestic violence are uncooperative in approximately eighty to ninety percent of cases... the victim will usually recant her prior statements...' (1996, pp. 367–68); Rutledge: 'False statements in domestic violence cases are a significant problem... with an estimated 40 to 90 percent of domestic violence victims recanting' (2009, p. 149); and Beloof and Shapiro: 'Non-cooperation by recantation or failure to appear at trial is an epidemic in domestic violence cases. Persons qualified to give expert testimony at trial on domestic violence, including psychologists, counselors, police detectives, directors of battered women's shelters, and victim advocates, consistently testify that, in their experience, it is commonplace for domestic violence victims to recant or minimize initial reports of abuse. The head of the Family Violence Division of the Los Angeles District Attorney's Office estimates that ninety percent of domestic violence victims recant. A psychologist specializing in the treatment of battered women has estimated the non-cooperation rate to be eighty percent. Similarly, one judge reports that in as many as eighty percent of domestic violence prosecutions the victim refuses to cooperate at trial.... Thus, recantation is the norm rather than the exception, in domestic violence cases. This is hardly surprising. Batterers put hydraulic pressures on domestic violence victims to recant, drop the case, or fail to appear at trial' (2002, pp. 3–4).

[44] See Ellison (2002), Lininger (2005), Camacho and Alarid (2008), and Bonomi et al. (2011).

[45] Lininger (2005). [46] Bonomi et al. (2011).

[47] Rutledge discusses three categories of reasons for recantations in domestic violence cases: '(1) psychological trauma, (2) self-motivated objectives, and (3) external pressure or coercion' (2009, p. 165).

[48] See Ellison (2002), Lininger (2005), Meier (2006), and Bonomi et al. (2011).

sort closes a victim out of a reasonable decision-making space. By putting an option on the table, such as the loss of one's life, that swamps all other relevant considerations, victims are left with only one viable path forward and that is to recant the report of abuse. Such a recantation does not involve the exercise of epistemic agency, as the victim's ability to be properly responsive to reasons has been subverted through the threat's screening off all of the other factors in her decision space.

While threats of retaliation lead to recantations that have been coerced, perpetrators also often use subtler forms of testimonial extraction. In a study of the decision-making process that leads to domestic violence victims recanting, Bonomi et al. found that two central factors associated with a victim's intention to ultimately recant are the perpetrator's minimization of the abuse event and the perpetrator's appeals to the sympathy of the victim.[49] Minimization of the abuse event involves 'resisting responsibility (V: "They think my cheek is broken; P: I'm really sorry, but I didn't even do anything"); denying the credibility of the victim's story ("I didn't push you like you think I pushed you"); and reminding the victim that she was to blame for the violence' (2011, p. 1057). This is a tactic that is clearly manipulative and deceptive. The perpetrators are attempting to influence their victims through lying—'I didn't do anything'—and gaslighting[50] them—'I didn't push you like you think I pushed you'—so as to achieve the desired end of extracting a recantation. In this way, perpetrators are not engaging in the giving and taking of reasons, as would happen if rational persuasion were operative, but instead they circumvent or bypass the epistemic agency of victims.

While minimization is effective in extracting recantations, the most significant tactic, and the one that was found 'consistently across all couples,' was the perpetrator's appeals to the victim's sympathy. This involved descriptions of his suffering from mental and physical problems, jail conditions that are intolerable, and how unbearable life is without her (Bonomi et al. 2011, p. 1054). In one case, a perpetrator 'screamed: "You're making me go crazy. They're telling me they're gonna' press charges then, damn. You wanna' see a motherfucker suicidal?"' (Bonomi et al. 2011, p. 1057). In another, a perpetrator 'began a call distraught, telling the victim "Oh my god, I love you. I haven't been able to call you." He then immediately instructed the victim to recant: "I'm goin' to the Supreme Court...you gotta' be there...you gotta' sit up front and tell them that what you wrote in the (police) report was a lie." The victim responded: "Uh huh, I will." He continued the sympathy appeal with "Oh my god, let me talk to my son...hi, baby...I don't wanna' be here"' (Bonomi et al. 2011, p. 1057). These sympathy

[49] Bonomi et al. (2011) found that there were three factors associated with a victim's intention to ultimately recant, with the third being the couple's expressed need to keep their relationship and family intact (p. 1057). I will focus only on the first two, however, since these are most directly related to the issue of recantations being extracted in domestic violence cases.

[50] For a discussion of gaslighting, see Abramson (2014 and forthcoming).

appeals are a 'sophisticated [form of] emotional manipulation' to achieve the perpetrator's desired end of 'getting out of jail' (Bonomi et al. 2011, p. 1060).[51] By targeting the victim's emotional responsiveness, the perpetrator is bypassing her rational faculties—those that are sensitive to truth and reasons[52]—and is instead extracting testimony that is influenced by her feelings of sympathy, guilt, and regret.[53]

Fascinatingly, Bonomi et al. draw a direct connection between the process whereby the victim ultimately recants and the erosion of her agency. They describe how in the early stages of the conversations, victims '"exercised agency" by "telling the truth about what happened" and even calling the perpetrator an "abuser"' (2011, p. 1057). While Bonomi et al. do not themselves specify this, it is interesting for our purposes that this clearly involves agency that is distinctively epistemic. The victims are initially offering testimony that is sensitive to the evidence provided by how the actual events of their abuse unfolded. This agency, however, is described by the authors of the study as 'fleeting,' with the version of the victim's story that is responsive to reasons 'unraveling' as the perpetrator engages in minimization and the eliciting of sympathy (2011, p. 1057). This is a powerful illustration of the extraction dimension of agential testimonial injustice. Coercive, manipulative, and deceptive tactics to bring about testimony bypass or

[51] Of course, there are many different ways in which victims of domestic violence are subject to coercion and manipulation by their abusers. As Donna Wills says, 'Batterers are "master manipulators." They will do anything to convince their victims to get the prosecution to drop the charges. They call from jail threatening retaliation. They cajole their victim with promises of reform. They remind her that they may lose their jobs and, hence, the family income. They send love letters, pledging future bliss and happiness. They have their family members turn off the victim's electricity and threaten to kick the victim and her children out into the street. They pay for the victim to leave town so that she will not be subpoenaed. They use community property to pay for an expensive lawyer to try to convince the jury that the whole thing was the victim's fault and that she attacked him. They prey on the victim's personal weaknesses, especially drug and alcohol abuse, physical and mental disabilities, and her love for their children. They negotiate financial and property incentives that cause acute memories of terror and pain to fade dramatically' (1997, pp. 179–80).

[52] I should note that I am not claiming that *all* appeals to sympathy and emotion bypass an agent's rational capacities, as emotion and reason can sometimes be closely intertwined. For instance, an emotional appeal may intend to engage a person's rational capacities by making salient certain reasons to her. (I am grateful to an anonymous reviewer for pressing this point.) In the cases discussed above, however, the appeals to sympathy of abusers are clearly being used in manipulative ways that circumvent the rational agency of their victims.

[53] There may also be multiple factors at work in a victim of domestic violence recanting. Kate Manne, for instance, discusses Lisa Henning's recantation of violent abuse inflicted on her by her then-husband, Andrew Puzder, who was tapped in 2016 to be President Donald Trump's pick for labor secretary: 'This assertion and recanting: any given instance could have any number of explanations, including the original testimony having in fact been false. But put these and other such cases together and one begins to suspect a pattern. Part of male dominance, especially on the part of the most privileged and powerful, seems to be seizing control of the narrative—and with it, controlling her, enforcing her concurrence. It is not exactly deference: rather, it closely resembles the moral aim of gaslighting....' (Manne 2017, p. 11). In the case of Henning, this male dominance includes not only the direct influence of her ex-husband—she reported in a 1990 appearance on *The Oprah Winfrey* show that he had 'vowed revenge,' saying 'I will see you in the gutter. This will never be over. You will pay for this' (Manne 2017, p. 9)—but also the broader social and political pressure imposed by the possibility of Puzder being a part of the Trump Administration.

undermine epistemic agency. Thus, as victims move from rational responsiveness to being under the sway or influence of their abusers, their epistemic agency erodes until the desired end of the recantation is fully extracted.

Once the recantation is extracted from victims of domestic violence, there are a number of systemic ways in which it is then afforded an excess of credibility, thereby resulting in victims of domestic violence also being victims of agential testimonial injustice. For instance, the Supreme Court ruled in *Crawford v. Washington* (124 S. Ct. 1354 (2004)) that testimonial hearsay violates the Confrontation Clause of the Sixth Amendment, according to which '[i]n all criminal prosecutions, the accused shall enjoy the right... to be confronted with the witnesses against him' (Sixth Amendment, United States Constitution). In particular, *Crawford* holds that 'testimonial' out-of-court statements are inadmissible unless the witness is presently available for cross-examination or was once available for cross-examination. Prior to this decision, many state legislatures had special hearsay exceptions for domestic violence cases and 'courts had liberally admitted hearsay statements by domestic violence victims under traditional hearsay exceptions' precisely because recantations are an epidemic in such cases (Lininger 2005, p. 751). The impact of *Crawford* on the prosecution of domestic violence cases, however, was massive: '[W]ithin days—even hours—of the *Crawford* decision, prosecutors were dismissing or losing hundreds of domestic violence cases that would have presented little difficulty in the past' (Lininger 2005, p. 749).

There is no doubt that this decision affords a deficit of credibility to the original testimony of domestic violence victims. If victims are unavailable or unwilling to testify at trial, *Crawford* requires that judges exclude their pretrial statements, ones that are often highly reliable and given shortly after the abuse occurred. Indeed, in *Ohio v. Roberts* (448 U.S. 56 (1980)), the Supreme Court held that an out-of-court statement made by a declarant who is unavailable to testify in court is still admissible if there are indications of reliability or if the circumstances under which the statement was offered indicate that the statement is trustworthy. In *Crawford*, however, Justice Scalia—writing for the majority—was highly critical of *Roberts*, shifting the focus away from questions of the reliability of the original testimony to the rights of the accused.[54] The sweeping rejection of pretrial statements in cases where victims are unavailable for cross-examination found in *Crawford*, then, results in a systemic deficit of credibility given to the original testimony of victims.

[54] 'In delivering the opinion of the Court, Justice Scalia was highly critical of *Roberts* and its focus on reliability for being not only lenient and malleable, but also misguided.... Thus, Justice Scalia's criticism of *Roberts* chipped away at the increased prosecutorial power that *Roberts* allowed for and instead, through *Crawford*, he empowered the accused with the opportunity he believed rightfully belongs to defendants per the Sixth Amendment' (Rouhanian 2017, pp. 7–8).

The flipside of this—one that is far too often ignored—is that the decision in *Crawford* also gives a massive excess of credibility to the recantations or silence of victims of domestic violence. Knowing full well that there is an epidemic of recantations and later silence in such cases, and that these victims are often coerced or manipulated into recanting or not testifying, the Supreme Court nonetheless ruled that later actions completely swamp earlier reports. Otherwise put, the terms for prosecution in domestic violence cases in the criminal legal system are being determined by victim recantations and silence, despite the fact that they are known to often be the result of threats and tactics employed by the very abusers who are being prosecuted. Indeed,

> during the summer of 2004, half of the domestic violence cases set for trial in Dallas County, Texas, were dismissed because of evidentiary problems under *Crawford*. In a survey of over 60 prosecutors' offices in California, Oregon, and Washington, 63 percent of respondents reported the *Crawford* decision has significantly impeded prosecutions of domestic violence. Seventy-six percent indicated that after *Crawford*, their offices are more likely to drop domestic violence charges when the victims recant or refuse to cooperate. Alarmingly, 65 percent of respondents reported that victims of domestic violence are less safe in their jurisdictions than during the era preceding the *Crawford* decision.
>
> (Lininger 2005, pp. 749–50)

When threats of violence and manipulative appeals to sympathy from abusers extract recantations from victims that are widely known to be false and unreliable in domestic violence cases, the criminal legal system is surely giving such testimony an excess of credibility when it systematically leads to the failure to prosecute.

Against this background, aggressively prosecuting domestic violence victims for perjury can also reflect an excess of credibility afforded to recantations. For instance, Njeri M. Rutledge writes, 'Allowing victims to use and manipulate the system for their own ends is unacceptable.... One way to encourage self-motivated victims to testify truthfully is to increase the potential costs. If prosecution of perjury becomes a real possibility for false complainants and some domestic violence victims, perjury should be deterred' (2009, p. 187).[55] Given that it is often difficult to determine whether recantations have been extracted, aggressive perjury prosecutions will surely end up punishing domestic violence victims for offering testimony that has been coerced or manipulated by their abusers. In this way, recantations are afforded an unwarranted elevated status within the criminal legal system, as statements that result, for instance, from

[55] Similarly, Aya Gruber argues that '[t]he criminal law should account for the victim, not only as a wronged actor, but also as a wrongful actor where appropriate' (2003, p. 651).

threats of bodily harm should not be regarded as reflecting the actual states of domestic violence victims. Consider, for instance, the trial court's treatment of a domestic violence victim in *Ohio v. Hancock* (No. C-030459, 2004 WL 596103 (Ohio Ct. App. Mar. 26, 2004)):

THE COURT: You willing to go to prison for—

[WITNESS]: No, I am not.

THE COURT: —for five years for perjury?

[WITNESS]: No.

THE COURT: Is that what—so what is the story going to be then? What is it?

[WITNESS]: That we were arguing.

THE COURT: Well, you were arguing—you said initially after it happened that he actually hit you twice. Now you're telling us that it is an accident. So, either he goes or you go, what is it going to be. You got kids?[56]

The trial court's weaponization of perjury charges fails to recognize the extracted nature of many recantations in domestic violence cases. By giving the victim two options—either send your abuser to prison or go to prison yourself—the court is treating the recantation as voluntary or otherwise reflective of the victim's agency. But recantations often result from the consequences of standing behind the truth of the original report of abuse being too great, including the loss of home, job, children, and even life itself. Perjury charges thus treat recantations as true, and the original testimony as thereby false, which afford them a massively elevated status when viewed within the broader context of the relationship between domestic violence victims and their abusers.

In addition, courtroom responses often reinforce the swamping effect that recantations have in domestic violence cases. For instance, James Ptacek (1999) extensively discusses how judges empower men who batter women by neglecting women's fears, having a condescending or harsh demeanor in the courtroom, minimizing, denying, and blaming the victim, engaging in intimidation in the courtroom, colluding with violent men, and furthering women's isolation. Such judicial responses, ranging from apathy to outright contempt,[57] often reflect negative stereotypes of domestic violence victims that are shared by other court professionals, including prosecutors and public defenders.[58] In a study involving survey and interview data collected in a large midwestern urban area from central courtroom officials, Hartman and Belknap found that when domestic violence victims pursued cases against their abusers, 'they were viewed as vindictive, crazy, or falsely charging domestic violence to meet their own selfish needs.... Indeed, many public defenders referred to this behavior as a "weekend divorce,"' where a

[56] Quoted in Rutledge (2009, p. 162).

[57] See Rutledge (2009, pp. 160–63).

[58] Hartman and Belknap (2003).

'woman gets her boyfriend or husband arrested for [domestic violence] so that she can be with her new boyfriend for the weekend' (2003, pp. 363–64). When the central figures in the courtroom are harboring attitudes and beliefs of this sort about victims of domestic violence, it is not surprising that the credibility of reports of abuse is deflated while that of recantations is inflated. More precisely, if women are perceived to be falsely reporting abuse for their own desire for a 'weekend divorce,' then of course their recantations—even those extracted through threats of violence—are going to be viewed as trustworthy. Given what is known about the prevalence of recantations in domestic violence cases, combined with the tactics abusers widely use to extract them, these responses reflect a massive excess of credibility afforded to recantations.

5. Conclusion

According to the multi-directional model, then, credibility assessments wrong testifiers in a multitude of directions and a variety of ways, all of which can be magnified by other factors at both the intrapersonal and interpersonal levels, such as myths and prejudices that target social identities, other biases, and the content of the testimony in question. The epistemic status of testimony is inflated when suspects confess to a crime and when eyewitnesses identify a suspect but deflated when they recant. Conversely, the credibility of statements of victims of sexual violence is discounted when they report being sexually assaulted, but elevated when they recant. These excesses and deficits are magnified, redirected, or even turned on their heads as social identities are added. The excess of credibility afforded to a confession or an eyewitness identification, for instance, can be even greater when the confessor or suspect is Black, and greater still when the victim is white. The discounting of the testimony of victims of sexual violence can be even greater when the victim is a Black woman but can be entirely redirected into a massive excess of credibility when the victim is white and the suspect is a Black man. Moreover, when deeply entrenched racist and sexist myths and prejudices are operative in the assessments of credibility, then conditions are ideal for confirmation bias and tunnel vision to be operative. What we have, then, is not a linear regression of deficits leading to an ever-increasing discounting of credibility, but a multi-directional attack that twists and turns and, in so doing, maximizes the epistemic wrongs perpetrated within the criminal legal system, especially against the most vulnerable suspects, defendants, witnesses, and victims.

6
Admissions of Guilt and Expressions of Remorse: Sentencing and Parole Hearings

This book began with an examination of how false confessions are a paradigmatic case of agential testimonial injustice—extracted through processes that are manipulative, deceptive, and coercive and then given a massively elevated evidential status, leading not only to wrongful convictions, but even to the execution of innocent people. I now want to close by turning to how this wrong persists until the final stages of the processes in the criminal legal system. In particular, I will argue that admissions of guilt and expressions of remorse are being extracted at sentencing hearings and in front of paroles boards in the United States, especially from those who are wrongfully convicted, and are then afforded an excess of credibility. This gives rise not only to acts of agential testimonial injustice being systematically perpetrated against defendants and those who are incarcerated, but also to a direct attack on their epistemic and moral agency and, ultimately, on their very status as persons.

1. Sentencing Hearings

Much of this book has focused on false testimony being extracted from suspects and defendants in the criminal legal system and then being weaponized against them to ground convictions and punishment. While such assertions have been shown to play a massively oversized evidential role, it is important to note that defendants otherwise rarely have the opportunity to use their own voices during the legal process. Alexandra Natapoff expresses this point powerfully when she writes, 'The United States's criminal justice system is shaped by a fundamental absence: Criminal defendants rarely speak' (Natapoff 2005, p. 1449). This is particularly significant in the present context. When testimony is extracted against a general background of silence and silencing,[1] defendants end up being reduced to nothing more than puppets of the State. Compare two systems, one where a defendant's testimony is extracted on an occasion, but where there are many other opportunities in the criminal legal process for him to speak and to exercise his

[1] See Natapoff (2005).

Criminal Testimonial Injustice. Jennifer Lackey, Oxford University Press. © Jennifer Lackey 2023.
DOI: 10.1093/oso/9780192864109.003.0007

epistemic agency, and another where a defendant uses his own voice only rarely and when he does so, his testimony is extracted by authorities. Unlike in the former case, any meaningful sense of epistemic agency, or substantive membership in an epistemic community, has been entirely stripped away from the defendant in the latter case. And yet this extraction of testimony coupled with systematic silencing is the stark reality for countless defendants in the United States criminal legal system.

It is against this background that we turn to an area in the criminal legal system where defendants have a seemingly robust role to play in their own destinies: sentencing hearings. The 'right of allocution,' which permits a criminal defendant to speak at his own sentencing hearing prior to the sentencing itself, is detailed in Rule 32 of the Federal Rules of Criminal Procedure: '[B]efore imposing sentence, the court must... address the defendant personally in order to permit the defendant to speak or present any information to mitigate the sentence' (32(i)(4)(A)(ii)). The importance of this right is clear: 'In a system where so few people go to trial, let alone testify, sentencing is often the only opportunity for defendants to speak during the legal process in a way that is even nominally unconstrained' (Burger-Caplan 2017, p. 41). As presented in the Federal Rules of Criminal Procedure, the central function or rationale of allocution is mitigation. Defendants are allowed to personally address the court and present information that might lessen their sentence prior to it being imposed. There may, however, be other, related purposes of allocution as well. In *United States v. Li*, for instance, the right of allocution is said to allow 'a defendant... [an] opportunity to plead for mercy....' (115 F.3d 125, 133 (2d Cir. 1997)), quoting *United States v. Barnes*, 948 F.2d 325, 328 (7th Cir. 1991). To the extent that pleading for mercy is distinct from the presentation of mitigating information, this is an additional function of allocution. A further purpose of allocution is the individualization or humanization of the defendant: 'The sentencing hearing, and the defendant's allocution in particular, is an opportunity for the court to learn details about the person to be sentenced. The court uses these nuances to impose a just sentence that is appropriate to the particular defendant' (Thomas 2007, p. 2644).[2]

Regardless of whether allocution's rationale is mitigation, mercy, or humanization, the actual innocence of a defendant ought to be relevant. Mitigating reasons, for instance, are those that show that the defendant should be viewed as less responsible for his acts or that the acts themselves should be seen as less severe.[3] A story of innocence should thus be understood as an extreme version of mitigation insofar as lack of guilt warrants neither responsibility nor punishment.[4] Moreover, when one has the power to punish or harm another, mercy involves showing that person compassion or forgiveness. If a defendant is actually innocent and yet has been wrongfully found to be guilty, then the court has a final

[2] See also Chan (2009). [3] Thomas (2007, p. 2655). [4] See Thomas (2007, p. 2661).

opportunity to hear that mercy may be called for before sentencing. And certainly individualization and humanization involve listening to a defendant's particular story of innocence. In *Williams v. New York* (1949), for instance, it is noted that '[h]ighly relevant—if not essential—to [a judge's] selection of an appropriate sentence is the possession of the fullest information possible concerning the defendant's life and characteristics' (337 U.S. 241, 246). That the innocent defendant is in fact innocent seems to be a feature about his life and characteristics that is relevant to his sentencing. Yet, this is not in any way the reality in the current criminal legal system. As Kimberly A. Thomas says, '[c]ourts do not want to hear allocution stories of innocence. Most judges assume, often consistent with the evidence they have heard, that the person before them actually has committed the offense and any innocence tale is fiction' (2007, p. 2661). Similarly, Mary Margaret Giannini writes, '[c]ourts appear willing to hear from remorseful and apologetic defendants, but are quick to cut off defendants who use their allocution right to reargue their case; to challenge the court, judicial system, or government; or to continue to protest their innocence' (2008, pp. 463–64).

From the perspective of epistemic agency and matters of testimonial justice, the mere fact that courts silence innocent defendants and their allocution stories of innocence is problematic by itself. Consider, for instance, the perspective of an innocent defendant who has just been wrongfully convicted of murder. The only point at which he has spoken in the process may have been in the interrogation room when a confession was extracted. After that, he may have been found guilty at trial because of the massive weight afforded to his false confession or pled guilty because he felt trapped by the manufactured evidence against him. In all of the proceedings since the confession or the guilty plea, he has been silent—spoken for and about—but never heard from by the court through his own, in-real-time voice. He finally arrives at the sentencing hearing and is aware that this is his final opportunity to make a case to the court for justice and mercy. And now he is told that no one wants to hear that he is actually innocent. As Natapoff says, '[s]entencing is the last stage of silencing: Between hostile judges, instrumentalist lawyers, and the threat of heightened punishment, the defendant's final day in court is one in which he will be told in numerous ways to be quiet.... Since this day will also often be his last day of freedom, for millions of defendants the silencing of the courtroom is the dress rehearsal for the silencing of incarceration' (2005, p. 1469). The defendant is thus told to swallow the truth, to silence his cries of innocence, and to bury the facts that would warrant no sentence at all. This, by itself, is an assault on his epistemic agency, as he is being prevented from having his testimony be appropriately guided by reasons. What is reasonable in a truth-directed sense, for instance, is that he make the case for receiving no punishment at all, as he is in fact not guilty of the crime in question. Being forced to leave this out of his allocution is to unwarrantedly curtail both his epistemic agency and his testimony.

But the violation doesn't stop here. In addition to being silenced about his actual innocence, the defendant is then essentially provided with a script of what he should say:

> [J]udges...have archetypes of ideal allocutions in mind. They want the allocution to express 'genuine remorse,' 'sincerity,' 'realistic and concrete plans for the future,' 'apology to the victims,' and an 'understanding of the seriousness of the offense.' They do not want to hear about 'how the defendant was the victim of circumstances,' how he or she has found religion, promises to never 'commit another crime,' or statements that the defendant cannot 'change the past.' With such clear goals for what should and should not be said in an allocution, continuously reinforced as judges gain more experience with allocutions and sentencing, it stands to reason that the further a defendant ventures from these archetypes, the angrier and less sympathetic that judge is likely to become.
>
> (Burger-Caplan 2017, p. 55)

Even if the defendant is in fact innocent and was the victim of unjust circumstances of a coercive interrogation or plea-bargaining process, the court does not want to hear this. Instead, the defendant should admit guilt, express remorse, be sincere, apologize to the victim and the community, and display an understanding of the seriousness of the crime. So, the innocent defendant is not only told to swallow the truth and eat his cries of innocence, he is also handed a script of what he should say to the court. More perversely, he is told, impossibly, to be both 'sincere' and yet to express life-shattering and identity-destroying falsehoods. He should somehow feign remorse for a crime he didn't commit—one that is often for him unimaginable to have committed—and to utter words that are in the shape of an apology but have no authenticity, as he cannot be truly sorry for doing something that he simply didn't do. This is an attack on both epistemic and moral agency, for he is being told to follow a script that has no grounding in truth and to repair fractured relationships in the moral community that he didn't disrupt in the first place.[5]

The assault on agency continues. He is then threatened with harsher punishment for failing to follow the script.[6] Defendants who maintain their innocence at sentencing hearings 'risk and receive harsher sentences because of their perceived failure to accept responsibility, lack of candor with the court, or failure to

[5] William Peeples, a student in the Northwestern Prison Education Program, powerfully describes the pain of following a script at his sentencing hearing for a crime he didn't commit: '[T]o stand before that judge and "perform" as this repentant "would be rapist" truly made me sick! My public defender literally coached me on how to stand, how to appear, what to say, and how to say it! I was terrified of doing 30 years. I wanted to be free, I missed my family, and the system played on that, coercing me to forever "brand" myself as someone I could never be, would never be' (personal correspondence).

[6] See Ward (2006) for a discussion of how both silence and professions of innocence are interpreted as a lack of remorse and aggravate the defendant's sentence.

acknowledge the validity of the fact-finder's decision' (Thomas 2007, p. 2661). In *United States v. Burgos-Andújar*, for instance, the defendant, who was a legislator in the Puerto Rican Senate, was found guilty of criminal trespass in United States naval territory. When she exercised her right to allocute, she maintained her innocence and challenged both the court's authority and the evidence it relied upon in her guilty conviction.[7] 'As a result of the defendant's allocution, the judge raised her sentence from that which the court had originally contemplated' (Giannini 2008, pp. 463–64). On appeal, the reviewing court supported this decision:

> Unfortunately for appellant, her statement did not have the intended effect of lowering her sentence. Rather, the judge increased her sentence. There are several reasons why the judge may have done this, all permissible within his discretion in sentencing. First, appellant essentially declared herself innocent of crime and thus was refusing to acknowledge the impact of her illegal action.... Her [statement] certainly suggest[s] a lack of remorse, an attempt to avoid responsibility for her actions, and even a likelihood of repeating her illegal actions. Any of these reasons may have legitimately led the sentencing judge to increase appellant's sentence. (275 F.3d 23, 30 (1st Cir. 2001)

What we see here is not only the pressure to silence claims of innocence, the imposing of a script, and the threat of a harsher punishment for failure to abide by it—we see the court following through on the threat. Moreover, this is not in any way unique or anomalous.[8] Indeed, harsher sentences are handed out not only for claims of innocence, but also for simply failing to follow the court's script to the judge's satisfaction. In an interview with a defendant who 'chose to incorporate speech into his allocution that went beyond areas typically thought of as acceptable,' Burger-Caplan notes that the 'gamble did not pay off':

> So being that I was arrogant, being that I challenged [the judge], being that I told him that this whole thing was like an illusion, okay, that this happened, dah, dah, dah, dah.... [S]o he actually says it... that he increased [the sentence] because of my arrogance, because he felt that I wasn't taking responsibility.

As Burger-Caplan says, 'because his expression did not comport with the judge's expectation or desires for the allocution, his sentence was increased' (2017, pp. 53–54). More generally, Weisman notes that in his observation of court conduct, '[t]here is... some evidence... of moral economism in which the more serious the

[7] Giannini (2008, pp. 463–64).

[8] 'If [the defendant] does speak outside the expected script of acquiescence and remorse, he will be punished more severely' (Natapoff 2005, p. 1469).

offense, the more dramatic must be the offender's suffering in order for it to be validated' (1999, p. 127). Thus, defendants are told not only what not to say, but also what to say and how to say it, and failure to comply will literally result in more time behind bars.

(Natapoff 2005) describes another case where the allocution of one of her clients deviated from the court's desires and expectations and resulted in severe consequences. Butch, who was charged with assaulting, resisting, or impeding a military police officer stationed at the entrance of a military base, was sorry for his role in the incident, but also 'had been insulted, pepper-sprayed, and, in his view, . . . had acted in a restrained way' (Natapoff 2005, p. 1468). In addressing the court, Butch said, 'I just want to say that I apologize for everything that happened . . . I've been trying to straighten my life out and that incident happened. I mean, it wasn't partially all my fault.' At this point in Butch's allocution, 'the judge's brow furrowed.' Butch continued, 'I mean, I know we can't get into it because I pled guilty,' but he then proceeded to provide his understanding of the facts, 'which differed significantly from that of the officer's.' He concluded by saying, 'It's just that incident occurred and I wish it never would have occurred. I apologize to the court. That's all I have to say' (Natapoff 2005, p. 1468). At this point, '[t]hunderclouds . . . were rolling over the judge's face' as he stated, 'I just don't hear a lot of remorse . . . and I don't hear in any expression he has made . . . any acceptance of responsibility for the incident . . . I don't hear that' (Natapoff 2005, p. 1468). The judge sentenced Butch to a month in prison, which wasn't the maximum, but was enough to ensure that he would lose his job and his house.[9]

Defendants are thus punished, often in life-altering ways, for deviating from the script handed to them by the court. What this means in practice, then, is that the vast majority of allocutions at sentencing hearings conform to the expectations and demands imposed on them so as to avoid harsher sentences. Burger-Caplan makes this clear when he writes, '[the] risk of increased punishment results, purposefully or not, in the truncating of defendants' stories to fit within the accepted range of expression. Defendants largely know what they are expected to say, and stay within these limits' (2017, p. 54). According to one of the defendants interviewed by Burger-Caplan:

> I was more, so like, accepting, and taking personal responsibility for my, for my actions at the sentencing. One, because . . . I figured, like, that is probably what they want to hear, but then also, like I said, like, I didn't have a very good education at that time. So I really thought that like, I was a bad person. (2017, p. 54)

Let's consider two different versions of an allocution of this sort. The first is where the defendant is in fact innocent but follows the script of the court to avoid an

[9] Natapoff (2005, p. 1468).

even more unjust punishment. This defendant is essentially being threatened with longer incarceration unless he admits guilt, expresses remorse, apologizes, and otherwise takes responsibility for the action of another person. This is paradigmatic coercion: 'Give us the remorse or face additional years of violence and dehumanization.' Two options are put on the table, both of which involve being violated, and the one that is typically chosen is fueled by the unfairness of the threat underlying the other. One of the defendants interviewed by Burger-Caplan expresses this point powerfully:

> It's tough, right, because it's like, you know, it is a desperate-ass time, and people are probably going to say anything that they can say. It's like, shit, somebody has a gun to your head, and you know, 'Tell me what you want me to say so....' Or, 'Tell me something, you know, why I should keep you alive.' You know what I mean? It's like, you'll say anything, you know, and this is like, a pretty similar situation. Like, you know, like, you're, 'We can give you anything from 0 to 20-some years, you know, like.... Talk.' (2017, p. 75)

As this passage notes, the desperation invoked at a sentencing hearing will drive a defendant to say just about anything, including admitting guilt when he is in fact innocent. Once it is made clear that the State essentially has a script to follow, a defendant can reasonably feel that the only option is to say what the State wants to hear. Moreover, the threat of additional years of incarceration for speaking the truth has both features of the account of coercion defended in Chapter 4. First, it is straightforwardly unfair to force someone to admit guilt for something he didn't do, to express remorse for another person's actions, to apologize when one has nothing to be sorry for, and to accept responsibility when one has no connection to the crime. Indeed, the tragic irony of such a situation is that the State ought to be following this script in its treatment of the defendant. Few harms are more destructive than wrongful convictions and so the innocent defendant is owed these reparative acts from the State, which is preparing to unjustly lock him up for years in violent and dehumanizing conditions. Second, this unfair threat of a harsher punishment swamps the normative force of all of the other considerations that a defendant may reasonably consider, such as whether it is epistemically appropriate to lie and admit guilt and whether it is morally acceptable to feign remorse and offer an inauthentic apology. In this way, there is clearly the extraction of testimony from innocent defendants via coercion at sentencing hearings.

But even the defendant who is guilty is being both silenced and coerced into following the script provided by the court. Many defendants might reasonably feel that it is inappropriate and inauthentic to simply admit guilt, express remorse, and apologize. A guilty defendant may have ended up in front of the judge for countless reasons, including in large part because he is poor, uneducated, a Black male, consistently profiled by police, a victim of abuse or neglect, or addicted to drugs. He may feel that he has been victimized himself by many people and systems in a multitude of ways. For instance, in a recent study of interviews with drug sellers in Philadelphia, all but one started selling drugs when they were between 11 and 17 years old and most reported 'facing dire economic circumstances such as food and housing insecurity, drug-addicted family members, and teen parenthood,' which forced them to assume adult economic responsibilities early in life (Fader 2019, p. 62). If one of these drug sellers were to be at a sentencing hearing, wouldn't it be understandable for him to not feel fully responsible for his actions? Moreover, perhaps his anger, sadness, and resentment at his own circumstances push out feelings of remorse or regret. Nevertheless, these facts and emotions should be swallowed so that the allocution story is one that fits the narrative prescribed by the court. To the extent that defendants follow the script because they feel cornered by the unfair threat of harsher punishment, their allocutions are coerced and therefore extracted.

Let's take a step back here and take stock. Defendants rarely speak throughout the entire criminal legal process, with some literally never uttering a single word to the courts in their own voices from the moment of arrest through their convictions. Sentencing hearings thus provide a rare and powerful moment for defendants to be agents exerting some control over their own destinies. As Justice Frankfurter says in *Green v. United States*, '[t]he most persuasive counsel may not be able to speak for a defendant as the defendant might, with halting eloquence, speak for himself' (365 U.S. 304 (1961)). So, here we have a rare moment for agency, one with life-altering consequences, and the court once again seizes control of the defendant's voice and turns him into a puppet of the State.

Once admissions of guilt, expressions of remorse, and apologies are extracted from defendants, they then play a normatively oversized role in sentencing. How, for instance, could the uttering of a string of words that are false, feigned, and coerced warrant fewer years in prison while a true insistence of innocence leads to more? Both the weight given to the former,[10] and the deficit given to the latter, defy any sort of epistemic or moral justification. To see this even more clearly, let's focus a bit more attention on remorse, as it not only plays a powerful role in sentencing decisions, but also poses some unique challenges.

While judges determine sentences in most criminal cases in the United States, juries generally determine both culpability and sentences in capital cases.[11] Yet remorse has been shown to be a very significant factor in the deliberations of both.[12] We saw this fact borne out in the sentencing by judges in some of the cases discussed earlier, but this is no less true with juries. For instance, the Capital Jury Project, which is a nationwide study of factors influencing jurors in capital

[10] Burger-Caplan (2017). [11] Bandes (2016).
[12] See Everett and Nienstedt (1999), Wood and MacMartin (2007), and Bandes (2016).

cases, found that juries weighed remorse very heavily at the penalty phase. In an article that draws on the project's data from California, Haney et al. found that jurors identified 'whether or not the defendant expressed remorse (based only on in-court observations of the defendant)' (1994, p. 163) as one of the most important factors underlying their decisions about life or death. Drawing on the same data, Sundby found that '69% of the jurors who voted for death... pointed to lack of remorse as a reason for their vote... many of those jurors cited it as the most compelling reason for their decision' (1998, pp. 1560–62). Moreover, with both judges and juries, demeanor plays a powerful role in determining remorse. Indeed, even when defendants offer verbal testimony, many judges regard demeanor as a *more reliable* indicator of remorse.[13] And (Sundby 1998) found that a defendant's demeanor and behavior at trial were the *most powerful* factors determining jurors' evaluation of remorse.

This raises a number of very important concerns. First, remorse is rarely defined in legal proceedings[14] and even when it is, there is no legal consensus about how to identify it.[15] Steven Keith Tudor characterizes remorse as the 'mental and emotional suffering a person experiences when and as she recognises that she has done a moral wrong, especially one that involves wronging another person' (2008, p. 242). In addition to feelings, Michael A. Simons understands remorse as involving other-directed actions of atonement:

> Remorse begins—but does not end—with a felt sense of guilt. In an ideal community, the wrongdoer will identify with the victim, and the pain inflicted on the victim will, in the wrongdoer, become self-directed anger that is guilt. Remorse takes guilt one step further. Where guilt is passive and self-centered, remorse is active and other-centered. The remorseful (as opposed to the merely guilty) wrongdoer will seek to atone for his wrong. (2003, p. 35)

Even with just these two notions of remorse on the table, it is clear that judges and juries might be looking for different factors in their assessments of defendants. Some might be expecting expressions of emotional anguish, others might be looking for identification with the victim, while still others might be requiring some actions of atonement. In the absence of a clear definition, defendants might be held to radically different expectations of what remorseful behavior ought to involve.

In addition, there is simply no reliable way for judges and juries to assess whether defendants in fact are remorseful. Given that there is at least agreement that remorse involves a critical emotional component, and it is not possible to have direct access to the emotional states of defendants, judges and juries

[13] Zhong et al. (2014). [14] Weisman (2014, pp. 26–27). [15] Bandes (2016, p. 14).

typically fall back on evaluations of demeanor in their determinations of remorse. Unfortunately, there is no evidence that remorse can be reliably evaluated based on facial expression, body language, or other nonverbal behavior.[16] Moreover, defendants are often in a 'no-win' situation where no matter how they look or act, they will be interpreted negatively. During Karla Faye Tucker's capital trial, for instance, her lawyer told her 'to try to look dignified and calm and so she was trying to look unmoved by the proceedings and when she did they said she was cold and when she looked out into the courtroom and smiled at [her father], the press reported that she had smiled at someone else, and so she never looked out in the courtroom again' (Lowry 2002, p. 71). As Weisman notes, it is a paradox that demeanor, the 'most elusive and least articulated of all criteria,' is 'perceived as the true window to the person's essence' (2014, p. 32). What this means in practice, then, is that remorse is often used as a justification for enhancing or reducing sentences based entirely on the 'gut instincts' of judges and juries.[17]

This then throws the door wide open to factors such as race, culture, gender, class, and mental impairment significantly prejudicing judges and juries in assessing demeanor for evidence of remorse.[18] For instance, the more stereotypically Black a person's physical traits appear to be, the more criminal that person is perceived to be.[19] When this is combined with the fact that demeanor plays an oversized role in evaluations of remorse, it is not surprising that studies found[20] that perceived stereotypicality correlated with the actual sentencing decisions of judges. Indeed, even when the criminal histories of defendants were statistically controlled, 'those defendants who possessed the most stereotypically Black facial features served up to 8 months longer in prison for felonies than defendants who possessed the least stereotypically Black features' (Eberhardt et al. 2006, p. 383). The data is even more concerning with respect to capital sentencing decisions, with 57.5% of more stereotypically Black defendants receiving a death sentence compared to 24.4% of those who are seen as less stereotypically Black.[21] Moreover, there are cross-racial problems with the identification of remorse. (Bowers et al. 2001), for instance, found that when assessing the same Black capital defendant's demeanor, white jurors saw deceptive behavior, coldness, and incorrigibility, while Black jurors saw sincerity and remorse.

What we see here, then, is utterly shocking. Remorse is rarely defined, it is impossible to reliably identify, and it is often a proxy for *de facto* racist stereotypes and biases to be operative, and yet it is one of the most important factors in sentencing decisions. When 69% of jurors who voted for death point to lack of remorse as a reason for their vote and many cite it as the most compelling reason for their decision, it is clear that an excess of credibility is being afforded to

[16] Bandes (2016, p. 15).
[17] Ward (2006, p. 166).
[18] Bronnimann (2020, pp. 348–52).
[19] Eberhardt et al. (2004).
[20] Blair et al. (2004).
[21] Eberhardt et al. (2006, p. 384).

expressions of remorse. Indeed, we ought to be appalled that literally life and death decisions are being made on the basis of such an ill-defined, elusive, and bias-driven factor.

It is clear, then, that expressions of remorse are being extracted at sentencing hearings and are then given a massive excess of credibility, thereby resulting in defendants being victims of agential testimonial injustice during their allocutions.

There is also a further epistemic and moral concern worth raising here. The State is policing not only what defendants do, say, and believe, but also what they feel. Because of this, they are placing many defendants in a literally impossible situation. One cannot feel genuine remorse for something one did not do, and so innocent defendants are being forced to follow a script that involves widespread deception. They need to utter certain words, behave in expected ways, and have particular facial expressions, all with the aim of convincing people that they feel something that they do not, should not, and could not, feel. So, they are violated twice over, first through the wrongful conviction and then through being forced to be deceptive to try to mitigate the effects of the first injustice. Notice, however, that this second violation brings with it an impact on one's epistemic and moral character. Expressing remorse is often a first step toward reconciliation with those who have been harmed by one's actions. But feigning remorse and offering an insincere apology is to not only lie and deceive, it is to engage in behavior that purports to be healing and restorative but is instead harmful and fracturing. Imagine, for instance, that the mother of a murdered child learned not only that the wrong person was convicted, but also that he then pretended to be deeply sorry and consumed with guilt for the murder despite having nothing to do with it. She would rightly feel further harmed and violated by such pretense and theater, especially against the background of the loss of her child. Despite the fact that the defendant capitulated to pressure by the court, he was nonetheless complicit in the perpetration of this wrong, and so the extraction of his remorse results in a stain on his epistemic and moral character. Wrongs beget further wrongs, and violations beget further violations.

2. Parole Hearings

The granting of parole in the United States criminal legal system 'is often viewed as an act of grace: the dispensation of mercy by the government to an individual prisoner deemed worthy of conditional release prior to the expiration of his sentence' (Medwed 2008, p. 493). The parole evaluation process in the United States has its roots in the rehabilitative ideal of punishment, with words and acts associated with rehabilitation, such as admissions of guilt, expressions of remorse, and acceptance of responsibility functioning as central aspects of parole determinations.[22] Parole officials are generally quite overt about the substantive role that admissions of guilt and expressions of remorse play in release decisions,[23] and some states are clear that these should be relevant factors. For instance, the 'preprinted "Rationale Sheet" that the Utah Board of Pardons and Parole uses in explaining its decision after each parole hearing expressly designates complete acceptance of responsibility as a mitigating factor and denial or minimization as an aggravating one' (Medwed 2008, p. 515). Similarly, California and Pennsylvania are explicit that remorse is a factor that should be taken into account, with California authorizing as relevant considerations 'past and present attitude toward the crime' and 'signs of remorse' (Bronnimann 2020, p. 335). But even in states whose statutes do not explicitly include such factors, parole boards still regularly assign enormous weight to them, which is revealed in both case law and regulations that either directly entail these considerations or can be understood as doing so.[24]

As may be recalled from Chapter 4, coercion involves the making of an unfair offer or threat that closes a person out of a reasonable decision-making space. What I now want to show is that people who have been wrongfully convicted in the United States are systematically coerced into admitting guilt, expressing remorse, and accepting responsibility for a crime they didn't commit in order to be released on parole.

To see this, notice first that there are really only two options on the table for Americans who are innocent and seeking parole:

> To put it bluntly, innocent inmates currently face a true 'prisoner's dilemma' when encountering parole boards. Choice A consists of proclaiming innocence and consequently hindering the possibility of parole; Choice B involves taking responsibility for a crime the prospective parolee did not commit and bolstering the chance for release, albeit with dire effects for any post-conviction litigation involving the underlying innocence claim. (Medwed 2008, p. 497)

This is clearly an unfair set of options to have in one's decision space: the first is to truly proclaim that one is innocent of what is often a violent crime that one cannot imagine having inflicted on another person, but in so doing to dramatically increase the likelihood that one will continue to be incarcerated, possibly indefinitely. Prisons 'are places where the principles on which human life and liberty depend are tested to the core. They are inherently depriving and painful' and have become increasingly inhumane and 'degrading' (Liebling 2011, p. 532). Incarceration in the United States, for instance, involves separation from loved ones, living in inhumane cells,[25] exposure to inescapable and traumatizing

[22] Medwed (2008, p. 513). [23] Medwed (2008, p. 515). [24] Bronnimann (2020, p. 335).
[25] https://eji.org/issues/prison-conditions/.

violence,[26] harmful isolation,[27] abysmal health care,[28] degrading and frequent strip searches,[29] overcrowded conditions,[30] and limited treatment, education, and rehabilitation opportunities.[31] The second option is to significantly increase the probability of being released from these daily violations and horrors of incarceration, but only by virtue of admitting guilt to a crime one did not commit. Not only does this involve a violation of one's own sense of self and authenticity, it also severely compromises one's actual claim of innocence, especially in any future litigation.

Some opt for Choice A. When Chester Weger was released from an Illinois prison in February of 2020, he had served 59 years behind bars for the murder of three Riverside, IL women in Starved Rock State Park in 1960. Despite professing his innocence for almost six decades, he was the State's longest held incarcerated person, a fact that was not disconnected from his resolute refusal to capitulate to the demands of the Illinois Prisoner Review Board: '[Weger] had long been aware that the board wanted him to express remorse and that not doing so would almost certainly doom his chance of early release. But year after year, over the course of 23 hearings since he became eligible for parole a half-century ago, he refused.'[32] This decision most likely cost him decades of freedom and time with his family, especially with his two children, who were three and one when he was first arrested. Nevertheless, he was clear and steadfast about not compromising his innocence: 'I don't want to die with people thinking I'm guilty of a crime I never committed.'[33]

Similarly, Joseph Gordon has spent nearly three decades in a New York prison for the 1991 murder of a 38-year-old neurologist in Elmsford, New York, though he insists that he did not kill the doctor. When Gordon went up for parole in March of 2021, he had an overwhelming amount of support, including from corrections officers, civilian prison employees, and a psychiatric social worker.[34] Nevertheless, he was denied parole, with 'board members focus[ing] chiefly on a single and apparently unforgivable flaw: He insists he is innocent of the crime that sent him to prison.... His refusal to admit guilt, the parole panels ruled, showed that he lacked remorse for his crime.'[35] This was the fifth parole denial that Gordon received since he completed the minimum term of his sentence in

[26] https://www.prisonpolicy.org/blog/2020/12/02/witnessing-prison-violence/.
[27] https://www.prisonpolicy.org/blog/2020/12/08/solitary_symposium/.
[28] https://www.prisonpolicy.org/blog/2021/06/23/jail_mortality/.
[29] https://www.themarshallproject.org/2021/02/04/i-ve-been-strip-frisked-over-1-000-times-in-prison-i-consider-it-sexual-assault.
[30] https://www.prisonpolicy.org/blog/2020/12/21/overcrowding/.
[31] https://eji.org/issues/prison-conditions/.
[32] https://www.chicagomag.com/chicago-magazine/march-2022/unmaking-a-murderer/.
[33] https://www.chicagomag.com/chicago-magazine/march-2022/unmaking-a-murderer/.
[34] https://www.nytimes.com/2021/12/02/nyregion/joseph-gordon-parole-murder.html.
[35] https://www.nytimes.com/2021/12/02/nyregion/joseph-gordon-parole-murder.html.

2017 of 25 years to life in prison. As Michelle Lewis, Executive Director of the Parole Preparation Project, says, 'The board expects them to accept responsibility and express remorse. People who maintain their innocence remain in an impossible situation.'[36]

Unsurprisingly, others opt for Choice B. Daniel S. Medwed makes vivid some of the forces at work in this decision: 'Given the stark reality of prison life—its everyday brutality and ample deprivations—the yearning to escape can overwhelm even the strongest and most stoic of people and prompt an innocent prisoner to surrender to the lure of "admitting" guilt before the parole board to boost the odds of a parole grant' (2008, p. 529). John Ramsey, for instance, spent 33 years in prison after being wrongfully convicted of the 1981 murder of Vernon Green during the robbery of a drug den in Flatbush. Despite the fact that the only evidence against him was the testimony of a single witness who admitted that he spent the day smoking angel dust, and that he consistently maintained his innocence for over three decades, he was denied parole six times. In 2015, he finally relented, lied, and expressed regret for the murder: 'I just admitted it. I was never getting out if I say it wasn't me.'[37] Elsewhere, Ramsey said, 'I'm walking back and forth before the hearing with tears in my eyes. It was more frustration than anything. I just couldn't take [prison] anymore.'[38]

It is clear that Ramsey's admission of guilt and expression of regret at his parole hearing were coerced. After surviving for 33 years in an environment 'where stabbings and slashings regularly occurred,'[39] he was given only two options: continue enduring this life-threatening violence and maintain your innocence, or falsely admit that you murdered Vernon Green, express remorse, and go home. For a person who is innocent, the unfairness of this offer is colossal: being forced to choose between the truth and inhumane living conditions or lying and freedom. Moreover, the threat of remaining in prison indefinitely functions as a swamping consideration that screens off the normative force of all of the other relevant factors. Ramsey makes this clear when he says that he chose to give the parole board what they wanted because he 'couldn't take prison anymore.' The conditions of incarceration in the United States will drive many people to acts of utter desperation. Suicide, for instance, is the leading cause of death for people in American jails, accounting for almost 30% of deaths.[40] A person in jail is more than three times as likely to die from suicide as is a person in the general population in the United States, and half of those who died by suicide in jail between

[36] https://www.nytimes.com/2021/12/02/nyregion/joseph-gordon-parole-murder.html.

[37] https://www.nytimes.com/2021/12/02/nyregion/joseph-gordon-parole-murder.html.

[38] https://www.nydailynews.com/new-york/ny-metro-brooklyn-saga-john-ramsey-three-decades-prison-20190207-story.html.

[39] https://www.nydailynews.com/new-york/ny-metro-brooklyn-saga-john-ramsey-three-decades-prison-20190207-story.html.

[40] https://www.prisonpolicy.org/blog/2021/06/23/jail_mortality/.

2000 and 2018 had been incarcerated for nine days or fewer.[41] When nearly 1/3 of those who die in jail take their own lives, often within a week or so of being detained, the overwhelming desire to escape the conditions of American incarceration is clear. This provides further support for seeing the coercive nature of the two options presented in the United State parole system. When one involves indefinite violence and deprivation that drives many people to acts of often unparalleled desperation, it is not surprising that it swamps all of the other considerations on the table. Notice, for instance, that Ramsey does not discuss the epistemic and moral factors that bear on whether he should admit guilt and express remorse when he decides to do so, such as whether it is true that he murdered Vernon Green or appropriate to express remorse for something he did not do. He instead focuses entirely on his overwhelming desire to be released from prison. Thus, Ramsey's false admission of guilt and feigned expression of remorse were extracted by a parole system that chose to subvert his epistemic agency rather than appeal to it.

In addition to this extraction, we see the other component of agential testimonial injustice at work here: an excess of credibility. Ramsey was denied parole six times but was granted it the first time he capitulated to the demands of the parole board by admitting guilt and remorse for a murder he didn't commit. Moreover, this is not an isolated or anomalous occurrence. As Medwed (2008) notes, 'surveying state parole release decisions demonstrates that a prisoner's willingness to "own up" to his misdeeds—to acknowledge culpability and express remorse for the crime for which he is currently incarcerated—is a vital part of the parole decision-making calculus' (p. 493). Indeed, he later makes an even stronger point: 'It may not be too farfetched to suggest that, in their modern incarnation, parole boards view sincere admissions of guilt at a hearing as evidence of that inmate's cooperation in his own rehabilitation and, thus, indicia of having been cured. Mea culpa meets medical restoration, so to speak' (Medwed 2008, p. 514). So not only is failure to admit guilt and remorse a barrier to being granted parole, it also seems to be the deciding factor in many cases. Otherwise put, such an admission is, at least in many cases, both a necessary and a sufficient condition for a person to be granted parole, regardless of his actual guilt or innocence.

This reveals two sides of the same credibility coin, so to speak. Given that assertions of innocence at parole hearings are so undermining of the aim to be released, they should be given far more weight as evidence of actual innocence than they in fact are. Indeed, rather than parole boards quickly and reliably taking such an assertion as indicating a failure of the person to be rehabilitated and a need for further incarceration, they should leave open the possibility that he may in fact have been the victim of a wrongful conviction. In light of the sheer number

[41] https://www.prisonpolicy.org/blog/2021/06/23/jail_mortality/.

of DNA exonerations in the United States[42] and existing 'doubts surrounding the fundamental accuracy of the criminal adjudicatory process' (Medwed 2008, p. 532), the deficit of credibility given to claims of innocence at parole hearings is especially evident. Medwed makes a similar point when he writes, '[t]he prison grapevine has presumably informed the parole hearing-bound population that remorse is essentially a quid pro quo for release, casting doubt on the sincerity of many pleas of repentance before the board, however contrite they may seem. In reality, considering the profound disincentive to claim innocence at parole hearings, logic suggests those assertions should be taken quite seriously' (2008, p. 496). The flip side of this deficit of credibility afforded to declarations of innocence is an excess of credibility given to admissions of guilt and remorse. When such an admission is bestowed with the power to be the sole factor standing between incarceration and freedom, its normative status is massively inflated, both epistemically and morally. In particular, despite professing innocence countless times, often for decades, including at the original trial, one admission of guilt—in the context of knowing full well that this is a quid pro quo for release—is taken to finally reflect the person's true, authentic self and to repair the fractured relationships in the community.

What happens at parole hearings thus parallels what we see with false confessions except at the opposite end of the criminal legal process. A confessing self is believed when he reports guilt only once, under conditions of manipulation, deception, and coercion, while a recanting self is regarded as a liar despite maintaining innocence for years, even decades, under conditions where epistemic agency has been exercised. Similarly, a denying self is regarded as a liar despite maintaining his innocence for years, even decades, while an admitting self expresses guilt and remorse only once, under coercive conditions at a parole hearing, and is then taken to be a truthteller. As we saw in earlier chapters, the criminal legal system is treating people as givers of knowledge only when their testimony is extracted and is thus not the product of the proper exercising of epistemic agency.

Kevin Smith's case provides another powerful illustration of the agential testimonial injustice at work in parole decisions. Smith served 27 years in New York for the 1986 murder of Gary Van Dorn in Bedford Stuyvesant, Brooklyn, despite the fact that the only evidence against him was the testimony of a single 'eyewitness,' Trent Richardson, whose identification was coerced. Richardson repeatedly said that he didn't recognize the two men who killed Van Dorn. After refusing to testify at Smith's trial, however, he was essentially 'kidnapped' by the Brooklyn District Attorney's offices, separated from his lawyer, 'placed in a cold and damp jail cell in the 81st precinct house,' 'allowed no phone call or other

[42] https://innocenceproject.org/dna-exonerations-in-the-united-states/.

communication,' and held this way for four days with no shower or toiletries.[43] He was then charged with perjury and was told that in order to avoid a seven-year sentence, he needed to cooperate with the prosecution and identify Smith as Van Dorn's murderer. '[T]ired of the isolation and needing treatment because of his addiction, [Richardson] finally agreed to identify the defendants even though he did not know who committed the crime.'[44]

Richardson's eyewitness identification of Smith was clearly extracted. Richard Leo, a leading expert on coerced confessions, is unequivocal: 'The conditions of Trent Richardson's interrogation were psychologically coercive, and contained interrogation techniques that are known to cause a person to perceive he or she has no choice but to comply with the demands and/or requests of his or her interrogators, and that are known to increase the risk of eliciting involuntary and/or unreliable statements, admissions and/or confessions.'[45] Similarly, Justin Bonus, Smith's attorney, said, '[i]n the years that I have practiced criminal law, involved with hundreds of cases, I have never seen a witness who was kidnapped and coerced in the manner that Trent Vernon Richardson was.'[46] That Richardson was kidnapped, isolated, denied treatment for his addiction, and charged with perjury overwhelmingly shows that the threat of seven years of incarceration was extraordinarily unfair and closed him out of a reasonable decision-making space. He was no longer able to consider the relevant epistemic and moral factors at issue—such as whether he recognized the two men who killed Van Dorn or the catastrophic impact of an erroneous identification—and was now simply trying to avoid the dire practical consequence of continued incarceration. Moreover, Richardson's extracted identification was afforded a massive excess of credibility. As Smith's attorney notes: 'The criminal justice community must resoundingly condemn the actions of the People in the case. Mr. Smith's conviction, which was solely obtained through the coerced testimony of Richardson, should be vacated and dismissed or a new trial should be ordered.'[47] Given that Smith's conviction was based solely on Richardson's identification, it is clear that it was weighed far too heavily epistemically, thereby giving rise to a paradigmatic case of agential testimonial injustice.

But what is particularly relevant for our purposes here is how this act of agential testimonial injustice begets further ones downstream. At his initial parole

[43] https://wrongfullyconvicted.info/kevin-smith-who-served-27-years-for-a-crime-he-did-not-commit-seeks-to-overturn-conviction/.

[44] https://wrongfullyconvicted.info/kevin-smith-who-served-27-years-for-a-crime-he-did-not-commit-seeks-to-overturn-conviction/.

[45] https://wrongfullyconvicted.info/kevin-smith-who-served-27-years-for-a-crime-he-did-not-commit-seeks-to-overturn-conviction/.

[46] https://wrongfullyconvicted.info/kevin-smith-who-served-27-years-for-a-crime-he-did-not-commit-seeks-to-overturn-conviction/.

[47] https://wrongfullyconvicted.info/kevin-smith-who-served-27-years-for-a-crime-he-did-not-commit-seeks-to-overturn-conviction/.

hearing, Smith insisted on his innocence of the murder of Van Dorn. However, after his mother became ill, he felt that he had no choice but to capitulate to the demands of the board. 'I couldn't stomach saying I did it, at first. But I went back before the board and made a false admission.'[48] Following this admission of guilt, Smith was approved for parole and returned home in 2012 to see his mother before she died. What we see here, then, is agential testimonial injustice layered on top of agential testimonial injustice. Smith was only in prison in the first place because of the extraction of Richardson's identification and the excess of credibility it received throughout the criminal legal system, culminating in his wrongful conviction. That Smith is then—27 years later—having an admission of guilt and expression of remorse extracted from him by the same system that wrongfully convicted him in order to be released is injustice on an epic scale. This is agential testimonial injustice[49] all the way up and all the way down.

Such admissions of guilt and expressions of remorse also give rise to further wrongs and harms suffered by those who have them extracted. As Medwed says, 'regardless of whether [an] admission accomplishes its objective, inculpatory statements at parole hearings can hamper the prisoner's later attempts to prove innocence through litigation and thus have long-term negative effects' (2008, p. 22). Indeed, this is precisely what happened to Ramsey and may very well impact Smith, both of whom are actively trying to get their original convictions overturned. 'In 2019, a Brooklyn Supreme Court judge dismissed Mr. Ramsey's request for a new trial, citing his admission of guilt to the board. He is appealing the decision.'[50]

3. Conclusion

What we see, then, is that from the beginning of the criminal legal process in the interrogation room, where false confessions and eyewitness identifications are extracted, to the very end, where innocent defendants are forced to admit guilt and express remorse for crimes they did not commit, the epistemic agency of Americans is being bypassed, exploited, and subverted to serve the interests of State power. Given the scale and scope of this assault on rational capacities, treating persons as tools or puppets for the desired ends of those in power seems to be woven into the fabric of the criminal legal system rather than an accidental or anomalous feature of it.

[48] https://www.nytimes.com/2021/12/02/nyregion/joseph-gordon-parole-murder.html.

[49] Of course, Smith and Richardson suffered many other kinds of injustice in addition to the agential testimonial kind.

[50] https://www.nytimes.com/2021/12/02/nyregion/joseph-gordon-parole-murder.html.

At sentencing hearings and in front of parole boards in particular, those who are innocent are pressured to assert not only that the State was right all along in convicting and incarcerating them, but also that the system effectively rehabilitated them. As if a wrongful conviction and being held captive in violent and dehumanizing conditions isn't injustice enough, the State extracts one further indignity and that is the wrongfully convicted's truth itself. Even someone like Ramsey, who withstood all of the tactics and pressures to falsely confess for decades, and maintained his innocence through six parole denials, was finally broken by a system designed to secure, protect, and flaunt its own righteousness. It is as if the system is saying, 'You have defied us up to this point, but you will admit that we were right all along before you step foot outside of these bars.'

Conclusion

Epistemic agency is fundamental to personhood. In bypassing or subverting the epistemic agency of those who enter the doors of the criminal legal system, the State is also thereby attacking their *autonomy* and *dignity* and ultimately their status as *persons*.

At the most basic level, autonomy involves self-governance, or the ability to be directed by desires and conditions that are part of one's authentic self rather than simply imposed externally.[1] Even among moral theories that are deeply opposed, autonomy is understood to be a central value, one that often occupies a foundational or otherwise prominent place within the overall framework.[2] And for those moral theories that center another normative concept, such as John Rawls's famous 'justice as fairness' view, autonomy often plays a crucial role. As Thomas Nagel says, 'The fundamental attitude toward persons on which justice as fairness depends is a respect for their autonomy' (1995, p. 125).

Of course, autonomy does not mean that we are not subject to any outside influence. Indeed, our beliefs, values, desires, and goals are often at least partially shaped by other people, events, and circumstances. Nevertheless, to be autonomous is to be governed by one's own will rather than that of another—it is to be the author of one's own life.[3] As Susser et al. note, '[a]utonomy is not the absence of influence, but the presence of self-government. To be autonomous... is to know that one's decision-making is conditioned, and yet, still, to take one's own reasons for acting as authoritative' (2019, p. 17, note 62). The connection between epistemic agency and autonomy is clear here: being guided by one's own reasons, rather than the will of another, is at the heart of being self-governed. Being the author of one's life in this sense enables people to act for reasons that they endorse as authentically their own.[4] Even if, for instance, my undergraduate teacher influenced me to become a professor, this choice was governed by my own reasons,

[1] There is a vast body of literature on autonomy. Autonomy is sometimes understood in procedural terms, where autonomy involves how people make decisions rather than anything about the content of them. (See, for instance, Christman (1991), Dworkin (1988), and Frankfurt (1998).) In contrast, substantive theories of autonomy are not content-neutral and hold that it is important to be able to regard as non-autonomous preferences that are the result of oppressive or otherwise harmful forms of socialization. (See, for instance, Babbitt (1996) and Stoljar (2000).) Indeed, liberation from oppressive social conditions is often regarded as a fundamental component of both autonomy and justice. (See Cornell (1998), Young (1990), and Hirschmann (2002).)

[2] See, for instance, Kant (1785/Kant 1983) and Mill (1859/Mill 1975).

[3] See Raz (1986).

[4] See Susser et al. (2019, p. 36).

Criminal Testimonial Injustice. Jennifer Lackey, Oxford University Press. © Jennifer Lackey 2023.
DOI: 10.1093/oso/9780192864109.003.0008

ones that I embrace as truly my own. My teacher's influence did not in any way constrain, or limit, my autonomy to act as a rational agent.

Without autonomy, there is no basis for properly attributing actions to people, which is central to understanding the behavior not only of others but of ourselves as well. Moreover, autonomy is the foundation of holding people responsible for their actions.[5] If they are not the authors of their own actions, then they cannot and should not be held accountable for them. Since the criminal legal system is largely in the business of holding people responsible for their actions, it is of central importance that autonomy be promoted and respected.

But even more fundamentally, protecting the autonomy of those in the criminal legal system is to recognize and respect their dignity as *persons*. Indeed, this is what truly lies at the heart of *Miranda v. Arizona*, the 1966 Supreme Court case grounding our conception of *Miranda* rights: 'All these policies point to one overriding thought: the constitutional foundation underlying the privilege is the respect a government—state or federal—must accord to the dignity and integrity of its citizens' (*Miranda v. Arizona*, 384 U.S. 436, 460 (1966)). Natapoff echoes this when she writes: 'It is precisely its ability to reveal thought-processes that makes testimonial speech expressive and makes its protection integral to defendants' dignity and autonomy as free, willing speakers' (Natapoff 2005, p. 1479). As noted in Chapter 2, in establishing the classic contours of the right to remain silent in *Miranda v. Arizona*, the Court was primarily concerned with the expressive or testimonial liberty of suspects and defendants.[6] Moreover, in discussing the aim of *Miranda* warnings, the Court notes that they enable 'the defendant under otherwise compelling circumstances to tell his story without fear, effectively, and in a way that eliminates the evils in the interrogation process' (*Miranda v. Arizona*, 384 U.S. 436, 466 (1966)). Some of these 'evils' include lengthy and frequent interrogations, especially of suspects who are cognitively impaired, whereby 'an...environment is created for no purpose other than to subjugate the individual to the will of his examiner' and where an atmosphere of intimidation is created that is 'equally destructive of human dignity' as physical intimidation is (*Miranda v. Arizona*, 384 U.S. 436, 457 (1966)). The Court is here clearly interested in ensuring that suspects are able to freely offer testimony that has not been brought under the sway of an interrogator. Thus, there is an important sense in which *Miranda* warnings are less about, say, the right to remain silent and more about protecting a defendant's right to 'speak in the unfettered exercise of his own will' (*Miranda v. Arizona*, 384 U.S. 436, 460 (1966)). As Natapoff notes, the privilege against self-incrimination is '[a]t bottom...not about silence but expressive choice' (2005, p. 1478).

[5] Susser et al. (2019, p. 36). [6] Natapoff (2005, p. 1477).

According to Kant, dignity is 'an unconditional' and 'incomparable' 'inner worth' that 'admits of no equivalent' and is grounded in the capacity of persons for rational agency or autonomy (1785/1983, 4: 434–36). This distinctive worth is possessed only by ends in themselves, and only and all persons are ends in themselves. Jeremy Waldron maintains that a person's dignity is 'their social standing…that entitles them to be treated as equals in the ordinary operation of society' (2012, p. 5). And according to the Universal Declaration of Human Rights, 'all human beings are born free and equal in dignity and rights' (Article 1). While there are clearly some differences here, there is broad convergence on dignity being a distinctive worth of humans or persons that is grounded in or connected to their rational agency and that entitles them to be treated as equals.

What we see, then, is that an attack on epistemic agency is therewith an attack on autonomy, dignity, and ultimately on personhood. To bypass, exploit, or subvert a person's ability to offer testimony grounded in reasons that she would endorse as her own is not only to fail to respect her autonomy and dignity, it is to treat her as less than a person. As Herbert Morris notes, 'to treat another as a person requires that we provide him with reasons for acting and avoid force or deception….' Moreover, the right to be treated as a person 'is a fundamental human right belonging to all human beings by virtue of their being human' (Morris 1968, p. 493). In a similar spirit, Robert Noggle writes that 'since a person's rational moral agency is crucial to her personhood, to fail to respect it is [to] degrade her; it is to treat her as less than a person. And for that reason it is wrong' (Noggle 1996, p. 52). Extracting testimony from a speaker is thus not only to wrong her as an epistemic agent—it is also crucially to violate her as a person.

Importantly, however, the compromising of epistemic agency—and therewith, of personhood—can vary dramatically in degree, kind, and impact. Advertising, for instance, is frequently regarded as manipulative and is, to this extent, circumventing or exploiting the rational capacities of those being targeted. But if advertising is a targeted attack, what is occurring in the criminal legal system is a full-scale war swallowing up combatants and civilians alike. From start to finish, with ignorance and malice, aimed similarly at defendants, witnesses, and victims, through small acts of influence and will-crushing threats, engulfing the innocent as well as the guilty, the State is treating its citizens as puppets to be shaped and molded to meet its desires and ends. This is not merely to accord people diminished respect and dignity or to regard them as less than persons. It is to treat them as *non-persons*, ones whose beliefs, words, actions, and even feelings are to be subjugated to the will of the State, often with life-destroying consequences.

Throughout this book, various reforms have been recommended. From replacing confrontational interrogation methods with information-gathering ones to providing expert testimony about eyewitness identifications, small steps can and should be taken to avoid wrongful convictions and to promote truth and justice. But at its core, there is a prior, deeper, and far more fundamental transformation that is needed in the United States criminal legal system: the recognition and respect of the personhood of all of those who enter its doors. Whether a suspect is being interrogated or a victim is reporting a sexual assault, an eyewitness is making an identification or a defendant is seeking parole, each speaker's agency and dignity should be seen, acknowledged, and centered. It is only through the hope and promise of respecting the personhood of each participant in the criminal legal system that we can truly grasp what justice demands and, in so doing, to reimagine what is possible.

References

Abramson, Kate. 2014. 'Turning Up the Lights on Gaslighting.' *Philosophical Perspectives* 28: 1–30.

Abramson, Kate Forthcoming. *On Gaslighting*. Princeton, NJ: Princeton University Press.

Alkon, Cynthia. 2014. 'The U.S. Supreme Court's Failure to Fix Plea Bargaining: The Impact of *Lafler* and *Frye*.' *Hastings Constitutional Law Quarterly* 41: 561–621.

Alkon, Cynthia 2017. 'Hard Bargaining in Plea Bargaining: When do Prosecutors Cross the Line?' *Nevada Law Journal* 17: 401–28.

Allen, Ronald J. and Alex Stein. 2013. 'Evidence, Probability, and the Burden of Proof.' *Arizona Law Review* 55: 557–602.

Alschuler, Albert W. 1968. 'The Prosecutor's Role in Plea Bargaining.' *The University of Chicago Law Review* 36: 50–112.

Alschuler, Albert W. 2003. 'Straining at Gnats and Swallowing Camels: The Selective Morality of Professor Bibas.' *Cornell Law Review* 88: 1412–24.

Anderson, Elizabeth. 1999. 'What is the Point of Equality?' *Ethics* 109: 287–337.

Anderson, Elizabeth. 2012. 'Epistemic Justice as a Virtue of Social Institutions.' *Social Epistemology* 26: 163–73.

Appleby, Sara C. and Saul M. Kassin. 2016. 'When Self-Report Trumps Science: Effects of Confessions, DNA, and Prosecutorial Theories on Perceptions of Guilt.' *Psychology, Public Policy, and Law* 22: 127–40.

Armbrust, Shawn. 2008. 'Reevaluating Recanting Witnesses: Why the Red-Headed Stepchild of New Evidence Deserves Another Look.' *Boston College Third World Law Journal* 28: 75–104.

Audi, Robert. 1997. 'The Place of Testimony in the Fabric of Knowledge and Justification.' *American Philosophical Quarterly* 34: 405–22.

Audi, Robert. 1998. *Epistemology: A Contemporary Introduction to the Theory of Knowledge*. London: Routledge.

Austin, J.L. 1962. *How to Do Things with Words*. Oxford: Clarendon Press.

Babbitt, Susan M. 1996. *Impossible Dreams: Rationality, Integrity, and Moral Imagination*. Boulder, CO: Westview Press.

Bandes, Susan A. 2016. 'Remorse and Criminal Justice.' *Emotion Review* 8: 14–19.

Barnhill, Anne. 2014. 'What is Manipulation?' in Christian Coons and Michael Weber (eds.), *Manipulation: Theory and Practice*. New York, NY: Oxford University Press, 51–72.

Baron, Marcia. 2003. 'Manipulativeness.' *Proceedings and Addresses of the American Philosophical Association* 77: 37–54.

Bazargan, Saba. 2014. 'Moral Coercion.' *Philosophers' Imprint* 14: 1–18.

Becker, Loftus. 1988. 'Plea Bargaining and the Supreme Court.' *Loyola of Los Angeles Law Review* 21: 757–841.

Beloof, Douglas E. and Joel Shapiro. 2002. 'Let the Truth Be Told: Proposed Hearsay Exceptions to Admit Domestic Violence Victims' out of Court Statements as Substantive Evidence.' *Columbia Journal of Gender and Law* 11: 1–37.

Benkler, Yochai, Robert Faris, and Hal Roberts. 2018. *Network Propaganda: Manipulation, Disinformation, and Radicalization in American Politics.* Oxford: Oxford University Press.

Berenstain, Nora. 2016. 'Epistemic Exploitation.' *Ergo* 3: 569–90.

Bergmann, Michael. 1997. 'Internalism, Externalism and the No-Defeater Condition.' *Synthese* 110: 399–417.

Berman, Mitchell. 2001. 'Coercion without Baselines: Unconstitutional Conditions in Three Dimensions.' *Georgetown Law Journal* 90: 1–112.

Bibas, Stephanos. 2004. 'Plea Bargaining Outside the Shadow of Trial.' *Harvard Law Review* 117: 2463–547.

Blackmon, Douglas A. 2009. *Slavery by Another Name: The Re-Enslavement of Black Americans from the Civil War to World War II.* New York, NY: Anchor Books.

Blair, Irene V., Charles M. Judd, and Kristine M. Chapleau. 2004. 'The Influence of Afrocentric Facial Features in Criminal Sentencing.' *Psychological Science* 15: 674–79.

Blumenthal, Jeremy A. 1993. 'A Wipe of the Hands, A Lick of the Lips: The Validity of Demeanor Evidence in Assessing Witness Credibility.' *Nebraska Law Review* 72: 1157–204.

BonJour, Laurence. 1980. 'Externalist Theories of Epistemic Justification.' *Midwest Studies in Philosophy* 5: 53–73.

BonJour, Laurence. 1985. *The Structure of Empirical Knowledge.* Cambridge, MA: Harvard University Press.

BonJour, Laurence and Ernest Sosa. 2003. *Epistemic Justification: Internalism vs. Externalism, Foundations vs. Virtues.* Oxford: Blackwell Publishing.

Bonomi, Amy E., Rashmi Gangamma, Chris R. Locke, Heather Katafiasz, and David Martin. 2011. 'Meet Me at the Hill Where We Used to Park: Interpersonal Processes Associated with Victim Recantation.' *Social Science & Medicine* 73: 1054–61.

Bowers, William J., Benjamin D. Steiner, and Marla Sandys. 2001. 'Death Sentencing in Black and White: An Empirical Analysis of the Role of Jurors' Race and Jury Racial Composition.' *University of Pennsylvania Journal of Constitutional Law* 3: 171–275.

Brewer, Marilynn. 1999. 'The Psychology of Prejudice. Ingroup Love or Outgroup Hate?' *Journal of Social Issues* 55: 429–44.

Bronnimann, Nicole. 2020. 'Remorse in Parole Hearings: An Elusive Concept with Concrete Consequences.' *Missouri Law Review* 85: 321–56.

Bruck, Maggie, Stephen J. Ceci, and Helene Hembrooke. 1998. 'Reliability and Credibility of Young Children's Reports: From Research to Policy and Practice. *American Psychologist* 53: 136–51.

Brunk, Conrad G. 1979. 'The Problem of Voluntariness and Coercion in the Negotiated Plea.' *Law & Society Review* 13: 527–53.

Burge, Tyler. 1993. 'Content Preservation.' *The Philosophical Review* 102: 457–88.

Burge, Tyler. 1997. 'Interlocution, Perception, and Memory.' *Philosophical Studies* 86: 21–47.

Burger-Caplan, Joshua I. 2017. 'Time of Desperation: An Examination of Criminal Defendants' Experiences of Allocuting at Sentencing.' *Columbia Journal of Law and Social Problems* 51: 39–77.

Burns, Casey M. 2018. 'Plea Bargaining: A Practice of Convenience or a Line-Crossing System of Coercion?' *Stetson Journal of Advocacy and the Law* 99: 3–18.

Buss, Sarah. 2005. 'Valuing Autonomy and Respecting Persons: Manipulation, Seduction, and the Basis of Moral Constraints.' *Ethics* 115 195–235.

Caldwell, Laura and Leslie S. Klinger. 2017. *Anatomy of Innocence: Testimonies of the Wrongfully Convicted.* New York: Liveright Publishing Corporation.

Camacho, Christina M. and Leanne F. Alarid. 2008. 'The Significance of the Victim Advocate for Domestic Violence Victims in Municipal Court.' *Violence and Victims* 23: 288–300.

Carlin, Amanda. 2016. 'The Courtroom as White Space: Racial Performance as Noncredibility.' *UCLA Law Review* 63: 452–84.

Carson, Thomas L. 2010. *Lying and Deception: Theory and Practice*. Oxford: Oxford University Press.

Carter, Dan T. 1969. *Scottsboro: A Tragedy of the American South*. Baton Rouge: Louisiana State University Press.

Cassidy, R. Michael. 2019. 'Plea Bargaining, Discovery, and the Intractable Problem of Impeachment Disclosures.' *Vanderbilt Law Review* 64: 1429–87.

Chan, Celine. 2009. 'The Right to Allocution: A Defendant's Word on Its Face or Under Oath?' *Brooklyn Law Review* 75: 579–625.

Chisholm, Roderick M. 1989. *Theory of Knowledge*, 3rd edn. Englewood Cliffs, NJ: Prentice-Hall.

Chisholm, Roderick M. and Thomas D. Feehan. 1977. 'The Intent to Deceive.' *The Journal of Philosophy* 74: 143–59.

Christman, John. 1991. 'Autonomy and Personal History.' *Canadian Journal of Philosophy* 21: 1–24.

Cloud, Morgan. 1996. 'Torture and Truth.' *Texas Law Review* 74: 1211–15.

Clow, Kimberley A. and Amy-May Leach. 2015. 'After Innocence: Perceptions of Individuals Who Have Been Wrongfully Convicted.' *Legal and Criminological Psychology* 20: 147–64.

Cohen, Shlomo. 2018. 'Manipulation and Deception.' *Australasian Journal of Philosophy* 96: 483–97.

Connery, Donald S. (ed.). 1996. *Convicting the Innocent: The Story of a Murder, A False Confession, and the Struggle to Free a Wrong Man*. Cambridge, MA: Brookline.

Coons, Christian and Michael Weber. 2014. 'Introduction' in Christian Coons and Michael Weber (eds.), *Manipulation: Theory and Practice*. New York, NY: Oxford University Press, 1–16.

Cornell, Drucilla. 1998. *At the Heart of Freedom*. Princeton, NJ: Princeton University Press.

Covey, Russell D. 2009. 'Signaling and Plea Bargaining's Innocence Problem.' *Washington and Lee Law Review* 66: 73–130.

Covey, Russell D. 2016. 'Recantations and the Perjury Sword.' *Albany Law Review* 79: 101–33.

Craig, Edward. 1990. *Knowledge and the State of Nature*. Oxford: Clarendon Press.

Crenshaw, Kimberlé. 1989. 'Demarginalizing the Intersection of Race and Sex: A Black Feminist Critique of Antidiscrimination Doctrine, Feminist Theory and Antiracist Politics.' *University of Chicago Legal Forum* 1989: 139–67.

Crespo, Andrew Manuel. 2018. 'The Hidden Law of Plea Bargaining.' *Columbia Law Review* 118: 1303–1424.

Cutler, Brian L. and Steven D. Penrod. 1988. 'Improving the Reliability of Eyewitness Identification: Lineup Construction and Presentation.' *Journal of Applied Psychology* 73: 281–90.

Davis, Angela Y. 1985. *Violence Against Women and the Ongoing Challenge to Racism*. Latham, NY: Kitchen Table.

Davis, Angela Y. 2013. 'In Search of Racial Justice: The Role of the Prosecutor.' *New York Journal of Legislation and Public Policy* 16: 821–51.

Davis, Emmalon. 2016. 'Typecasts, Tokens, and Spokespersons: A Case for Credibility Excess as Testimonial Injustice.' *Hypatia* 31: 485–501.

Davis, Emmalon. 2018. 'On Epistemic Appropriation.' *Ethics* 128: 702–27.
Deffenbacher, Kenneth A., Brian H. Bornstein, Steven D. Penrod, and Kiernan E. McGorty. 2004. 'A Meta-Analytic Review of the Effects of High Stress on Eyewitness Memory.' *Law and Human Behavior* 28: 687–706.
De Sanctis, Lisa Marie. 1996. 'Bridging the Gap Between the Rules of Evidence and Justice for Victims of Domestic Violence.' *Yale Journal of Law and Feminism* 8: 359–407.
Douglass, John G. 2007. 'Can Prosecutors Bluff—*Brady v. Maryland* and Plea Bargaining.' *Case Western Reserve Law Review* 57: 581–92.
Dotson, Kristie. 2011. 'Tracking Epistemic Violence, Tracking Practices of Silencing.' *Hypatia* 26: 236–57.
Dotson, Kristie. 2014. 'Conceptualizing Epistemic Oppression.' *Social Epistemology* 28: 115–38.
Drizin, Steven A. and Beth A. Colgan. 2004. 'Tales from the Juvenile Confession Front: A Guide to How Standard Police Interrogation Tactics Can Produce Coerced and False Confessions from Juvenile Suspects,' in G. Daniel Lassiter (ed.), *Interrogations, Confessions, and Entrapment* (*Perspectives in Law & Psychology* 20). New York, NY: Kluwer Academic/Plenum Publishers: 127–62.
Drizin, Steven A. and Richard A. Leo. 2004. 'The Problem of False Confessions in the Post-DNA World.' *North Carolina Law Review*: 891–1008.
Dunning, David and Justin Kruger. 1999. 'Unskilled and Unaware of It: How Difficulties in Recognizing One's Own Incompetence Lead to Inflated Self-Assessments.' *Journal of Personality and Social Psychology* 77: 1121–34.
Dworkin, Gerald. 1988. *The Theory and Practice of Autonomy*. Cambridge: Cambridge University Press.
Dysart, Jennifer E., R.C.L. Lindsay, Robin Hammond, and Paul Dupuis. 2001. 'Mug Shot Exposure Prior to Lineup Identification: Interference, Transference, and Commitment Effects.' *Journal of Applied Psychology* 86: 1280–84.
Eberhardt, Jennifer L., Phillip Atiba Goff, Valerie J. Purdie, and Paul G. Davies. 2004. 'Seeing Black: Race, Crime, and Visual Processing.' *Journal of Personality and Social Psychology* 87: 876–93.
Eberhardt, Jennifer L., P.G. Davies, Valerie J. Purdie-Vaughns, and Sherri Lynn Johnson. 2006. 'Looking Deathworthy: Perceived Stereotypicality of Black Defendants Predicts Capital-Sentencing Outcomes.' *Cornell Law Faculty Publications* 41. https://scholarship.law.cornell.edu/lsrp_papers/41.
Ehrhard, Susan. 2008. 'Plea Bargaining and the Death Penalty: An Exploratory Study.' *The Justice System Journal* 29: 313–25.
Ellison, Louise. 2002. 'Prosecuting Domestic Violence without Victim Participation.' *The Modern Law Review* 65: 834–58.
Erickson, William H. 1973. 'The Finality of a Plea of Guilty.' *Notre Dame Law Review* 48: 835–49.
Everett, Ronald S. and Barbara C. Nienstedt. 1999. 'Race, Remorse, and Sentence Reduction: Is Saying You're Sorry Enough?' *Justice Quarterly* 16: 99–122.
Faden, Ruth R. and Tom L. Beauchamp. 1986. *A History and Theory of Informed Consent*. Oxford: Oxford University Press.
Fader, Jamie J. 2019. '"The Game Ain't What It Used to Be": Drug Sellers' Perceptions of the Modern Day Underground and Legal Markets.' *Journal of Drug Issues* 49: 57–73.
Faison, Lakia and Laura Smalarz. 2020. 'Perceptions of Exonerees: A Review of the Psychological Science.' *Albany Law Review* 83: 1021–58.
Fehr, Ernst and Klaus M. Schmidt. 1999. 'A Theory of Fairness, Competition, and Cooperation.' *The Quarterly Journal of Economics* 114: 817–68.

Feinberg, Joel. 1986. *Harm to Self*. New York, NY: Oxford University Press.

Findley, Keith A. and Michael S. Scott. 2006. 'The Multiple Dimensions of Tunnel Vision in Criminal Cases. *Wisconsin Law Review* 2006: 291–398.

Firstman, Richard and Jay Salpeter. 2008. *A Criminal Injustice: A True Crime, a False Confession, and the Fight to Free Marty Tankleff*. New York, NY: Ballantine Books.

Frankfurt, Harry. 1998. *The Importance of What We Care About: Philosophical Essays*. Cambridge: Cambridge University Press.

Fricker, Elizabeth. 1987. 'The Epistemology of Testimony.' *Proceedings of the Aristotelian Society* 61: 57–83.

Fricker, Elizabeth. 1994. 'Against Gullibility,' in Bimal Krishna Matilal and Arindam Chakrabarti (eds.), *Knowing from Words*. Dordrecht: Kluwer Academic Publishers, 125–61.

Fricker, Miranda. 2007. *Epistemic Injustice: Power & the Ethics of Knowing*. Oxford: Oxford University Press.

Fricker, Miranda. Forthcoming. "Institutionalized Testimonial Injustice: The Construction of a Confession Myth." *Journal of Dialectics of Nature*.

Frowe, Helen. 2021. 'The Moral Irrelevance of Moral Coercion.' *Philosophical Studies* 178: 3465–82.

Gagarin, Michael. 1996. 'The Torture of Slaves in Athenian Law.' *Classical Philology* 91: 1–18.

Gaubatz, Kathlyn Taylor. 1995. *Crime in the Public Mind*. Dearborn, MI: University of Michigan Press.

Geraci, Alessandra and Luca Surian. 2011. 'The Developmental Roots of Fairness: Infants' Reactions to Equal and Unequal Distributions of Resources.' *Developmental Science* 14: 1012–20.

Giannini, Mary Margaret. 2008. 'Equal Rights for Equal Rites?: Victim Allocution, Defendant Allocution, and the Crime Victims' Rights Act.' *Yale Law & Policy Review* 26: 431–84.

Goldberg, Sanford C. 2017. 'Should Have Known.' *Synthese* 194: 2863–94.

Goldman, Alvin. I. 1986. *Epistemology and Cognition*. Cambridge, MA: Harvard University Press.

Gonzales Rose, Jasmine B. 2016. 'Toward a Critical Race Theory of Evidence.' *Minnesota Law Review* 101: 2243–311.

Goodin, Robert E. 1980. *Manipulatory Politics*. New Haven: Yale University Press.

Gorin, Moti. 2014*a*. 'Towards a Theory of Interpersonal Manipulations' in Christian Coons and Michael Weber (eds.), *Manipulation: Theory and Practice*. New York, NY: Oxford University Press, 73–97.

Gorin, Moti. 2014*b*. 'Do Manipulators Always Threaten Rationality' *American Philosophical Quarterly* 51: 51–61.

Granhag, Pär Anders and Leif A. Strömwall (eds.). 2004. *The Detection of Deception in Forensic Contexts*. Cambridge: Cambridge University Press.

Greco, John. 2007. 'The Nature of Ability and the Purpose of Knowledge.' *Philosophical Issues* 17: 57–69.

Greenspan, Stephen and John H. Driscoll. 2016. 'Why People with FASD Fall for Manipulative Ploys: Ethical Limits of Interrogators' Use of Lies,' in Monty Nelson and Marguerite Trussler (eds.), *Fetal Alcohol Spectrum Disorders in Adults: Ethical and Legal Perspectives. International Library of Ethics, Law, and the New Medicine* 63, DOI 10.1007/978-3-319-20866-4_16, 23–38.

Greenwald, Anthony G. and Linda Hamilton Krieger. 2006. 'Implicit Bias: Scientific Foundations.' *California Law Review* 94: 945–67.

Greenwald, Anthony G. and Thomas F. Pettigrew. 2014. 'With Malice Toward None and Charity for Some: Ingroup Favoritism Enables Discrimination.' *American Psychologist* 69: 669–84.

Grisso, Thomas, Laurence Steinberg, Jennifer Woolard, Elizabeth Cauffman, Elizabeth Scott, Sandra Graham, Fran Lexcen, N. Dickson Reppucci, and Robert Schwartz. 2003. 'Juveniles' Competence to Stand Trial: A Comparison of Adolescents' and Adults' Capacities as Trial Defendants.' *Law and Human Behavior* 27: 333–63.

Gross, Samuel R., Kristen Jacoby, Daniel J. Matheson, and Nicholas Montgomery. 2005. 'Exonerations in the United States 1989 Through 2003.' *Journal of Criminal Law and Criminology* 95: 523–60.

Gross, Samuel R., Maurice Possley, and Klara Stephens. 2017. 'Race and Wrongful Convictions in the United States,' in *The National Registry of Exonerations*. Newkirk Center for Science and Society.

Gruber, Aya. 2003. 'Victims Wrongs: The Case for a General Criminal Defense Based on Wrongful Behavior in an Era of Victims' Rights.' *Temple Law Review* 76: 645–738.

Grundmann, Thomas. 2021. 'Preemptive Authority: The Challenge from Outrageous Expert Judgments.' *Episteme* 18: 407–27.

Gudjonsson, Gisli H. 2003. *The Psychology of Interrogations and Confessions: A Handbook*. New York, NY: Wiley.

Gudjonsson, Gisli H. and Jon F. Sigurdssonb. 1999. 'The Gudjonsson Questionnaire-Revised (GCQ-R) Factor Structure and its Relationship with Personality.' *Personality and Individual Differences* 27: 953–68.

Guillory, James Denny. 1968. 'The Pro-Slavery Arguments of Dr. Samuel A. Cartwright.' *Louisiana History: The Journal of the Louisiana Historical Association* 9: 209–27.

Hale, Chelsea and Meghan Matt. 2019. 'The Intersection of Race and Rape Viewed through the Prism of a Modern-Day Emmett Till.' American Bar Association. https://www.americanbar.org/groups/litigation/committees/diversity-inclusion/articles/2019/summer2019-intersection-of-race-and-rape/.

Haney, Craig, Lorelei Sontag, and Sally Constanzo. 1994. 'Deciding to Take a Life: Capital Juries, Sentencing Instructions, and the Jurisprudence of Death.' *Journal of Social Issues* 50: 149–76.

Harding, David J. 2003. 'Jean Valjean's Dilemma: The Management of Ex-Convict Identity in the Search for Employment.' *Deviant Behavior* 24: 571–95.

Hartman, Jennifer L. and Joanne Belknap. 2003. 'Beyond the Gatekeepers: Court Professionals' Self-Reported Attitudes about and Experiences with Misdemeanor Domestic Violence Cases.' *Criminal Justice and Behavior* 30: 349–73.

Hawthorne, John. 2004. *Knowledge and Lotteries*. Oxford: Oxford University Press.

Hieronymi, Pamela. 2008. 'Responsibility for Believing.' *Synthese* 161: 357–73.

Hirji, Sukaina. 2021. 'Oppressive Double Binds.' *Ethics* 131: 643–69.

Hirschfield, Paul J. and Alex R. Piquero. 2010. 'Normalization and Legitimation: Modeling Stigmatizing Attitudes Toward Ex-Offenders.' *Criminology* 48: 27–55.

Hirschmann, Nancy. 2002. *The Subject of Freedom: Toward a Feminist Theory of Freedom*. Princeton, NJ: Princeton University Press.

Hodson, Gordon, John F. Dovidio, and Samuel L. Gaertner. 2002. 'Processes in Racial Discrimination: Differential Weighting of Conflicting Information.' *Personality and Social Psychology Bulletin* 28: 460–71.

Hoffman, Kelly M., Sophie Trawalter, Jordan R. Axt, and M. Norman Oliver. 2016. 'Racial Bias in Pain Assessment and Treatment Recommendations, and False Belief about Biological Differences between Blacks and Whites.' *Proceedings of the National Academy of Sciences of the United States of America* 113: 4296–301.

Honoré, Tony. 1990. 'A Theory of Coercion.' *Oxford Journal of Legal Studies* 10: 94–105.

Inbau, Fred E., John E. Reid, Joseph P. Buckley, and Brian C. Jayne. 2001. *Criminal Interrogation and Confessions*, 4th edn. Gaithersberg, MD: Aspen.

Inbau, Fred E., John E. Reid, Joseph P. Buckley, and Brian C. Jayne. 2013. *Criminal Interrogation and Confessions*, 5th edn. Burlington, MA: Jones & Bartlett Learning.

Innocence Project. 2009. 'Reevaluating Lineups: Why Witnesses Make Mistakes and How to Reduce the Chance of a Misidentification.' 1–33.

Jacobs, Michelle S. 2017. 'The Violent State: Black Women's Invisible Struggle Against Police Violence.' *William & Mary Journal of Women and the Law* 24: 39–100.

Janssens, M.J.P.A., M.F.A.M. Van Rooij, H. A. M. J ten Have, F.A.M. Kortmann, and F.C.B. Van Wijmen. 2004. 'Pressure and Coercion in the Care for the Addicted: Ethical Perspectives.' *Journal of Medical Ethics* 30: 453–58.

Jensen, Keith, Brian Hare, Josep Call, and Michael Tomasello. 2006. 'What's in It for Me? Self-Regard Precludes Altruism and Spite in Chimpanzees.' *Proceedings of the Royal Society of London B* 273: 1013–21.

Johnson, Sheri Lynn. 1996. 'The Color of Truth: Race and the Assessment of Credibility.' *Michigan Journal of Race and Law* 1: 263–346.

Jones, Karen. 2002. 'The Politics of Credibility,' in Louise Antony and Charlotte Witt (eds.), *A Mind of One's Own: Feminist Essays on Reason and Objectivity*. Boulder, CO: Westview Press, 154–76.

Jordan, Jan. 2004. 'Beyond Belief? Police, Rape, and Women's Credibility.' *Criminal Justice* 4: 29–59.

Joselow, Margaux. 2019. 'Promise-Induced False Confessions: Lessons from Promises in Another Context.' *Boston College Law Review* 60: 1641–87.

Kant, Immanuel. 1785 [1983]. *Grounding for the Metaphysics of Morals*, in Immanuel Kant, *Ethical Philosophy*, James W. Ellington (trans.). Indianapolis, IA: Hackett Publishing Co.

Kasel, Lisa E. and Saul M. Kassin. 2009. 'On the Presumption of Evidentiary Independence: Can Confessions Corrupt Eyewitness Identifications?' *Psychological Science* 20: 122–26.

Kassin, Saul M. 2005. 'On the Psychology of Confessions: Does Innocence Put Innocents at Risk?' *American Psychologist* 60: 215–28.

Kassin, Saul M., Steven A. Drizin, Thomas Grisso, Gisli H. Gudjonsson, Richard A. Leo, and Allison D. Redlich. 2010. 'Police-Induced Confessions: Risk Factors and Recommendations.' *Law and Human Behavior* 34: 3–38.

Kassin, Saul M. and Katherine L. Kiechel. 1996. 'The Social Psychology of False Confessions: Compliance, Internalization, and Confabulation.' *Psychological Science* 7: 125–28.

Kassin, Saul M., Richard A. Leo, Christian A. Meissner, Kimberly D. Richman, Lori H. Colwell, Amy-May Leach, Dana La Fon. 2007. 'Police Interviewing and Interrogation: A Self-Report Survey of Police Practices and Beliefs.' *Law and Human Behavior* 31: 381–400.

Kassin, Saul M. and Karlyn McNall. 1991. 'Police Interrogations and Confessions: Communicating Promises and Threats by Pragmatic Implication.' *Law and Human Behavior* 15: 233–51.

Kassin, Saul M. and Rebecca J. Norwick. 2004. 'Why People Waive Their *Miranda* Rights: The Power of Innocence.' *Law and Human Behavior* 28: 211–21.

Kassin, Saul M. and Lawrence S. Wrightsman. 1985. 'Confession Evidence,' in Saul M. Kassin and Lawrence S. Wrightsman (eds.), *The Psychology of Evidence and Trial Procedure*. Beverly Hills, CA: Sage: 67–94.

King, Nancy J. 2013. 'Plea Bargains that Waive Claims of Ineffective Assistance—Waiving Padilla and Fry.' *Duquesne Law Review* 51: 647–72.

King, Nancy J. 2014. 'Judicial Review: Appeals and Postconviction Proceedings,' in Allison D. Redlich, James R. Acker, Robert J. Norris, and Catherine L. Bonventre (eds.), *Examining Wrongful Convictions: Stepping Back, Moving Forward.* Durham, NC: Carolina Academic Press, 217–36.

King, Nancy J. and Michael E. O'Neill. 2005. 'Appeal Waivers and the Future of Sentencing Policy.' *Duke Law Journal* 55: 209–61.

Kipnis, Kenneth. 1976. 'Criminal Justice and the Negotiated Plea.' *Ethics* 86: 93–106.

Klaver, Jessica R., Zina Lee, and V. Gordon Rose. 2008. 'Effects of Personality, Interrogation Techniques and Plausibility in an Experimental False Confession Paradigm.' *Legal and Criminal Psychology* 13: 71–88.

Klein, Richard. 2004. 'Due Process Denied: Judicial Coercion in the Plea Bargaining Process.' *Hofstra Law Review* 32: 1349–423.

Kohlberg, Lawrence. 1969. 'Stage and Sequence: The Cognitive Development Approach to Socialization,' in David A Goslin (ed.), *Handbook of Socialization Theory.* Chicago, IL: Rand McNally, 347–480.

Kozinski, Wyatt. 2018. 'The Reid Interrogation Technique and False Confessions: A Time for Change.' *Seattle Journal for Social Justice* 16: 301–45.

Kramer, Greg M., Melinda Wolbransky, and Kirk Heilbrun. 2007. 'Plea Bargaining Recommendations by Criminal Defense Attorneys: Evidence Strength, Potential Sentence, and Defendant Preference.' *Behavioral Sciences & the Law* 25: 573–85.

Lackey, Jennifer. 1999. 'Testimonial Knowledge and Transmission.' *The Philosophical Quarterly* 49: 471–90.

Lackey, Jennifer. 2007. 'Norms of Assertion.' *Noûs* 41: 594–626.

Lackey, Jennifer. 2008. *Learning from Words: Testimony as a Source of Knowledge.* Oxford: Oxford University Press.

Lackey, Jennifer. 2012. 'Group Knowledge Attributions,' in Jessica Brown and Mikkel Gerken (eds.), *Knowledge Ascriptions.* Oxford: Oxford University Press, 243–69.

Lackey, Jennifer. 2013. 'Lies and Deception: An Unhappy Divorce.' *Analysis* 73: 236–48.

Lackey, Jennifer. 2016. 'Pitted Against Yourself: Credibility and False Confessions.' *Blog of the American Philosophical Association.*

Lackey, Jennifer. 2018*a*. 'Credibility and the Distribution of Epistemic Goods,' in Kevin McCain (ed.), *Believing in Accordance with the Evidence: New Essays on Evidentialism.* Cham, Switzerland: Springer Publishing, 145–68.

Lackey, Jennifer. 2018*b*. 'The Duty to Object.' *Philosophy and Phenomenological Research* 101: 35–60.

Lackey, Jennifer. 2018*c*. 'Experts and Peer Disagreement,' in Matthew Benton, John Hawthorne, and Dani Rabinowitz (eds.), *Knowledge, Belief, and God: New Insights in Religious Epistemology.* Oxford: Oxford University Press, 228–45.

Lackey, Jennifer. 2020*a*. 'False Confessions and Testimonial Injustice.' *Journal of Criminal Law and Criminology* 110: 43–68.

Lackey, Jennifer. 2020*b*. 'Epistemic Duties Regarding Others,' in Kevin McCain and Scott Stapleford (eds.), *Epistemic Duties: New Arguments, New Angles.* New York: Routledge, 281–94.

Lackey, Jennifer. 2021. *The Epistemology of Groups.* Oxford: Oxford University Press.

Langbein, John H. 1978. 'Torture and Plea Bargaining.' *The University of Chicago Law Review* 46: 3–22.

LeBel, Thomas P. 2008. 'Perceptions of and Responses to Stigma.' *Sociology Compass* 2: 409–32.

Lee, Youngjae. 2018. 'Multiple Offenders and the Question of Desert' in Jesper Ryberg, Julian V. Roberts, and Jan W. de Keijser (eds.), *Sentencing Multiple Crimes.* Oxford: Oxford University Press, 113–36.

Lee, Youngjae. 2019. 'Proportionality in Punishment,' in Larry Alexander and Kimberly Kessler (eds.), *The Palgrave Handbook of Applied Ethics and the Criminal Law*. Cham, Switzerland: Springer Verlag, 549–69.

Leipold, Andrew D. 2005. 'How the Pretrial Process Contributes to Wrongful Convictions.' *American Criminal Law Review* 42: 1123–65.

Leipold, Andrew D. and Hossein A. Abbasi. 2006. 'The Impact of Joinder and Severance on Federal Criminal Cases.' *Vanderbilt Law Review* 59: 349–404.

Leo, Richard A. 2009. 'False Confessions: Causes, Consequences, and Implications.' *The Journal of the American Academy of Psychiatry and the Law* 37: 332–43.

Leo, Richard A. and Richard J. Ofshe. 1997. 'The Social Psychology of Police Interrogation: The Theory and Classification of True and False Confessions.' *Studies in Law, Politics, and Society* 16: 189–251.

Leo, Richard A. and Richard J. Ofshe. 1998. 'Consequences of False Confessions: Deprivations of Liberty and Miscarriages of Justice in the Age of Psychological Interrogation.' *Journal of Criminal Law and Criminology* 88: 429–96.

Leo, Richard A. and Richard J. Ofshe. 2008. 'The Decision to Confess Falsely: Rational Choice and Irrational Action.' *Denver University Law Review* 74: 979–1122.

Leydon-Hardy, Lauren. 2021. 'Predatory Grooming and Epistemic Infringement,' in Jennifer Lackey (ed.), *Applied Epistemology*. Oxford: Oxford University Press, 119–47.

Li, Jing, Wen Wang, Jing Yu, and Liqi Zhu. 2016. 'Young Children's Development of Fairness Preference.' *Frontiers in Psychology* 7: 1274. doi: 10.3389/fpsyg.2016.01274.

Liebling, Alison. 2011. 'Moral Performance, Inhuman and Degrading Treatment and Prison Pain.' *Punishment & Society* 13: 530–50.

Lindsay, R. C. and Gary L. Wells. 1985. 'Improving Eyewitness Identifications from Lineups: Simultaneous Versus Sequential Lineup Presentation.' *Journal of Applied Psych*ology 70: 556–64.

Lininger, Tom. 2005. 'Prosecuting Batterers After Crawford.' *Virginia Law Review* 91: 748–822.

List, Christian, and Phillip Pettit. 2011. *Group Agency: The Possibility, Design, and Status of Corporate Agents*. Oxford: Oxford University Press.

Loftus, Elizabeth F. 1979. *Eyewitness Testimony*. Cambridge, MA: Harvard University Press.

Loftus, Elizabeth F. 1980. 'Impact of Expert Psychological Testimony on the Unreliability of Eyewitness Identification.' *Journal of Applied Psychology* 65: 9–15.

Loney, Danielle M. and Brian L. Cutler. 2016. 'Coercive Interrogation of Eyewitnesses Can Produce False Accusations.' *Journal of Police and Criminal Psychology* 31: 29–36.

Lowell, A. Lawrence. 1897. 'The Judicial Use of Torture. Part I.' *Harvard Law Review* 11: 220–33.

Lowry, Beverly. 2002. *Crossed Over: A Murder, A Memoir*. New York, NY: Knopf Doubleday.

Lyons, Daniel. 1975. 'Welcome Threats and Coercive Offers.' *Philosophy* 50: 425–36.

McAdoo, Ryan M. and Scott D. Gronlund. 2016. 'Relative Judgment Theory and the Mediation of Facial Recognition: Implications for Theories of Eyewitness Identification.' *Cognitive Research: Principles and Implications* 1: 1–12.

McConkie, Daniel S. 2017. 'Structuring Pre-Plea Criminal Discovery.' *The Journal of Criminal Law and Criminology* 107: 1–64.

McDowell, John. 1994. 'Knowledge by Hearsay,' in Bimal Krishna Matilal and Arindam Chakrabarti (eds.), *Knowing from Words*. Dordrecht: Kluwer Academic Publishers, 195–224.

McHugh, Conor. 2013. 'Epistemic Responsibility and Doxastic Agency.' *Philosophical Issues* 23: 132–57.

McKee, Duff. 1996. 'Challenge to Eyewitness Testimony through Expert Testimony.' Proof of Facts 3rd Index. Rochester, NY: Lawyers Cooperative Publishing.

McKinney, Rachel Ann. 2016. 'Extracted Speech.' *Social Theory and Practice* 42: 258–84.
McMurtrie, Jacqueline. 2015. 'The Unindicted Co-Ejaculator and Necrophilia: Addressing Prosecutors' Logic-Defying Responses to Exculpatory DNA Result.' *Journal of Criminal Law and Criminology* 105: 853–80.
Maitra, Ishani. 2010. 'The Nature of Epistemic Injustice.' *Philosophical Books* 51: 195–211.
Manne, Kate. 2017. *Down Girl: The Logic of Misogyny*. Oxford: Oxford University Press.
Marcus, Paul. 2006. 'It's Not Just About *Miranda*: Determining the Voluntariness of Confessions in Criminal Prosecutions.' *Valparaiso University Law Review* 40: 601–44.
Marion, Stéphanie B., and Jeff Kukucka, Carisa Collins, Saul M. Kassin, and Tara M. Burke. 2016. 'Lost Proof of Innocence: The Impact of Confessions on Alibi Witnesses.' *Law and Human Behavior* 40: 65–71.
Marlowe, Jen, Martina Davis-Correia, and Troy Davis. 2013. *I Am Troy Davis*. Chicago, IL: Haymarket Books.
Martin, Dianne L. 2002. 'Lessons about Justice from the Laboratory of Wrongful Convictions: Tunnel Vision, the Construction of Guilt and Informer Evidence.' *UMKC Law Review* 70: 847–64.
Materni, Mike C. 2013. 'Criminal Punishment and the Pursuit of Justice.' *British Journal of American Legal Studies* 2: 263–304.
Medina, José. 2011. "The Relevance of Credibility Excess in a Proportional View of Epistemic Injustice: Differential Epistemic Authority and the Social Imaginary. *Social Epistemology* 25: 15–35.
Medwed, Daniel S. 2005. 'Up the River Without a Procedure: Innocent Prisoners and Newly Discovered Non-DNA Evidence in State Courts.' *Arizona Law Review* 47: 655–718.
Medwed, Daniel S. 2008. 'The Innocent Prisoner's Dilemma: Consequences of Failing to Admit Guilt at Parole Hearings.' *Iowa Law Review* 93: 491–557.
Meier, Joan S. 2006. '*Davis/Hammon*, Domestic Violence, and the Supreme Court: The Case for Cautious Optimism.' *Michigan Law Review First Impressions* 105: 22–27.
Meissner, Christian A., Allison D. Redlich, Stephen W. Michael, Jacqueline R. Evans, Catherine R. Camilletti, Sujeeta Bhatt, and Susan Brandon. 2014. 'Accusatorial and Information-Gathering Interrogation Methods and their Effects on True and False Confessions: A Meta-Analytic Review.' *Journal of Experimental Criminology* 10: 459–86.
Memon, Amina, Lorraine Hope, and Ray Bull. 2003. 'Exposure Duration: Effects on Eyewitness Accuracy and Confidence.' *British Journal of Psychology* 94: 339–54.
Memon, Amina, Aldert Vrij, and Ray Bull. 2003. *Psychology and Law: Truthfulness, Accuracy and Credibility*. London: Jossey Bass.
Mill, John Stuart. 1859 [1975]. *On Liberty*, David Spitz (ed.), New York, NY: Norton.
Mills, Charles. 2007. 'White Ignorance,' in Shannon Sullivan and Nancy Tuana (eds.), *Race and Epistemologies of Ignorance*. Albany, NY: SUNY Press, 13–38.
Mills, Claudia. 1995. 'Politics and Manipulation.' *Social Theory and Practice* 21: 97–112.
Miranda, Mario J. 2008. 'Determinants of Shoppers' Checkout Behavior at Supermarkets.' *Journal of Targeting, Measurement, and Analysis for Marketing* 16: 312–21.
Moore, Timothy E., Brian L. Cutler, and David Shulman. 2014. 'Shaping Eyewitness and Alibi Testimony with Coercive Interview Practices.' *The Champion*, October: 34–40.
Morris, Herbert. 1968. 'Persons and Punishment.' *The Monist* 52: 475–501.
Moss, Sarah. 2015. 'Time-Slice Epistemology and Action under Indeterminacy.' *Oxford Studies in Epistemology* 5: 172–94.
Moston, Stephen, Geoffrey M. Stephenson, and Thomas M. Williamson. 1992. 'The Effects of Case Characteristics on Suspect Behaviour During Police Questioning.' *British Journal of Criminology* 32: 23–39.

Munroe, Wade. 2016. 'Testimonial Injustice and Prescriptive Credibility Deficits.' *Canadian Journal of Philosophy* 46: 924–47.
Nagel, Thomas. 1995. 'Rawls on Justice,' in *Other Minds*. New York, NY: Oxford University Press, 121–36.
Nash, Robert A. and Kimberly A. Wade. 2009. 'Innocent but Proven Guilty: Eliciting Internalized False Confessions Using Doctored-Video Evidence.' *Applied Cognitive Psychology* 23: 624–37.
Nash, Jennifer C. 2009. 'Black Women and Rape: A Review of the Literature.' Brandeis University Feminist Sexual Ethics Project. https://www.brandeis.edu/projects/fse/slavery/unitedstates/slav-us-articles/nash2009.pdf.
Natapoff, Alexandra. 2005. 'Speechless: The Silencing of Criminal Defendants.' *New York University Law Review* 80: 1449–504.
Neta, Ram. 2006. 'Epistemology Factualized: New Contractarian Foundations for Epistemology.' *Synthese* 150: 247–80.
New York State Association of Criminal Defense Lawyers. 2021. 'The New York State Trial Penalty: The Constitutional Right to Trial Under Attack.'
Nickerson, Raymond S. 1998. 'Confirmation Bias: A Ubiquitous Phenomenon in Many Guises.' *Review of General Psychology* 2: 175–220.
Nobles, Richard and Davis Schiff. 2019. 'Criminal Justice Unhinged: The Challenge of Guilty Pleas.' *Oxford Journal of Legal Studies* 39: 100–23.
Noggle, Robert. 1996. 'Manipulative Actions: A Conceptual and Moral Analysis.' *American Philosophical Quarterly* 33: 43–55.
Nozick, Robert. 1969. 'Coercion,' in Sidney Morgenbesser, Patrick Suppes, and Morton White (eds.), *Philosophy, Science, and Method: Essays in Honor of Ernest Nagel*. New York, NY: St. Martin's Press, 440–72.
Nozick, Robert. 1981. *Philosophical Explanations*. Cambridge, MA: The Belknap Press.
O'Brien Patricia and Robin Bates. 2003. 'Negotiating the Waves: Challenges of Conducting In-Prison and Follow-Up research with Women.' *Affilia* 18: 210–25.
Ojanuga, Durrenda. 1993. 'The Medical Ethics of the "Father of Gynaecology", Dr J Marion Sims.' *Journal of Medical Ethics* 19: 28–31.
Oliver, Mary Beth. 2003. 'African American Men as "Criminal and Dangerous": Implications of Media Portrayals of Crime on the "Criminalization" of African American Men.' *Journal of African American Studies* 7: 3–18.
O'Neill, Onora. 1991. 'Which are the Offers *You*, Can't Refuse?' in R. G. Frey and Christopher Morris (eds.), *Violence, Terrorism, and Justice*. Cambridge: Cambridge University Press, 170–95.
Page, Amy Dellinger. 2008. 'Gateway to Reform? Policy Implications of Police Officers' Attitudes Toward Rape.' *American Journal of Criminal Justice* 33: 44–58.
Pager, Chet K.W. 2005. 'Blind Justice, Colored Truths and the Veil of Ignorance' *Willamette Law Review* 41: 373–434.
Pager, Devah. 2007. *Marked: Race, Crime, and Finding Work in an Era of Mass Incarceration*. Chicago, IL: The University of Chicago Press.
Pallikkathayil, Japa. 2011. 'The Possibility of Choice: Three Accounts of the Problem with Coercion.' *Philosophers' Imprint* 11: 1–20.
Patton, Tracey Owens and Julie Snyder-Yuly. 2007. 'Any Four Black Men Will Do: Rape, Race, and the Ultimate Scapegoat.' *Journal of Black Studies* 37: 859–95.
Peet, Andrew. 2015. 'Epistemic Injustice in Utterance Interpretation.' *Synthese* 194: 3421–43.
Peters, Edward. 1985. *Torture*. Philadelphia, PA: University of Pennsylvania Press.
Piaget, Jean. 1965. *The Moral Judgment of the Child*. New York, NY: The Free Press.

Pilcher, June J. and Allen I. Huffcutt. 1996. 'Effects of Sleep Deprivation on Performance: A Meta-Analysis.' *Sleep* 19: 318–26.

Plantinga, Alvin. 1993. *Warrant and Proper Function*. Oxford: Oxford University Press.

Pollock, John. 1986. *Contemporary Theories of Knowledge*. Totowa, NJ: Rowman and Littlefield.

Pornpitakpan, Chanthika. 2004. 'The Persuasiveness of Source Credibility: A Critical Review of Five Decades' Evidence.' *Journal of Applied Social Psychology* 34: 243–81.

Ptacek, James. 1999. *Battered Women in the Court Room*. Boston, MA: Northeastern University Press.

Radelet, Michael L., Hugo Adam Bedau, and Constance E. Putnam. 1994. *In Spite of Innocence: Erroneous Convictions in Capital Cases*. Boston, MA: Northeastern University Press.

Raeder, Myrna. 2003. 'What Does Innocence Have to Do with It: A Commentary on Wrongful Convictions and Rationality.' *Law Review of Michigan State University Detroit College of Law* 2003: 1315–36.

Rakoff, Jed S. 2014. 'Why Innocent People Plead Guilty.' *The New York Review* November Issue.

Rand, Joseph W. 2000. 'The Demeanor Gap: Race, Lie Detection, and the Jury.' *Connecticut Law Review* 33: 1–76.

Range, Friederike, Lisa Horn, and Zsófia Viranyi, and Ludwig Huber. 2009. 'The Absence of Reward Induces Inequity Aversion in Dogs.' *Proceedings of the National Academy of Sciences of the United States of America* 106: 340–45.

Rawls, John. 1958. 'Justice as Fairness.' *The Philosophical Review* 67: 164–94.

Raz, Joseph. 1986. *The Morality of Freedom*. Oxford: Clarendon Press.

Reed, Baron. 2001. 'Epistemic Agency and the Intellectual Virtues.' *Southern Journal of Philosophy* 39: 507–26.

Reed, Baron. 2006. 'Epistemic Circularity Squared? Skepticism about Common Sense.' *Philosophy and Phenomenological Research* 73: 186–97.

Reed, Baron. 2013. 'Fallibilism, Epistemic Possibility, and Epistemic Agency.' *Philosophical Issues* 23: 40–69.

Repka, Janice J. 1986. 'Rethinking the Standard for New Trial Motions Based upon Recantations as Newly Discovered Evidence.' *University of Pennsylvania Law Review* 134: 1433–59.

Roberts, Dorothy. 1997. *Killing the Black Body: Race, Reproduction, and the Meaning of Liberty*. New York, NY: Pantheon Books.

Rouhanian, Anoosha. 2017. 'A Call for Change: The Detrimental Impacts of *Crawford v. Washington* on Domestic Violence and Rape Prosecutions.' *Boston College Journal of Law & Social Justice* 37: 1–72.

Rudinow, Joel. 1978. 'Manipulation.' *Ethics* 88: 338–47.

Rutledge, Njeri M. 2009. 'Turning a Blind Eye: Perjury in Domestic Violence Cases.' *New Mexico Law Review* 39: 149–94.

Rutledge, John P. 2001. 'They All Look Alike: The Inaccuracy of Cross-Racial Identification.' *American Journal of Criminal Law* 28: 207–28.

Savage, Meaghan E., Kimberley A. Clow, Regina A. Schuller, and Rosemary Ricciardelli. 2018. 'After Exoneration: Attributions of Responsibility Impact Perceptions.' *Canadian Journal of Law and Society* 33: 85–103.

Saywitz, Karen J., Rebecca Nathanson, Lynn S. Snyder. 1993. 'Credibility of Child Witnesses: The Role of Communicative Competence.' *Topics in Language Disorders* 13: 59–78.

Scheffler, Samuel. 2003. 'What is Egalitarianism?' *Philosophy and Public Affairs* 31: 5–39.

Schehr, Robert. 2018. 'Standard of Proof, Presumption of Innocence, and Plea Bargaining: How Wrongful Conviction Data Exposes Inadequate Pre-Trial Criminal Procedure.' *California Western Law Review* 54: 51–102.

Schelling, Thomas C. 1966. *Arms and Influence*. New Haven: Yale University Press.

Seigel, Michael L. and Christopher Slobogin. 2005. 'Prosecuting Martha: Federal Prosecutorial Power and the Need for a Law of Counts.' *Penn State Law Review* 109: 1107–32.

Shaw, John S. and Kimberly A. McClure. 1996. 'Repeated Postevent Questioning Can Lead to Elevated Levels of Eyewitness Confidence.' *Law and Human Behavior* 20: 629–53.

Sides, John and Kimberly Gross. 2013. 'Stereotypes of Muslims and Support for the War on Terror.' *The Journal of Politics* 75: 583–98.

Simons, Michael A. 2003. 'Retribution for Rats: Cooperation, Punishment, and Atonement.' *Vanderbilt Law Review* 56: 1–54.

Sinnott, Christopher J. 1993. 'When Defendant Becomes the Victim: A Child's Recantation as Newly Discovered Evidence.' *Cleveland State Law Review* 41: 569–98.

Smiley, Calvin John and David Fakunle. 2016. 'From "Brute" to "Thug:" The Demonization and Criminalization of Unarmed Black Male Victims in America.' *Journal of Human Behavior in the Social Environment* 26: 350–66.

Smoyer, Amy B., Kim M. Blankenship, and Brandis Belt. 2009. 'Compensation for Incarcerated Research Participants: Diverse State Policies Suggest a New Research Agenda.' *American Journal of Public Health* 99: 1746–52.

Sorensen, Roy. 2007. 'Bald-Faced Lies! Lying without the Intent to Deceive.' *Pacific Philosophical Quarterly* 88: 251–64.

Stalnaker, Robert. 2014. *Context*. Oxford: Oxford University Press.

Steblay, Nancy Mehrkens. 1992. 'A Meta-Analytic Review of the Weapon Focus Effect.' *Law and Human Behavior* 16: 413–24.

Steblay, Nancy K. and Elizabeth F. Loftus. 2013. 'Eyewitness Identification and the Legal System,' in Eldar Shafir (ed.), *The Behavioral Foundations of Public Policy*. Princeton, NJ: Princeton University Press, 145–62.

Stephens, Rebecca. 2013. 'Disparities in Postconviction Remedies for Those Who Plead Guilty and Those Convicted at Trial: A Survey of State Statutes and Recommendations for Reform.' *Journal of Criminal Law and Criminology* 103: 309–42.

Stevens, Robert. 1988. 'Coercive Offers.' *Australasian Journal of Philosophy* 66: 83–95.

Stoljar, Natalie. 2000. 'Autonomy and the Feminist Intuition,' in Catriona Mackenzie and Natalie Stoljar (eds.), *Relational Autonomy: Feminist Perspectives on Autonomy, Agency, and the Social Self*. New York, NY: Oxford University Press, 94–111.

Stuntz, William J. 2011. *The Collapse of American Criminal Justice*. Cambridge, MA: The Belknap Press of Harvard University Press.

Sundby, Scott E. 1998. 'The Capital Jury and Absolution: The Intersection of Trial Strategy, Remorse, and the Death Penalty.' *Cornell Law Review* 83: 1557–98.

Sunstein, Cass R. 2015. 'Fifty Shades of Manipulation.' *Journal of Marketing Behavior* 1: 213–44.

Susser, Daniel, Beate Roessler, and Helen Nissenbaum. 2019. 'Online Manipulation: Hidden Influences in a Digital World.' *Georgetown Law Technology Review* 4: 1–45.

Sussman, David. 2005. 'What's Wrong with Torture?' *Philosophy and Public Affairs* 33: 1–33.

Taslitz, Andrew E. 2006. 'Wrongly Accused: Is Race a Factor in Convicting the Innocent?' *Ohio State Journal of Criminal Law* 4: 121–33.

Taylor, Richard B. 2020. 'The Epistemology of Plea Bargaining.' *Social Epistemology* 34: 501–12.

Thomas, Kimberly A. 2007. 'Beyond Mitigation: Towards a Theory of Allocution.' *Fordham Law Review* 75: 2641–83.

Timony, James P. 2000. 'Demeanor Credibility.' *Catholic University Law Review* 49: 903–43.

Trawalter, Sophie, Kelly M. Hoffman, and Adam Waytz. 2012. 'Racial Bias in Perceptions of Other's Pain.' *PLOS ONE* 7. doi: 10.1371/journal.pone.0048546.

Trivedi, Somil and Nicole Gonzalez Van Cleve. 2020. 'To Serve and Protect Each Other: How Police-Prosecutor Codependence Enables Police Misconduct.' *Boston University Law Review* 100: 895–933.

Tudor, Steven Keith. 2008. 'Why Should Remorse be a Mitigating Factor in Sentencing?' *Criminal Law and Philosophy* 2: 241–57.

Tuerkheimer, Deborah. 2014. *Flawed Convictions: 'Shaken Baby Syndrome' and the Inertia of Injustice*. Oxford: Oxford University Press.

Tuerkheimer, Deborah. 2017. 'Incredible Women: Sexual Violence and the Credibility Discount.' *University of Pennsylvania Law Review* 166: 1–58.

Vallas, George. 2011. 'A Survey of Federal and State Standards for the Admission of Expert Testimony on the Reliability of Eyewitness.' *American Journal of Criminal Law* 39: 97–146.

Vrij, Aldert. 2000. *Detecting Lies and Deceit: The Psychology of Lying and the Implications for Professional Practice*. London: Wiley.

Waldron, Jeremy. 2012. *The Harm in Hate Speech*. Cambridge, MA: Harvard University Press.

Ward, Bryan H. 2006. 'Sentencing without Remorse.' *Loyola University Chicago Law Journal* 38: 131–68.

Ware, Alan. 1981. 'The Concept of Manipulation: Its Relation to Democracy and Power.' *British Journal of Political Science* 11: 163–81.

Warren, Jonathan M. 2018. 'Hidden in Plain View: Juries and the Implicit Credibility Given to Police Testimony.' *DePaul Journal for Social Justice* 11: 2–32.

Weber, Michael. 2019. 'The Persistence of the Leveling Down Objection.' *Erasmus Journal for Philosophy and Economics* 12: 1–25.

Weigend, Thomas. 2011. 'Should We Search for the Truth, and Who Should Do It?' *North Carolina Journal of International Law* 36: 389–416.

Weisman, Richard. 1999. 'Detecting Remorse and Its Absence in the Criminal Justice System.' *Studies in Law, Politics, and Society* 19: 121–38.

Weisman, Richard. 2014. *Showing Remorse: Law and the Social Control of Emotion*. Farnham: Ashgate Press.

Wells, Gary L. 1984. 'The Psychology of Lineup Identifications.' *Journal of Applied Social Psychology* 14: 89–103.

Wells, Gary L. 2006. 'Eyewitness Identification: Systemic Reforms.' *Wisconsin Law Review* 2006: 615–44.

Wells, Gary L., Roy S. Malpass, R.C.L. Lindsay, Ronald P. Fisher, John W. Turtle, and Solomon M. Fulero. 2000. 'From the Lab to the Police Station: A Successful Application of Eyewitness Research.' *American Psychologist* 55: 581–98.

Wells, Gary L. and Elizabeth A. Olson. 2001. 'The Other-Race Effect in Eyewitness Identification: What Do We Do About It?' *Psychology, Public Policy, and Law* 7: 230–46.

Wells, Gary L., Steven D. Penrod, Roy S. Malpass, Solomon M. Fulero, and C. A. E. Brimacombe. 1998. 'Eyewitness Identification Procedures: Recommendations for Lineups and Photospreads.' *Law and Human Behavior* 22: 603–47.

Wells, Gary L. and John W. Turtle. 1986. 'Eyewitness Identification: The Importance of Lineup Models.' *Psychological Bulletin* 99: 320–29.

Wendler, David and Alan Wertheimer. 2017. 'Why is Coerced Consent Worse Than No Consent and Deceived Consent?' *Journal of Medicine and Philosophy* 42: 114–31.

Westen, Peter. 2008. 'Individualizing the Reasonable Person in Criminal Law.' *Criminal Law and Philosophy* 2: 137–62.

Wertheimer, Alan. 1987. *Coercion*. Princeton, NJ: Princeton University Press.

Williams, Bernard. 1973. *Problems of the Self*. Cambridge: Cambridge University Press.

Williams, Michael. 1999. *Groundless Belief: An Essay on the Possibility of Epistemology*, 2nd edn. Princeton, NJ: Princeton University Press.

Wills, Donna. 1997. 'Domestic Violence: The Case for Aggressive Prosecution.' *UCLA Women's Law Journal* 7: 173–82.

Winston, Kenneth I. 1974. 'On Treating Like Cases Alike.' *California Law Review* 62: 1–39.

Wise, Richard A., Kristen A. Dauphinais, and Martin A. Safer. 2007. 'A Tripartite Solution to Eyewitness Error.' *Journal of Criminal Law and Criminology* 97: 807–72.

Wise, Richard A., Clifford S. Fishman, and Martin A. Safer. 2009. 'How to Analyze the Accuracy of Eyewitness Testimony in a Criminal Case.' *Connecticut Law Review* 42: 435–513.

Wise, Richard A. and Andre Kehn. 2020. 'Can the Effectiveness of Eyewitness Expert Testimony Be Improved?' *Psychiatry, Psychology and Law* 27: 315–30.

Wise, Richard A. and Martin A. Safer. 2003. 'A Survey of Judges' Knowledge and Beliefs About Eyewitness Testimony.' *Court Review: The Journal of the American Judges Association* 40: 6–16.

Wixted, John T. and Gary L. Wells. 2017. 'The Relationship Between Eyewitness Confidence and Identification Accuracy: A New Synthesis.' *Psychological Science in the Public Interest* 18: 10–65.

Wood, Allen. 2014. 'Coercion, Manipulation, Exploitation,' in Christian Coons and Michael Weber (eds.), *Manipulation: Theory and Practice*. Oxford: Oxford University Press, 17–50.

Wood, Linda A. and Clare MacMartin. 2007. 'Constructing Remorse: Judges' Sentencing Decisions in Child Sexual Assault Cases.' *Journal of Language and Social Psychology* 26: 343–62.

Wriggins, Jennifer. 1983. 'Race, Racism, and the Law.' *Harvard Women's Law Journal* 6: 103–41.

Wynbrandt, Katie. 2016. 'From False Evidence Ploy to False Guilty Plea: An Unjustified Path to Securing Convictions.' *The Yale Law Journal* 126: 545–63.

Yancy, George. 2008. 'Elevators, Social Spaces and Racism: A Philosophical Analysis.' *Philosophy & Social Criticism* 34: 843–76.

Yarbrough, Marilyn, and Crystal Bennett. 2000. 'Cassandra and the Sistahs: The Peculiar Treatment of African American Women in the Myth of Women as Liars.' *Journal of Gender, Race and Justice* 3: 625–58

Young, Iris Marion. 1990. *Justice and the Politics of Difference*. Princeton, NJ: Princeton University Press.

Young, Jock. 1999. *The Exclusive Society: Social Exclusion, Crime and Difference in Late Modernity*. Thousand Oaks, CA: Sage.

Zagzebski, Linda. 2012. *Epistemic Authority: A Theory of Trust, Authority, and Autonomy in Belief*. Oxford: Oxford University Press

Zhong, Rocksheng, Madelon Baranoski, Neal Feigenson, Larry Davidson, Alec Buchanan, and Howard V. Zonana. 2014. 'So You're Sorry? The Role of Remorse in Criminal Law.' *Journal of the American Academy of Psychiatry and the Law* 42: 39–48.

Zimmerman, David. 1981. 'Coercive Wage Offers.' *Philosophy and Public Affairs* 10: 121–45.

Index

For the benefit of digital users, indexed terms that span two pages (e.g., 52–3) may, on occasion, appear on only one of those pages.